BUSINESS ANALYTICS

This book provides a first-hand account of business analytics and its implementation and an account of the brief theoretical framework underpinning each component of business analytics. The themes of the book include (1) learning the contours, scope, and boundaries of business analytics; (2) understanding the design aspects of an analytical organization; (3) providing knowledge focusing on developing business activities for financial impact through functional analysis; and (4) deriving a whole gamut of business use cases in a variety of situations to apply business analytics techniques. The book gives a complete and insightful understanding of developing and implementing analytical solutions by analyzing concrete use cases.

Dinabandhu Bag is Associate Professor in Finance at the School of Management, the National Institute of Technology in Rourkela, India. He teaches finance and economics and specializes in risk capital and financial modelling. Dr Bag has over thirteen years of industry experience implementing enterprise analytic applications for banks and financial institutions. He has worked with Oracle Financial Services Software Ltd, Bangalore; Citibank NA Global Decision Management; GE Capital International Services, Bangalore; and the Reserve Bank of India, Mumbai.

BUSINESS ANALYTICS

Dinabandhu Bag

LONDON AND NEW YORK

First published 2017
by Routledge
2 Park Square, Milton Park, Abingdon, Oxon OX14 4RN

and by Routledge
711 Third Avenue, New York, NY 10017

Routledge is an imprint of the Taylor & Francis Group, an informa business

© 2017 Dinabandhu Bag

The right of Dinabandhu Bag to be identified as author of this work has been asserted by him in accordance with sections 77 and 78 of the Copyright, Designs and Patents Act 1988.

All rights reserved. No part of this book may be reprinted or reproduced or utilised in any form or by any electronic, mechanical, or other means, now known or hereafter invented, including photocopying and recording, or in any information storage or retrieval system, without permission in writing from the publishers.

Trademark notice: Product or corporate names may be trademarks or registered trademarks, and are used only for identification and explanation without intent to infringe.

British Library Cataloguing in Publication Data
A catalogue record for this book is available from the British Library

Library of Congress Cataloging in Publication Data
Names: Bag, Dinabandhu, author.
Title: Business analytics / by Dinabandhu Bag.
Description: Abingdon, Oxon ; New York, NY : Routledge, 2017. |
　Includes bibliographical references and index.
Identifiers: LCCN 2016019619 | ISBN 9781138916111 (hardback) |
　ISBN 9781138916128 (pbk.) | ISBN 9781315464695 (ebook)
Subjects: LCSH: Management—Statistical methods. | Decision making—Statistical methods.
Classification: LCC HD30.215 .B345 2017 | DDC 658.4/013—dc23
LC record available at https://lccn.loc.gov/2016019619

ISBN: 978-1-138-91611-1 (hbk)
ISBN: 978-1-138-91612-8 (pbk)
ISBN: 978-1-315-46469-5 (ebk)

Typeset in Bembo
by Apex CoVantage, LLC

CONTENTS

List of figures — vii
List of tables — viii
Preface — xii
Acknowledgements — xiii
Helping you learn — xiv
Abbreviations — xv

1 Introduction — 1

2 Business roles — 9

3 Functional analytics — 15

4 Human resource analytics — 22

5 Supply chain analytics — 34

6 Customer analytics — 61

7 Business process analytics — 82

8 Financial analytics — 104

9 Implementing business analytics — 149

10 Use cases and business applications — 162

Appendix 1 Formulae and derivations   *201*
Appendix 2 Sample test data on banking customers   *205*
Appendix 3 Sample test data on GSM subscribers   *208*
Appendix 4 Sample test data on household purchases from stores   *213*
Appendix 5 Sample test data on learning in manufacturing   *216*
Appendix 6 Sample test data on general insurance   *217*
Glossary   *221*

FIGURES

1.1	Choice-making process in business organizations	5
5.1	Supply network strategy	41
5.2	Weibull distribution of ordering volume A(.)	50
5.3	Benefits of inventory control	55
5.4	Rational distribution model	56
6.1	Contextual factors	62
6.2	Social nurturing of a customer	75
7.1	Fishbone diagram – customer delay in logistics	95
7.2	Pareto chart of cause attributes	96
8.1	Weibull distribution of contingent pricing	123
9.1	Plan of analytics implementation	153
10.1	Distribution of segments	164

TABLES

1.1	Contours of business analytics	6
1.2	Engagement map of business analytics	7
2.1	Business roles in analytics: first-level users	10
2.2	Business roles in analytics: second-level users	11
2.3	Business roles in analytics: third-level users	12
2.4	Business roles and reporting requirements	14
3.1	Types of functional analytics	16
3.2	Uses of human resources analytics	18
3.3	Uses of supply chain analytics	18
3.4	Uses of customer analytics	19
3.5	Uses of business process analytics	20
3.6	Uses of financial analytics	21
4.1	Engagement map of human resource analytics	23
4.2	Nature of engagement	23
4.3	Attrition analysis	25
4.4	Performance appraisal analytics	26
4.5	Engagement analysis	27
4.6	Training and development	27
4.7	Compensation and benefit analysis	28
4.8	Recruitment and induction	29
4.9	Manpower forecast model estimates	30
5.1	Engagement map of supply chain analytics	35
5.2	Supply chain core excellence	37
5.3	E-supply chain finance modalities	39

5.4	Supply chain finance components	40
5.5	Supplier model rating model estimates	45
5.6	Challenges to advanced distribution planning	46
5.7	Supplier performance review	48
5.8	Minimization of project overrun	54
5.9	Cost planning options	57
6.1	Customer analytics users	63
6.2	Engagement map of customer analytics	63
6.3	Churn analysis	66
6.4	Movement and migration of segments	67
6.5	Focus on new customers	72
6.6	Cross-sell summary	72
6.7	Value proposition in FMCG	75
6.8	Segment optimization report	77
6.9	Focus on social media	79
7.1	Engagement map of business process analytics	83
7.2	New business branch outlook	85
7.3	New business product outlook	85
7.4	Engagement in the collection process	86
7.5	Swap set analysis	87
7.6	Engagement in marketing process	88
7.7	Focus area in the sales process	91
7.8	Forms of dynamic pricing and differential pricing	92
7.9	Service resolution report	94
7.10	Restaurant Pareto analysis	95
7.11	Simulation trials of branch banking tellers	98
7.12	Simulation summary of branch banking tellers	98
7.13	Focus in new operations	101
8.1	Simple financial measures	105
8.2	Engagement map of financial analytics	106
8.3	Ratio analysis	106
8.4	Product sales data of garden furniture products	109
8.5	Cash flow ratios	110
8.6	Component ALM computation	117
8.7	Example for calculation of risk weight	120
8.8	Parameters of PD computation	122
8.9	FMI computation	122
8.10	Acceptance rates of warranty	123
8.11	Retail credit risk analysis	125

8.12	Estimates of a retail credit risk delinquency model	125
8.13	Population stability view	126
8.14	Characteristics analysis report	127
8.15	Examples of acquisitions in biotechnology	130
8.16	Operating performance after merger	131
8.17	Target selection scale	132
8.18	Projection of financials	133
8.19	Matched non-merging firm fundamentals (long term)	134
8.20	Scenarios of growth on firm value	134
8.21	Loss and gain to each player	139
8.22	Earnings dilution after acquisition	139
8.23	Ranking of financing options	141
8.24	Impact after spin-off	143
8.25	Post-merger impact	144
8.26	Engagement in insurance	145
8.27	General insurance analytics	146
8.28	Life insurance analytics	146
9.1	Business roles in implementation	154
9.2	Implementation plan of analytics	154
9.3	Initiatives in banking implementation of analytics	156
9.4	Initiatives in insurance implementation of analytics	157
9.5	Initiatives in manufacturing implementation of analytics	158
9.6	Initiatives in telecom implementation of analytics	159
9.7	Initiatives in retail implementation of analytics	160
10.1	Expected segment NPV summary	163
10.2	Segment profile	165
10.3	Response score profile	166
10.4	Response segmentation report	167
10.5	Classification table report	168
10.6	Segment optimization report	168
10.7	Offer affinity analysis	168
10.8	Life stage clusters for insurance marketing	171
10.9	Scheduling of jobs in manufacturing	177
10.10	Variation in traffic density ($\rho\star$)	179
10.11	Yield from traffic intensities	180
10.12	Balanced traffic after acceptance	180
10.13	GSM clusters	182
10.14	Parameter estimates from satisfaction models	185
10.15	Causes of food quality dissatisfaction	186

10.16	Operating parameters of the cab company	187
10.17	Fleet expansion choices for the cab company	188
10.18	Daily scheduling of cabs	189
10.19	Allocation of cabs to segments	191
10.20	Survival analysis	194
10.21	Usage of products by customers over time	195
10.22	Workforce scheduling	196
10.23	Manpower scheduling for the week	197
10.24	Logistic regression model for males	198
10.25	Follow-up cost of multi-disciplinary heart failure	199
A.1	Exemplary estimates	204
A.2	Sample test data on banking customers	206
A.3	Sample test data on GSM subscribers	209
A.4	Sample test data on household purchases from stores	214
A.5	Sample test data on learning in manufacturing	216
A.6	Sample test data on general insurance	218

PREFACE

Business Analytics indicates the practices and competencies for exploration and introspection of business performance to make purposive, intuitive, and expedient business decisions. Business analytics involves a plethora of analysis around business data to draw information that could be used by the managers at various levels in an organization. Business analytics enables fact-based decision making while extending accountability in decision making. Business analytics is defined as the process of looking at and summarizing data with the intent of extracting hidden predictive information. Numerous studies and much evidence exist on the benefits of business analytics for organizations[1]. Analytical projects improving productions had a median ROI of 277%; those involving financial management had a median ROI of 139%, involving customer relationship management had a median ROI of 55%. Similarly, the median ROI of predictive analytics projects were 145% compared to non-predictive projects at 89%.

Thus, this book deals with the science and art of business analytics with special emphasis on financial analytics and also provides the theoretical foundations and context for various elements of business analytics in specific situations. To highlight aspects of implementation, this book will show the reader how leading companies use the power of analytics to improve their investments. Often scientific knowledge alone cannot make good decisions unless combined with knowledge of the business with the best information available. Quantitative methods can help managers evaluate more strategic choices using tools. While many traditional academic texts mostly focus on quantitative methods, very few cover analytics for non-quantitative managers, which this book aims to correct.

Note

1 International Data Corporation. (2003). *The Financial Impact of Business Analytics: Key Findings* (IDC No. 28689, January 2003). Framingham, MA: International Data Corporation.

ACKNOWLEDGEMENTS

I am thankful to all those who directly or indirectly encouraged me complete this story, which was waiting to be written for a few years. I am also thankful to all who guided me directly or indirectly to finish this book. I am grateful to the revered business organizations that facilitated working on the implementation of analytics applications and provided me with the intuition to write this book. I am thankful to my current employer the National Institute of Technology in Rourkela, India, and visiting faculty assignments to multiple universities that provided me with the intensive opportunity of classroom lectures to understand the curiosity of class participants better. I am thankful to all those industries located in US and India spanning service industries, manufacturing, technology, telecom, and media that inspired me to learn from them.

I am also grateful to all the researchers who have contributed to the literature and guided the direction of this study. I am thankful to leading professional magazines and sources that provide periodic industry reviews and highlight the impending needs of business.

All errors and omissions remain the sole responsibility of the author.

HELPING YOU LEARN

Key features

- Highlights of functional analytics that cover components of major business areas and industries
- Focus on specific topics of human resource management, purchase, delivery, production, fulfilment, trading, investment, risk management, collections, marketing, audits, retail stores, etc.
- Concrete use cases with step-by-step calculations and detailed interpretations
- Discussion of common issues in implementation
- Sample field data to illustrate business analytics at work

End-of-chapter resources

- Summary and key questions
- Examples
- Test questions
- Selected bibliography

End-of-book resources

- Appendixes with sample data
- Glossary with definition of terms

ABBREVIATIONS

B2B	business to business
B2C	business to customer
CAR	capital adequacy ratio
ELS	economic level of stocking
EOQ	economic order quantity
ER	exchange ratio
FCFR	free cash flow ratio
G2B	government to business
IPO	initial public offering
IRR	internal rate of return
LBO	leverage buy-out
LLR	log likelihood ratio
MBO	management buy-out
MLE	maximum likelihood estimate
NWC	net working capital
P/E	price to earnings ratio
ROI	return on investment
ROTA	return on total assets
SKU	stocking unit

1
INTRODUCTION

Traditionally, business choices have been considered purely as an art, an erudite talent that is acquired over a period of time through experience. It has been so regarded because a variety of individual styles can be observed in the handling and successful solving of common business problems in actual businesses. However, the environment in which management must operate is more complex and fast changing. This calls for driving the art of business processes by scientific and objective methods. A theoretical and methodical business approach to business processes is necessary because today's business environments are far more intricate and heterogeneous than in the past and because the cost of making errors is far too high. Conventional tools are intuitional and judgmental so long as they rely on individual opinions. Common sense may be misleading, and snap judgments may have painful consequences. The conviction of individual opinions is strengthened by using business analytics to avoid the repercussions of costly errors across the enterprise. Therefore, the business problem can be articulated well by collecting relevant facts, by experimenting with potentially fruitful alternatives, and by implementing disruption.

Plan of the book

As the title suggests, this book is an introduction to business analytics and a theoretical aid to business decision making. Descriptions of business problems, important analytical techniques that can be deployed by managers in business situations, and the results of alternatives are embodied in the text of this book. There are ten chapters in this book, which are arranged in accordance with the functional depth of learning. Chapter 2 is devoted to describing business roles in an organization and presents an overview of the variety and levels of functional consumers of analytics, their end uses, and the hierarchical relationships of their consumption and intensity. Chapter 3 focuses on the aspects of functional analytics and the nature, intensity, engagement, periodicity, and strategic benefits that a business derives from using each of the independent components of functional analytics. Chapters 4 through 8 cover four major and critical functional areas in analytics that are suitable for businesses. Businesses may adopt one or all of the domains of analytics mentioned in Chapters 4 through 8. For example Chapter 4 starts with a detailed discussion on human resources analytics, which covers the "people" element of an organization, including employee life cycle, performance, and retention; talent management, rewards and compensation, and satisfaction. Chapter 5 covers supply chains and e-financial supply chains in business, with a special emphasis on inventory, distribution, working capital, stock planning, demand planning, and a plethora of inquiries around procurement cycles of a business. Chapter 6 covers customer analytics for a business, which encompasses details about customer acquisition, product holding, cross-selling, satisfaction, lifetime value, retention, and the customer resolution aspects of the business. Chapter 7 covers business processes that are critical for the smooth functioning of the business, such as operations, branches, campaigns, sales, marketing, quality, IT services, service resolutions, and re-engineering, which are applicable across both the service and manufacturing industries. Chapter 8 elaborates on financial analytics and on a host of tools around measuring the incremental financial impact of business decisions, such as pricing, mergers-demergers, valuation, spread, liquidity, asset liability, interest rate analysis, etc., to empower modern-day managers to understand incremental value from investments. Chapter 9 is especially focused on the implementation aspects of analytics, which are aimed at the skills, generating evidence and demonstrating the utility, organizing teams and handling the hurdles preventing the implementation of analytical solutions in a business. Chapter 10 supplements the text by giving use cases with detailed reports of results and their interpretation aimed at five industrial sectors, such as banking, financial services, and insurance (BFSI), manufacturing, services, hotel chains, retail chains, etc. The Appendixes give an overview of the formulae, derivations, measures in business and statistics, and example data.

This first chapter introduces the subject of business analytics by giving simple definitions of business analytics and by also explaining the goals, characteristics, and domains of business analytics.

Business analytics

Business analytics is defined as the process of understanding the data-driven activities of a business to draw inferences to make calculated decisions with higher certainty. Business analytics encompasses a gamut of analysis around business data to draw information that could be used by the managers at various levels in an organization. Business analytics enables fact-based decision making while extending accountability in decision making. Business analytics is *defined as* the process of exploring, experimenting, simulating, and summarizing data to extract information.

With the advent of real-time warehousing and web capabilities in business systems, business analytics has evolved as a practical choice for strategic business decisions. Is there any difference between business analytics and business intelligence? Business intelligence is generic and applies to any situation of discovery using data. Business analytics goes well beyond mere presentation of data and statistics. The essence of analytics lies in the application of logic and processes to find meaning in data. Through these processes, managers create activities that define intelligence, including the ability to identify, locate, predict, relate, innovate, and learn to recommend choices, which also encompass statistical analysis. Business analytics needs drivers, leaders, or business analysts who would apply the logic and processes described here in the text. Business analytics is one portion or component of business intelligence. Conventional data warehousing and reporting ends at the stage of report delivery. Business analytics extends through the value-added knowledge stage, which in turn supports decisions and makes life easier for businesses. Hence, business analytics measures the results that are produced and provides a feedback loop that facilitates organizational learning. With its ever-increasing popularity, business analytics has become more important and useful to a business manager.

Goals of business analytics

Business analytics encompasses the entire key informational and decisional attributes of any business, and it is vitally important that business analytics features in the overall strategic vision of all businesses.

The major goals of business analytics include:

- Providing real-time, actionable information aimed at superior business decision making.
- Providing tools at all levels of an organization to help decision making around customer goals and profits while comparing performance.
- Providing analysis that helps the business forecast the future with greater objectivity and accuracy.
- Providing the insight and understanding to support informed decisions and confident actions and providing the feedback that is needed to create a learning organization.

The following characteristics of business analytics identify its uniqueness:

- *Purposive:* Business analytics needs to purposefully know why we make deliveries and perform the analytics. The understanding derived from analysis must align with business functions (finance, marketing, sales, etc.) and with the issues and objectives of management (performance, growth, compliance, risk, profitability, etc.).
- *Intuitive:* Business analytics are insightful, and they help uncover new facts or information and help managers become aware of previously hidden patterns.

Cause-and-effect association is often the most valuable in business decision making. Analytics that simply confirm the status quo or reaffirm conventional wisdom offer no insight.
- *Expedient:* An expedient output or action plan makes an application doable and possible, which means a business manager should be able to act upon the recommendations of an insight.

Domains of business analytics

Domains refer to the variety of activities within a business. The business analytics is built around (but not limited to) the following analytical domains:

- Human resource analytics
- Supply chain analytics
- Customer analytics
- Business processes analytics
- Financial analytics

Human resource analytics is defined as the analysis of human resources (employees), which embodies the entire life cycle of an employee, such as recruitment, managing performance, incentives, and employee engagement. Using the right metrics can improve policies and procedures, increase team members' satisfaction and retention, focus employee training and support, improve morale, reduce costs, and increase productivity. The activities impacted by human capital involve recruitment, training, employee relationships, employee satisfaction, and turnover.

Supply chain analytics refers to the analysis of a firm's delivery processes, which includes acquisition of vendors, the sourcing of factors, inventory analytics, transportation and customer delivery network efficiency, vendor management, and sourcing efficiency. The baseline for strategic sourcing initiatives is as an enabler for process improvement. Further, supply chain analytics is a measurement device for cost-reduction programs, providing comprehensive spend visibility of both direct and indirect expenses on commodities and services, significant cost-saving opportunities through supplier and commodity consolidation and enhanced compliance through effective spend and supplier monitoring.

Customer analytics is an understanding of customers, the customer life cycle, their product needs, and customer satisfaction. Customer analytics is the systematic interpretation of a business's customer information to retain profitable customers and proactively build relationships with them. Customer behavioural analysis seeks to identify and weigh the relative importance of the factors customers use to choose one product over another. Customer profiling is a tool that helps business better understand customers so they can increase sales and grow their business. Customer profiles can also help develop targeted marketing plans and ensure that products meet the needs of their intended audience. By understanding the variables that influence individual decisions, businesses are more able to influence their outcome. Customer decision making will rely heavily on considerations using individuals as the unit of analysis.

Business process analytics refers to the activity flows of product or service deliveries within an organization to improve processes and productivity. Much of what will follow in this chapter will reply on the systems perspectives on the decision-making process described in Figure 1.1.

Financial analytics is defined as the analysis of the financial impact of business analytics. One aspect of financial analytics is the opportunity of working with net (final) figures, which are derived after taxes, duties, levies and penalties, or capital charges are charged to the business. It embodies the versatility of the risks of doing business and also translates such risks to net turnout. Financial analytics enables business to maintain cash flow, spread and liquidity; manage pricing value acquisitions; control investments in new products and working capital; and plan funds and directed investments. Improving financial performance and expense control, through organized monitoring of expenses, drives profitability across business units, geographic locations, products, or channels.

Therefore, the flavours of analytics encompass both simple buy-and-sell decisions in a treasury and larger buy-and-sell decisions, i.e. for valuations in a corporate merger and in an acquisition. Therefore, business choices are driven by goals that are set by top management (e.g. chief experience officers [CXOs] or the board of directors [BOD]), and functional managers, including the agents (e.g. analysts), act upon a tactical situation to freeze on a choice. Newer choices are generated

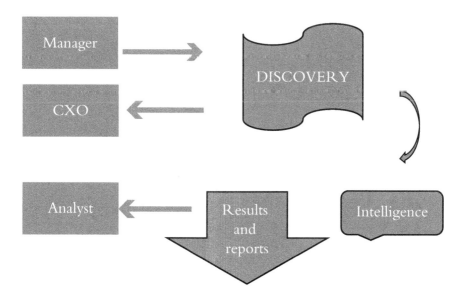

FIGURE 1.1 Choice-making process in business organizations

when a fixed set of choices do not suffice to fulfil the given goals, which is an iterative process, and this requires exchange transfer of information among all three. Discovering a feasible choice will be implemented only when it is visualized by CXOs, and hence the process of decision making is well understood in the context of a system shown in Figure 1.1. The onus of action lies with the agents, and whether they have acted successfully or not is displayed from the results and reports.

Tables 1.1 and 1.2 summarize the contours of business analytics and the engagement map of business analytics. The contours shown in Table 1.1 present the principal goals of a given type of analytics, which are no different from the goals of the business. Each type of analytics will ensure skilled teams comprising of personnel to attain primarily the goals of analytics (e.g. HR, marketing, finance, etc.), which in aggregate condenses to a larger business goal. This means the alignment of analytics' focus should be in tune with the target goals of business, and in no situation is the period of review or the maturity of the impact or the investment unmatched with the strategy.

Table 1.2 presents the engagement map of analytics by describing individual components in each analytics type (e.g. sourcing, retention, sales force, etc.) and the associated benefits to end users. End users could be internal or external to the business, and this simplifies the justification of the rationale for investments in people, resources, processes, data infrastructure, and support systems, which will hold the foundation of analytical competency within the business. Somewhere or another, the business gets sufficient reason to build a newer value proposition for its stakeholders, such as customers, suppliers, employees, regulators, or others.

TABLE 1.1 Contours of business analytics

Analytics	Objectives
Human resource analytics	To gain focus on employee engagement, deployment, performance evaluation and attrition management
Supply chain analytics	To manage cost savings with better sourcing by allocating sourcing channels to superior performance tasks
Customer analytics	To manage the customer life cycle, customer intelligence, customer service and satisfaction
Business processes analytics	To drive the business processes to deliver quality under timeliness with superior performance targets on collections, credit underwriting, production, conversion, machining, seasoning and so on
Financial analytics	To measure the financial impact of business decisions such as pricing, mergers and demergers, valuation, spread, liquidity, asset liability, interest rate management, etc. to empower modern-day managers to understand the incremental value of investments

TABLE 1.2 Engagement map of business analytics

Analytics type	Purpose
Human resource analytics	Managing human capital
Employee performance	Managing employee performance
Staffing and scheduling	Managing employee productivity
Supply chain analytics	Managing supply networks better
Sourcing analytics	Vendor management
Supplier rating	Vendor risk management
Inventory analytics	Inventory management
Customer analytics	Unified customer value management
New business and acquisition	New portfolio management
Business process analytics	Resilience, response and agility of delivery
Collections and recovery analytics	Recovery management
Risk analytics	Risk management
Marketing analytics	Marketing process
Portfolio analytics	Business management
Sales analytics	Sales planning and sales force management
Spatial analytics	Accuracy and timeliness in delivery
Channel analytics	Improve channel efficiency and return on investments and brand equity

In each of these domains, the following relevant thoughts are explored to achieve the goals outlined:

- What does the analytics imply for or impact on the business?
- What do the results of the analytics indicate for the manager responsible on the ground?
- Is analytics validated?
- Does analytics comply with the values of the company?
- Should analytics be used independently or in conjunction with other related aspects?

Applied questions

Which of the domains of business analytics is the most appropriate for ensuring "people" strength in a business? What are the engagement areas for satisfying such needs in a business?

The people in a business form its human capital and are the regular employees of the business who provide the strength and contribute to meeting the business goals mandated by top management. The focus of people management aims at human resources analytics, and the suggested areas of engagement are staffing, scheduling, employee productivity, etc. The distinct focus of engagement can ensure the completeness in achieving the "people" goals of a business.

References

Amaral, L.A.N., and B. Uzzi. (2007). Complex Systems – A New Paradigm for the Integrative Study of Management, Physical, and Technological Systems. *Management Science, 53*(7): 1033–1035.

Bartlett, R. (2013). *A Practitioner's Guide to Business Analytics: Using Data Analysis Tools to Improve Your Organization's Decision Making and Strategy.* New York: McGraw-Hill.

Davenport, T.H. (2007). *Competing on Analytics.* Cambridge, MA: Harvard Business School Press.

Gummesson, E. (2002). *Total Relationship Control.* Boston, MA: Butterworth-Heinemann.

Jacobides, M.G. (2007). The Inherent Limits of Organizational Structure and the Unfulfilled Role of Hierarchy: Lessons from a Near-War. *Organization Science, 18*(3): 455–477.

Lewis, M. (2004). *Moneyball: The Art of Winning an Unfair Game.* New York: W.W. Norton & Co.

Lim, M., G. Griffiths, and S. Sambrook. (2010). Organizational Structure for the Twenty-First Century. Presented the annual meeting of the Institute for Operations Research and the Management Sciences, Austin, Texas.

McDonald, M., and T. Nunno. (2007). *Creating Enterprise Leverage: The 2007 CIO Agenda.* Stamford, CT: Gartner, Inc.

Miles, R.E., and C.C. Snow. (1992, Summer). Causes of Failure in Network Organizations, *California Management Review, 28*: 62–73.

Pugh, D.S., ed. (1990). *Organization Theory: Selected Readings.* Harmondsworth, UK: Penguin.

Ranadive, V. (2006). *The Power to Predict: How Real Time Businesses Anticipate Customer Needs, Create Opportunities, and Beat the Competition.* New York: McGraw-Hill.

Robbins, S.F., and T.A. Judge. (2007). *Organizational Behavior.* 12th ed. New York: Pearson Education Inc.

Stubbs, E. (July 2011). *The Value of Business Analytics.* Hoboken, NJ: John Wiley & Sons.

Thareja, P. (2007). A Total Quality Organisation thru' People: Each One Is Capable. Retrieved from www.foundry-planet.com.

Zabin, J., and G. Brebach. (2004). *Precision Marketing.* Hoboken, NJ: John Wiley.

2
BUSINESS ROLES

This chapter describes various roles in a business organization and how each of these roles demands analytics. It is critical to understand the roles and responsibilities of business functionaries and kinds of engagement, which determine their intensity of use. This would help determine the requirements of a kind of analytics that is purposive, intuitive, and expedient.

Who consumes analytics?

Business analytics involves three major levels of users in an organization. These three levels are actually based on whether the user is the front-end user, a middle or back office worker, or a senior or top management user. Front-end users are called Level 1 users here, and they are the first group of users who actually need and gather real-time, first-hand information from the business to make routine decisions and take the necessary action onsite for any given incident or transaction. These users actually need the capability to see both customer transaction-level and portfolio-level information. Level 2 users need and gather information, which is processed with the input and a combination of the information gathered at the first level. This information is also used for periodic planning and is more tactical and strategic in nature. Level 3 users demand information that is strategic in nature and is needed to assess the strengths of the organization and also to look at the time ahead. However, certain information measures (e.g. daily balance changes at account levels) are confidential in nature, and some Level 1 or Level 2 users may not have access.

Details of consumer analytics include their daily, periodic, and ad hoc reporting requirements, which are described in subsequent sections. The nature of required analytics would vary by periodicity.

TABLE 2.1 Business roles in analytics: first-level users

Designation	Key responsibility	Analysis needs
Operations/technical/engineering manager	Monitor processes ensure that all operations are handled. Work planning for the entire unit, keeping in mind shift rotation.	Functional metrics
Customer fulfillment manager	Ensure the delivery of the transaction happens at the end of the customer transaction in a successful manner and to the satisfaction of the customer.	Delivery metrics
Quality manager	Responsible for ensuring good service to the branch customers. Benchmark turnaround times (TATs) on servicing. Implement best practices. Develop and implement a service plan. Communicate service initiatives and expectations to staff.	Quality metrics
Relationship manager	Achieving the business targets assigned in terms of cross-selling and enhancing and upgrading relationships. Ensure the highest levels of service to the customers. Serve as one point of contact for all requirements of customers in servicing of customers. Initiates and recommends corrective action including redressing grievances/issues as required.	Relationship metrics
Branch area manager	Manage branch operations and all functions within the branch area including staffing, procuring, delivery, sales, operations and channels.	Branch-level metrics
Unit manager/supervisor	Manage unit operations, staffing, scheduling, time study, motion study, etc. Serve as the first level supervisor to ensure the transactions are individually accounted for by respective representatives.	Unit level metrics

Daily: Shorter-term information generated within 24 hours that typically involves new products, compliance, new employees, promotional campaigns, and the like. The viewers are scattered over many locations of a business and have a big stake in the accuracy and timeliness of such information.

Weekly: Short-term information generated within 5 working days that typically involves sales cycle, quality, transportation, procurement, new teams, sales force, campaigns, and the like. This information may be shared internally for review meetings or status updates and may be escalated to Level 2 and higher.

Bi-weekly: Medium-term, analytical insights that involve longer-cycle sales, procurement, sourcing, recruitment, IT services, project evaluations, new business and branch operations, etc. This information may be shared internally for review meetings or status updates and may be transmitted downwards with suggested actions for agents.

Monthly: Period analytical outputs that are required for internal compliance, review, or external consumption across multiple levels within the company. It involves a whole gamut of products, campaigns, teams, and functions with richer information to help managers stay on their toes. Managers demand such analysis to be delivered systematically whether they decide to recommend the findings to agents or escalate to superiors internally. Therefore, monthly analytical outputs are the most needed and circulated pieces throughout the company. They ensure validation of evidence pointed to in analysis by employees within the business.

TABLE 2.2 Business roles in analytics: second-level users

Designation	*Key responsibility*	*Analysis needs*
Sales managers	Conceptualizing and creating a sales channel to deliver and distribute products across one or more regions. Deliver annual target goals while meeting qualitative metrics laid down by the regional head/product. Work with operations unit in each market to seamlessly drive business. Function as the primary coordinator and the one point of contact for customers.	New business metrics
Product managers	Overall responsibility for product planning, product positioning, product development, pricing strategy and structure for the relevant products. Managing new developments and enhancements to the current product line to meet market demands.	New business metrics
Campaign managers	Launch campaigns as per the specifications of the product manager and ensure successful delivery of campaign working with vendors and also preparing and communicating campaign tracking results.	Campaign metrics
Retention managers	Retain customers, obtain attrition alerts. Work with product manager planning retention offers, provide retention P&Ls. Identify causes of attrition and improve customer satisfaction levels.	Retention metrics
Financial analysts/ accounts and finance officers	Financial analysis of existing and new businesses. Assess the health of business portfolio.	Financial metrics

12 Business roles

Ad hoc: Engagement of a team of analysts to undertake a focused, specific, impromptu, and instinctive project, possibly without any planning. For example, an assignment to figure out the seasonality in customer returns in the past 12 months for a particular model of a product. The team may not be able to cover this for all customers handled by the business since it will be time consuming. The team will need a stratified random sample (e.g. a pilot sample) to churn an analysis and share the findings. Many times, the success of ad hoc analytical engagements has resulted in sustainable competency in near future and also the design of period analytical outputs.

The first-level users include:

- Channel sales managers
- Field sales managers
- Operations managers
- Unit managers
- Branch managers
- Supervisors
- Relationship managers
- Team leaders

TABLE 2.3 Business roles in analytics: third-level users

Designation	Key responsibility	Analysis
Heads of service	Establish and communicate customer service goals across the cluster and manage service officers	Customer service metrics
Marketing communications officers	Design creatives and obtain feedback on creatives from campaign managers	Creative metrics
Chief financial officer	Manage the financial health of the organization and board members	Financial analysis
Legal (compliance) officers	Customer/employee profile by gender, race, location, age, product processing, and environmental compliance; Norms and social responsibilities	Legal compliance metrics
Corporate strategy officers	Strategic objectives of the business; long-term directions	Strategic metrics
Business heads	Manage the overall value and net worth of the company	Strategic metrics
Chief marketing officers	Communications and branding, market planning, product management and partnership operations	Marketing campaign, new business metrics
Chief sales officers	Head of sales	New business analysis
Chief risk officers	Head of compliance, credit risks, market risk, operation risk, and other risks	Credit and enterprise risk analysis

The second-level users include:

- Sales managers
- Purchase officers
- Marketing managers
- Pricing analysts
- Product managers
- Accountants
- Campaign managers
- Marketing/pricing analysts
- Financial analysts

The third-level users include:

- Heads of service
- Chief financial officers
- Chief risk officers
- Legal officers
- Strategy officers
- Business heads

Applied questions

Business users in a company may find it hard to distinguish between the urgency and frequency of conducting supplier analysis to satisfy the periodic and ad hoc needs of the middle and top management for the procurement verticals in the business.

The first-level users interested in supply function include:

- Operations managers
- Unit managers

The second-level users include:

- Purchase officers
- Financial analysts

The third-level users include:

- Chief financial officers
- Strategy officers
- Business heads

Table 2.4 shows measures of interest for the three groups.

TABLE 2.4 Business roles and reporting requirements

Real-time	Level
Daily	Level 1
Weekly	Level 1
Bi-weekly	Level 2
Monthly	Level 2 and Level 3
Ad hoc	Level 3

References

Boje, D. M., R. P. Gephert Jr., and T. J. Thatchenkery, eds. (1996). *Post-Modern Management and Organization Theory*. Thousand Oaks, CA: Sage.

Cherrington, D. J. (1994). *Organizational Behavior: The Management of Individual and Organizational Performance*. Boston, MA: Allyn and Bacon.

Galbraith, J. R. (1994). *Competing with Flexible Lateral Organizations*. 2nd ed. Reading, MA: Addison-Wesley.

Gortner, H. F., J. Mahler, and J. B. Nicholson. (1997). *Organization Theory: A Public Perspective*. 2nd ed. Orlando, FL: Harcourt.

Hamilton, J. D. (1994). *Time Series Analysis*. Princeton, NJ: Princeton University Press.

Harris, D. (2012). Like Your Data Big? How about 5 Trillion Records? Gigaom.com. Retrieved from https://gigaom.com/2012/01/04/like-your-data-big-how-about-5-trillion-records/.

Hatch, M. J. (2006). *Organization Theory: Modern, Symbolic, and Postmodern Perspectives*. New York: Oxford University Press.

Hull, J. C. (1997). *Options, Futures, and Other Derivatives*. New York: Prentice Hall.

Madsen, L. (2012). *Healthcare Business Intelligence: A Guide to Empowering Data Reporting and Analytics*. Hoboken, NJ: John Wiley and Sons.

Pfeffer, J. (1997). *New Directions for Organization Theory: Problems and Prospects*. New York: Oxford University Press.

3
FUNCTIONAL ANALYTICS

This chapter provides a foundation in the functional components of business analytics and presents an overview of business analytics with brief descriptions for business managers. Many managers responsible for building strategy underestimate the importance of operational information for achieving strategic outcomes. Sales, logistics, customer service agents, field agents, and marketing representatives make decisions all the time, and the quality, accuracy, and timelines of those decisions have vital consequences for the business. When operational decisions are interwoven into strategic actions, they generate synergy towards the growth of the business. This brief outline of functional analytics will be elaborated upon with the specific uses of functional analytics that can be interwoven with strategic choices.

Definition

Functional analytics comprise the components of business areas that drive the critical functions of a business, including human resources (HR), production, fulfilment, trading, treasury, purchase, delivery, risk management, collections, marketing, audits, stores, finance, etc. These functions enable the greater need for a corporation to meet its business goals and provide both the foundation and pillars of strength for the business.

Types of functional analytics

Table 3.1 provides an engagement map showing the wide variety of functional analytics with end user benefits for various business roles. Analytics is an elaboration of the analysis type that is identified for that sub-function. The list of analytics mentioned here conforms to a given domain or sub-domain of functional analytics and therefore is mapped to analytics that benefit the end user.

16 Functional analytics

TABLE 3.1 Types of functional analytics

Analytics type	Analytics	End user benefit
Human resource analytics	Retention, compensation, reward analysis	Manage human capital
Employee performance	Vintage, performance appraisal, attrition, efficiency	Manage employee performance
Staffing and scheduling	Bench size, growth, deployment, utilization, allocation	Manage employee productivity
Supply chain analytics	Sourcing, supplier rating, working capital, inventory, transport and transshipment	Manage supply networks better
Sourcing analytics	Best buy analysis, savings due to auction, spend	Vendor management
Supplier rating	Vendor scoring, quality	Vendor management
Inventory analytics	Economic order quantity, lead time	Inventory management
Customer analytics	Engagement mix of customers	Unified customer value management
New business and acquisition	Scanning and locating eligible targets, health check of new business	New portfolio management
Business process analytics	Servicing, lead times, cycle time, unit costs, risks in enterprise, compliance	Resilience, response, and agility of delivery
Collections and recovery analytics	Rolls, delinquency, write-offs	Recovery management
Risk analytics	Delinquency, default and capital reserves	Risk management
Marketing analytics	Campaigns, offers, and new products	Marketing
Portfolio analytics	Portfolio churning	Business management
Sales analytics	Win–loss, lead analysis, sales force effectiveness	Sales planning and sales force management
Spatial analytics	Geo-positioning, minimal distance, circular time, best location for business centres	Accuracy and timeliness in delivery
Channel analytics	Differences across channels and migration towards value adding or alternate channels	Improve channel efficiency and return on investments and brand equity

Uses of functional analytics

The most common and expected functional benefits of deploying functional analytics do impact related aspects of the business, such as better design of portfolios, better understanding of consumer behaviour, responding to changes in consumer tastes more quickly, product portfolio optimization, intervening to prevent employee attrition, and re-negotiating with suppliers against changed marketplaces. Top benefits that could also be derived include efficient choice making, better alignment of available resources with short-term business goals, realizing cost savings, meeting user needs, etc. Meeting regulatory compliance and sharing information with external users (e.g. customers and suppliers) are also enabled. To simplify the variety of impacts that are sustained, the business can mainly reduce costs, improve the bottom line, and manage risk. When decision making is automatically delegated and transferred downwards, the benefits of transparency, simplicity, and a unified picture is made available to all users in a company. To make these possible, companies need to invest in functional infrastructure by creating specialized divisions with competencies that provide core analytics as a managed service to the rest of the business. Such outcome measures capture the extent to which a problem exists and should provide an indication of the extent to which actions taken by the business are successful. A more effective approach is to start with the problems or opportunities faced by the organization and develop an understanding of what information is likely to be useful. An understanding of these problems permits organizations to determine effectively the analytics that are most likely to be useful in improving organizational effectiveness. The difference in these two approaches is dramatic. The latter is targeted at specific decisions situations while the former does not have this focus.

Uses of human resources analytics

The core functions of HR include the management of the workforce, acquiring, developing, remunerating, and retaining their productivity. A manpower planner assesses the headcount level and turnover trends so that workforce capacity can be forecasted. Managers can factor in workforce compensation and vary the workforce cost structure, building an efficient, cost-effective, and scalable recruiting process. A talent manager can assess skills and experience levels and organizational strengths and weaknesses and can ensure engagement. The HR strategist can determine the top performers and identify their training needs. Correlating employee pay with employee performance, or employee pay with employee retention, and joining bonuses to attract new hires are choices that can be exercised by managers. Thus, managers can predict the effect of compensation on retention and performance and prepare the business towards higher market power.

The modern-day challenges for HR managers are:

- Higher salary expectations
- Lack of security
- Lack of social interaction
- Monotonous work
- Unusual working hours
- Pressure to perform

This has led to disillusioned employees, stress, and lack of motivation; substandard performance; uncongenial organizational cultures; and mystified career paths. A workforce could be segregated into four categories, namely the *disgruntled*, who are highly involved but demotivated individuals; *performers*, who are highly involved and highly motivated individuals; *laggards*, who are uninvolved but highly motivated employees; and the *detached*, who are uninvolved and demotivated employees. The degree of difficulty in satisfying all four groups of employees varies a lot and so do the incentives. Therefore, a business needs well-chosen incentives that can transform the disgruntled and the laggards more than others.

Uses of supply chain analytics

Businesses need to manage their business operations, delivery, and fulfilments cost-effectively, so that they meet their revenue and profitability targets. Managers need to visualize the key factors of production costs, inventory management, customer operations and total overheads, etc. To add greater value to the customer, a business need not refrain from providing widely diversified goods and services to its customers as a one-stop shop that adds to the simplicity of the supply chain. The supply chain is dependent on functional units, such as the manufacturing (assembly) unit, which desires longer product conversion cycles and the lowest procurement costs. Marketing prefers a finished goods inventory and a wide variety of offerings to the customer. Larger batch sizes of a product will reduce the set-up costs, and assortments increase inventory costs. The allocation of various types of inventories in supply chains is the critical goal of a manager. Shortage costs and inventory holding costs are to be measured and considered for planning. This ensures no loss of customers due to inappropriate stock levels. It involves engaging suppliers,

TABLE 3.2 Uses of human resources analytics

Compensation	*Bonus and reward*
Attrition	Stock option
Talent management	Promotion
Recruitment	Job rotation and engagement
Re-hiring	Employee satisfaction
Performance appraisal	Benefit administration

TABLE 3.3 Uses of supply chain analytics

Working capital	*Cost reduction*
Inventory	Responsive supply chain
Manufacturing size	Safety stock
Distribution	E-finance
Customization	Planning
Vendor scoring	Outsourcing

distributors, and customers to improve efficiency. Few critical areas of order management, supply returns, channels, and customer category, sales divisions, and destinations are attended to. Supply chains are not specific to manufacturing, and a business by itself could be a pure trading and distribution company rather than a producer and a distributor.

Uses of customer analytics

Customers feel empowered, which businesses cannot afford to forgo. Businesses put a lot of effort into getting to know their customers as well as possible. Businesses should derive *full 360-degree views of their customers across all channels* and a strategy for accessing and integrating customer footprints, devising a strategy to anticipate customer behaviour, and respond proactively with the design of suitable offerings to cross-sell or upgrade from a base vanilla offer to a superior experience. *Accuracy in targeting customers* can be enhanced by customizing campaigns and engagements and by tailoring the timing and content for customers, since supply chain response refers to the ability of the complete supply chain to react to changes in the market, which can be quantified by the ability, speed, and extent of adaptations. For example, upside production flexibility can be determined by the number of days needed to adapt to an unexpected 20% growth in demand. Resolving issues with customer complaints and designing products towards a more intensive marketing function are plausible. There are no options for the businesses to make premium gains, but no stones should remain unturned to doubly satisfy a customer. The product life cycle is critical and is imparted by brand awareness, conversion and activation, product loyalty, revenue per customer, channel costs per customer, cross-selling, customer satisfaction, churn and lifetime value, etc.

Uses of business process analytics

Business process analytics is a process that champions new ways of acquiring insights into an enterprise's business processes, which may cut across employee processes, supplier processes, customer processes, IT processes, the core activity of production, conversion, delivery, and fulfilment. The principal uses include new businesses and acquisitions analytics, which gives the general performance of new businesses and

TABLE 3.4 Uses of customer analytics

Customer acquisition	*Promotion strategy*
Marketing mix	Branding
Customer retention	Pricing strategy
Social media	Service strategy
Segmentation	Product strategy
New product development	Multi-channel and digital marketing

TABLE 3.5 Uses of business process analytics

Collection	Workforce planning
Marketing	Scheduling
Conversion	Operations management
Failure analysis	Forecasting
Campaign management	Simulation

insight into them, and risk analytics, which is key to the credit approval process and provides insight into new account profiles. Similarly, collections analytics involves various stages of delinquency. Fraud operations analytics is how fraud engines detect business fraud and fraud rate at the point of interception and includes the sources of recovery due to employee, customer, supplier, or third party fraud. Marketing analytics provides the better control of sales force effectiveness, sales efficiency and sales incentive design, sales planning, new product design, and forecasting. Campaign operations analytics includes campaign performance, campaign efficiency, profitability, sourcing, and campaign life cycles for the business. Business processes that can be explained in a few key repetitive activities can lead to the evaluation of business process analytics, which makes the task of the manager simpler than ever. For example, a few dials on a car's dashboard can reveal many invisible quandaries with the car's components.

Uses of financial analytics

Businesses may face increased pressure to grow revenues while holding costs under control. This means ensuring that money spent on marketing, acquisitions, sales, and customer service will return the best possible results. Traditional accounting managers do monitor routine financial performance, analyze financial statements, conduct audits, and compare them to budgets. Financial analytics enables business to maintain cash flow, spread, and liquidity; manage pricing value acquisitions; control investments in new products, working capital; and plan funds and directed investments. Improving financial performance and expense control can be through the organized monitoring of expenses, driving profitability across business units, geographic locations, products, and channels. It also drives the investment analysis of the firm, which could be for short-term, long-term, strategic, or inorganic growth drives. A spin-off or the resale of assets may effectively minimize the weighted average cost of capital, etc. Routine financial statements, which are prepared for regulatory and internal reporting, are much simpler than a confounding, dimensional view of final (netted) output, which a business must attempt to collate. A much larger use is the essential worthiness the business provides to shareholders, lenders, and society at large.

TABLE 3.6 Uses of financial analytics

Fund management	Costing
Weighted average cost of capital	Mergers
Liquidity analysis	Demergers
Cash flow forecasting	Credit risk
Risk management	Economic capital
Compliance	Spread

Applied questions

What is functional analytics, and what is its importance? How will the business end user benefit from sales planning?

Functional analytics is defined as the components of business areas that drive the critical functions of a business and includes people, operations, procurement, customers, and regulators. It is important because it enables core excellence in HR, production, fulfilment, trading, treasury, purchase, delivery, risk management, collections, marketing, audits, stores, finance, etc. It is easy to achieve sales planning by deploying activities that result in better and efficient sales outcomes such as win–loss analysis, lead generation, and sales force effectiveness, which are elements of the sales cycle.

References

Boje, D. M., R. P. Gephert Jr., and T. J. Thatchenkery, eds. (1996). *Post-Modern Management and Organization Theory*. Thousand Oaks, CA: SAGE.
Cherrington, D. J. (1994). *Organizational Behavior: The Management of Individual and Organizational Performance*. Boston, MA: Allyn and Bacon.
Davenport, T., J. Harris, and J. Shapiro (2010). Competing on Talent Analytics. *Harvard Business Review*, 88(10), 52–58.
Galbraith, J. R. (1994). *Competing with Flexible Lateral Organizations*. 2nd ed. Reading, MA: Addison-Wesley.
Gortner, H. F., J. Mahler, and J. B. Nicholson. (1997). *Organization Theory: A Public Perspective*. 2nd ed. Orlando, FL: Harcourt.
Hamilton, J. D. (1994). *Time Series Analysis*. Princeton, NJ: Princeton University Press.
Harris, D. (2012). Like Your Data Big? How about 5 Trillion Records? Gigaom.com. Retrieved from https://gigaom.com/2012/01/04/like-your-data-big-how-about-5-trillion-records/.
Hatch, M. J. (1997). *Organization Theory: Modern, Symbolic, and Postmodern Perspectives*. Oxford: Oxford University Press.
Hull, J. C. (1997). *Options, Futures, and Other Derivatives*. New York: Prentice Hall.
Madsen, L. (2012). *Healthcare Business Intelligence: A Guide to Empowering Data Reporting and Analytics*. Hoboken, NJ: John Wiley and Sons.
Pfeffer, J. (1997). *New Directions for Organization Theory: Problems and Prospects*. New York: Oxford University Press.

4
HUMAN RESOURCE ANALYTICS

This chapter describes human resource analytics by presenting a whole gamut of analysis that is widely used across the various functions and sub-functions of human resource units.

Human resource analytics is defined as the analytics of human resources (employees), which includes the entire life cycle of employees such as hiring, engaging, managing performance, and developing incentives and strategies for employee retention. It empowers HR managers to be conversant with the idiosyncrasies of teams, which may be built upon people at multi-location workplaces. In a retail chain, a "customer-first" program was increasing overall store revenue, but it was not working in a few stores. Similarly, a new leadership program at a travel company was gender specific and working only for men. A new induction program showed an increase in initial performance, but the benefit rapidly disappeared after the first 6 months. An automobile giant's new customer care centre training program successfully increased sales but also increased per-customer handling time. The turnover at an IT company was concerning to business leaders, who found that the high turnover could be broken down into "desirable" or "undesirable" to justify the warning bells of attrition, etc. Therefore, HR analytics can go a long way toward sensitizing people towards building upon employee relations and creating an employee-centric organization. Table 4.1 provides the engagement map of HR analytics, and Table 4.2 describes the nature of engagement in HR by audience.

The key questions around employee analytics include:

- How can one manage employee performance?
- How can one optimize deployment and staffing?
- How can one manage employee attrition and engagement?
- How should one provide for employee incentives?

- How do employees rate their satisfaction with their jobs?
- How many hours did employees spend sitting in training classes?
- How does the benefit administration compare vis-à-vis employee performance?
- What is employee productivity?
- How many accidents occur, and how much time is lost due to safety issues?

There is no definite and single answer to all these questions. Further, one should not attempt to find separate answers to these questions on a standalone basis. Managers must find a reasonably standard, unified approach to solve problems within a

TABLE 4.1 Engagement map of human resource analytics

Type of human resource analytics	Brief description	Audience
Appraisal analytics	Characterize the distribution of in-house talent and drill down to the causes of high performance vs. low performance	Chief people officer (CPO)
Employee reward	Objectively driven reward score for an employee irrespective of his/her location or role, where the reward is an incentive linked to the last appraisal. A promotion to the next level is translated into the cash equivalent cost of reward.	Chief human resources officer staff (CHRO)
Talent inventory	The new hires for all skills and the top deciles of existing employees. These belong to the segment of employees who fulfilled the listed skills and achieved maximum scores in their roles.	Chief people officer (CPO) staff
Involuntary attrition	Bottom performers or the last decile of existing employees for whom PIP cannot be recommended because skill gaps not met are flushed.	Chief people officer (CPO)

TABLE 4.2 Nature of engagement

Type	Audience
Appraisal analytics	Managers
Employee reward	CPO
Talent inventory	CPO
Involuntary attrition	CPO

few dimensions. A categorical answer is preferred. However, conditional opinions are more desirable where the advantages prevail. For example, when it comes to attrition, it may not be worthwhile to look at attrition just by products or clusters or periods of acquisitions, but attrition should be visualized against the profitability segment, the usage segment, or the financial viability segment to which the employee belongs.

The next few sections succinctly describe a series of people processes that could be used as significant differentiators of human resources functions.

Workforce planning

Workforce planning streamlines employee-related operations day by day such as work schedules and employee hours, the distribution of skilled and semi-skilled workers among units, identifying functional needs and hiring new workers to meet those needs, identifying non-value-adding tasks from value-adding ones, re-assigning workers, and ensuring workers' job satisfaction. For example, a level strategy is the manager's choice to keep the workforce constant and can vary its utilization to match the demand forecast via overtime, undertime, and vacation planning. A constant workforce can be sized at many levels, or smaller workforces can be planned for slack periods. A chase strategy could mean maximizing the utilization of the available workforce to improve upon the targets.

Attrition analysis

Employee turnover is a major phenomenon that is important to businesses. Retention is the percentage of employees remaining in the organization. Tenure, loyalty, experience levels, and average salary levels are possible drivers of attrition. There exist costs due to attrition in the form of productivity loss, business opportunity loss, service quality issues, loss of talent, and loss of expertise. Businesses need to obtain likely attrition and map it with performance appraisal scores to manage retention. The job characteristics model (Hackman 1976) focuses on the interaction between the psychological states of employees, the job characteristics that are believed to determine these states, and the attributes of individuals that determine how positively a person will respond to a complex and challenging job. A large percentage of attrition could be prevented during the hiring stage itself. Depending on the size of the company and the nature of newly recruited employees, some amount of attrition is desirable.

A few relevant questions are:

- What are the expected attrition rates by division and by unit?
- How costly is it to retain employees?
- Can one forego retention against minimized re-hiring costs, training costs, etc.?
- Can we prevent attrition by training, job rotation, or employee benefit programs?

TABLE 4.3 Attrition analysis

Voluntary termination rate	Average termination costs value
New hire turnover	Involuntary termination rate
Retention rate	Termination costs per full-time employee (FTE)
Turnover by performance rating	Turnover cost per new employee
Departure costs	Average turnover tenure

For each employee, the employee benefits score is vitally important. The benefits administration index may be calculated as the total health benefits costs for the past 12 months. Divide the result by total employee compensation for the past 12 months. A few of the critical indices covered are the voluntary termination rate, involuntary termination rate, average termination costs value, new hire turnover, retention rate, termination costs per full-time employee (FTE), turnover by performance rating, turnover cost per new employees and average turnover tenure, which are defined in the Glossary.

Employee performance management

A good performance management system needs to be based upon actually recognizing attributes of employee performance, such as vintage, time spent, engagement rate, utilization, project impact, goals versus actual results, etc. Analytics on employees' performance management reconciles the competing uses of assessment and appraisal in organizations. These analytics, with a measurement culture, could improve effectiveness.

The reasons for conducting employee appraisals are the following:

- to review past performance
- for training and development needs
- to improve current performance
- for future promotion and band movement
- for career planning decisions
- for incentives and rewards

Although performance and potential are two axes of employee appraisal, a qualitative rating scale is aptly chosen to describe their adeptness and proficiency. For example, during goal setting, the number of tasks handled and the duration of each assignment are parameters. Individual traits of responsiveness, inputs to workplace changes, satisfying a customer, and consistency in attendance are valued and make up an employee's average performance appraisal rating, employee turnaround rate, employee upgrade rate, promotion rate, average duration of promotion by band, performance appraisal participation rate, performance rating distribution, lateral mobility, promotion rate, promotion time duration by band, etc. The median

TABLE 4.4 Performance appraisal analytics

Average performance appraisal rating
Employee turnaround rate
Employee upgrade rate
Promotion rate
Average duration of promotion by band
Performance appraisal participation rate
Performance rating distribution
Lateral mobility
Promotion rate
Promotion time duration by band

shift in the performance rating of a business division across bands is a measure of improvement in talent. The rising proportion of "average" employees is a concern for the business. Alternatively, performance-rating scales of a multi-dimensional nature (5-point scales) are used with weightings for honesty, productivity, work quality, technical skills, enthusiasm, cooperation, attitude, initiative, creativity, punctuality, attendance, dependability and communication skills, etc. Table 4.4 explains these attributes, which are defined in the Glossary.

Reward management and incentive design

The design and management of reward systems for employees constitute a difficult task for HR managers. Economic and social factors present further challenges. HRM seeks to design rewards to meet the organization's strategic goals and meet the goals of individual employees. A growing need is towards the construction of an individually oriented reward rather than a group reward. Lastly, how can rewards be aligned towards performance?

Talent management and engagement

Employee engagement is defined as a stage in the work life of an employee that combines his or her commitment, pride, loyalty, and sense of responsibility to achieve an outcome that he or she has asked for. Although engagement is measured in hours, it also means the alignment of the perception of the individual with the tasks that have been assigned to them. Engagement leads to productivity only when the individual is self-motivated and supported. A number of tasks of fixed or variable duration can be assigned to employees to occupy them with opportunities to perform. Organizations realize positive outcomes from improved employee engagement such as quality, productivity, attendance, innovation, reduction in turnover, etc. A few of the measures focused on include diversity of engagement, offer fitment, depth of engagement, and duration of engagement. The definitions to each are given in the Glossary.

TABLE 4.5 Engagement analysis

Employee commitment
Employee engagement
Employee retention
Diversity of engagement
Offer fit
Depth of engagement
Duration of engagement

TABLE 4.6 Training and development

Employee satisfaction with training
Training course content breakdown
Training expense per employee
Training hours per FTE
Training hours per occurrence
Training penetration rate
Training quality
Training staff ratio
Training total compensation
Training expense rate
Training method delivery mix

Employee productivity and training

Declines in employee productivity and lack of identifying training needs add cost to the business organization. Measuring productivity is critical for organizational knowledge to pre-empt over-staffing and reduce the size of the bench. In the case of service organizations, it can lead to the successful deployment of skill sets for an upcoming project. Training culture is imbibed in a business to impart forward-looking skills to employees, which is not only intended to improve productivity in the short run but also to fight the tide of business cycles. We must align and measure training towards productivity, and competency mapping is needed to identify evolving skills to maintain competitiveness.

Compensation and benefits planning

Benefits programs are most effective in attracting, motivating, and retaining employees if they are part of a complete compensation strategy targeted for the employer's workforce. The aim is to provide meaningful benefits that aid in recruiting and retaining key employees. In a competitive market such as analytics, drawing talent requires suitable compensation design, and there exist trade-offs

TABLE 4.7 Compensation and benefit analysis

Direct compensation expense per FTE	Benefits expense per FTE
Bonus compensation rate	Benefits expense type
Bonus eligibility rate	
Bonus receipt rate	Average number of options per FTE
Overtime expense per FTE	Reimbursement (family benefits) rate
Development program participation rate	Equity incentive value per FTE
Reimbursement (tuition/professional examination) rate	Upward salary increment rate
Total compensation expense per FTE	Stock incentive participation rate

between an ideal package and realizing the desired results of the business. The three factors in compensation planning are:

- What benefits can the employer afford?
- What benefits will best attract and retain the employees needed to execute the organization's business strategy?
- What beneficial vendors provide quality and consistent products now and will continue to do so in the future?

Advantages may arise from offering new benefits beyond health, disability, life insurance plans, and retirement plans as well as stock purchases in instalments, stock options, health club memberships, pension policies that accumulate wealth, home loans, auto loans, personal loans, free family insurance, charge cards for purchases, or long-term care insurance. Which option would work best for their workforce? Local tax laws impact the design of incentives for employers, including childcare and medical expense reimbursement or flexible benefit programs to increase participation rates and reduce per capita administrative costs. The selected measures represent the business's general ability to deal with the changing requirements of its workforce and realize the potential of a talented workforce. For example, pension policies strongly influence workers' behaviours, encouraging younger workers to work longer and older workers to avoid premature retirement. Retirements are earned benefits, and hence, productivity increases with accrued retrials in a company. Businesses need to value the right workforce compensation and need to attract, retain, and engage the workforce.

Recruitment analytics

Recruitment refers to the process of sourcing skilled candidates from an internal or external source to fill a vacancy arising out of attrition or retirement. External sources include print media, consultants, online job listings, employee referrals, and social media, which do impact the average costs to the company, time

TABLE 4.8 Recruitment and induction

New position recruitment rate	Sign-on bonus expense
Recruitment source breakdown	Average time to fill
Recruitment cost per hire	Average time to start hiring
Recruitment expense	Interviewee offer rate
Referral conversion rate	Interviewee ratio
Employee referral rate	New hire satisfactory performance
Sign-on bonus expense rate	Offer acceptance rate
External hire rate	Applicant ratio

to fill, performance of new hires, cultural fit of the candidate, and type of skill. When market compensation for certain skills rises more than benchmark costs, the manager may increase the cycle time of hiring or may postpone the process. A larger population of applicants can help the HR team to draw quality hires against competitors. Using dimensional rating models, such as one with job criteria weights and interview assessment scores together, can be used to select candidates. The rating criteria may include technical skills, responsibility, analytical skills, cost consciousness, initiative, problem-solving ability, results orientation, time management, antecedent verification, etc.

Table 4.8 describes recruitment analytics, which primarily looks at measures such as time duration to fill, sourcing type, cost to company, new position recruitment rate, sign-on bonus expense, recruitment source breakdown, time to fill, recruitment cost per hire, time to start hiring, recruitment expense, interviewee offer rate, referral conversion rate, employee referral rate, new hire satisfactory performance, sign-on bonus expense rate, offer acceptance rate, external hire rate, etc. The definitions for each are given in the Glossary.

Manpower forecasting

Manpower demand is the need for skill based changes in a company that varies over projects that are executed by managers. The demand for labour tends to fluctuate enormously with the type and kind of projects. Rosenfeld and Warszawski (1993) point out that, even with the pace of technology and automation implemented in industries, a large portion of labour demand continues to prevail even in the construction industry, for example, regarding building methods, complexity of projects, number of project sites, and the demand for professional knowledge and management skills. The determinants of labour demand, therefore, includes project cost, project type, pre-fabrication, mechanization or automation, material cost, E&M services, project management skills, project size, physical conditions of the construction site, coordination between the design and construction team, etc. Table 4.9 provides estimates of manpower demand for major skill types undertaken for construction industry. It provides parameter estimates for each of the project variables, which could be used by HR managers to conduct manpower planning.

TABLE 4.9 Manpower forecast model estimates

Dependent variable	Total labour demand		
Variable	Estimate	t-statistics	Probability
Intercept	6.539	38.645	0.000
Labour trade type			
Labourer	6.371		
Bar bender and fixer	0.169		
Carpenter (form work)	3.758		
Concreter	2.495		
Electrician/electrical fitter	2.251		
Excavator	0.815		
Metal worker/welder	0.0604		
Plant and equipment operator	3.286		
Plasterer			
Log (COST)	+0.884	28.727	0.000
COM (Complexity)	−0.092	−3.280	0.002
PHYS (Physical conditions of the site)	0.059	2.335	0.024
TYPE (Building)	−0.178	−1.713	0.094
PREFAB (Pre-fabrication)	−0.262	2.5	0.013
CORD (Co-ordination)	0.275	2.10	0.021
RM (Raw material cost)	+0.195	1.85	0.066
MECH (Mechanization)	−0.119	1.95	0.052
N (No. of observations)		185	
SSE	0.301	MSE	0.05
R-square	0.95	Adj. R	0.94

Source: Wong, Chan, and Chiang 2008.

The principal categories of labour by trade type include labourer, bar bender and fixer, carpenter (form work), concreter, electrician/electrical fitter, excavator, metal worker/welder, plant and equipment operator, plasterer, or truck driver.

Applied questions

How does the chief people officer (CPO) attribute the employee compensation aspect of the business? Are there any control factors or indicators?

The CPO is the audience of the human resources analytics, which comprises the consumption of employee reward and benefit results. The CPO demands from its staff information related to employee costs, employee rewards, employee compensation analysis, cost to company, and other specific details. This information thus forms the control indicators.

References

Allaire, Y., and M. E. Firsirotu. (1984). Theories of Organizational Culture. *Organization Studies* 5: 193–226.

Allen, R. W., et al. (1979). Organizational Politics: Tactics and Characteristics of Its Actors. *California Management Review*, 22, 77–83.

Andrews, K. (1989, Sept–Oct). Ethics in Practice. *Harvard Business Review*, 99–104.

Argyris, C. (1987, Sept–Oct). Double Loop Learning in Organizations. *Harvard Business Review*, 115–125.

Ashforth, B. E., and F. Mael. (1989). Social Identity Theory and the Organization. *Academy of Management Review* 14(1): 20–39.

Ashmos, D. P., and G. P Huber. (1987). The Systems Paradigm in Organizational Theory: Correcting the Record and Suggesting the Future. *Academy of Management Review* 12(4): 607–621.

Augustine, N. R. (1987). Reshaping an Industry: Lockheed Martin's Survival Story. *Harvard Business Review* 75(3): 83–94.

Barrick, M. R., and M. K. Mount. (1991). The Big Five Personality Dimensions and Job Performance: A Meta-Analysis. *Personnel Psychology*, 44, 1–26.

Bass, B. M. (1985). *Leadership and Performance Beyond Expectation*. New York: Free Press.

Becker, H. S., and B. Geer. (1960). Latent Culture. *Administrative Science Quarterly*, 5, 303–313.

Bennis, W. (1989). *On Becoming a Leader*. Reading, MA: Addison-Wesley Publishing Co., Inc.

Bennis, W., and B. Nannus. (1985). *Leaders: The Strategies for Taking Charge*. New York: Harper and Row.

Bhide, A., and H. H. Stevenson. (1990). Why Be Honest If Honesty Doesn't Pay? *Harvard Business Review* 68(5): 121–129.

Blau, P. M. (1964). *Exchange and Power in Social Life*. New York: John Wiley.

Bolman, L. G., and T. E. Deal. (1991). *Reframing Organizations: Artistry, Choice, and Leadership*. San Francisco, CA: Jossey-Bass Publishers.

Bourgeois, L. J., III. (1985). Strategic Management and Determinism. *Academy of Management Review*, 9, 586–596.

Briggs Myers, I., and M. McCauley. (1985). *Manual: A Guide to the Development and Use of the Myers-Briggs Type Indicator*. Palo Alto, CA: Consulting Psychologists Press, Inc.

Brilhart, J. K., and G. J. Galanes. (1989). *Effective Group Decisions*. Dubuque, IA: William C. Brown Publishers.

Briscoe, G. (1989). *Construction Occupations Review of the Economy and Employment: Institute for Employment Research*. Coventry, UK: University of Warwick.

Briscoe, G., and R. Wilson. (1993). Employment Forecasting in the Construction Industry. Aldershot, UK: Avebury.

Broadbent, D. E. (1977). Levels, Hierarchies, and the Locus of Control. *Quarterly Journal of Experimental Psychology*, 29, 181–201.

Brown, L. D. (1983). *Managing Conflict at Organizational Interfaces*. Reading, MA: Addison-Wesley.

Brusilov, A. A. (1931). *A Soldier's Notebook: 1914–1918*. Westport, CT: Greenwood Press, Publishers.

Builder, C. H. (1989). *The Masks of War: American Military Styles in Strategy and Analysis*. Baltimore, MD: The Johns Hopkins University Press.

Caminiti, S. (1995, Feb. 20). What Team Leaders Need To Know. *Fortune*, 94, 100.

Chaloupka, M. G. (1987, Winter). Ethical Responses: How to Influence One's Organization. *Naval War College Review*, 80–90.

Cherrington, J.O., and D.J. Cherrington. (1992). A Menu of Moral Issues: One Week in the Life of the *Wall Street Journal*. *Journal of Business Ethics*, 11(4): 255–265.

Church, A.H. (1997). Managerial Self-Awareness in High Performing Individuals in Organizations. *Journal of Applied Psychology*, 82(2): 281–292.

Clark, K.B., and S.C. Wheelwright. (1992, Spring). Organizing and Leading 'Heavyweight' Development Teams. *California Management Review*, 9–28.

Collins, J.C., and J.I. Porras. (1991, Fall). Organizational Vision and Visionary Organizations. *California Management Review*, 30–52.

Colosi, T.R. (1993). *On and Off the Record: Colosi on Negotiation*. Dubuque, IA: Kendall/Hunt Publishing Company.

Conger, J.A. (1989). *The Charismatic Leader: Behind the Mystique of Exceptional Leadership*. San Francisco, CA: Jossey-Bass Publishers.

Cosier, R.A., and C.R. Schwenk. (1990). Agreement and Thinking Alike: Ingredients to Poor Decisions. *Academy of Management Executive*, 4(1): 69–74.

Costa, P.T., and R.R. McCrae. (1992). Trait Theory Comes of Age. In T.D. Sonderegger (ed.), *Psychology and Aging: Current Theory and Research in Motivation* (vol. 30). Lincoln: University of Nebraska Press.

Daft, R.L., J. Sormunen, and D. Parks. (1988). Chief Executive Scanning, Environmental Characteristics, and Company Performance: An Empirical Study. *Strategic Management Journal*, 9, 123–139.

Dess, G.G. (1987). Consensus on Strategy Formulation and Organizational Performance: Competitors in a Fragmented Industry. *Strategic Management Journal*, 8, 259–277.

Drucker, P.E. (1974). *Management: Tasks, Responsibilities, Practices*. New York: Harper and Row.

Eisenhardt, K.M., and M.J. Zbarecki. (1992). Strategic Decision Making. *Strategic Management Journal* 13: 20–22.

Fine, G.A., and S. Kleinman. (1979). Rethinking Subculture: An Interactionist Analysis. *American Journal of Sociology*, 85(1): 1–20.

Franks, F.G., S.G. Isaksen, and D.J. Treffinger. (1985). *Creative Problem Solving: The Basic Course*. Buffalo, NY: Bearly Limited.

Gabriel, R.A. (1985). *Military Incompetence: Why the Military Doesn't Win*. New York: The Noonday Press.

Goldberg, R.A. (1997). *Talking about Change. Issues and Observations 17*. Greensboro, NC: The Center for Creative Leadership.

Goodfellow, B. (1985). The Evolution and Management of Change in Large Organizations. *Army Organizational Effectiveness Journal*, 1, 25–29.

Gran, L. (1997, April 14). Monsanto's Bet: There's Gold in Going Green. *Fortune*, 116–118.

Hackman, J.R., ed. (1990). *Groups That Work and Those That Don't*. San Francisco, CA: Jossey-Bass Publishers.

Hunt, J.G. (1991). *Leadership: A New Synthesis*. Newbury Park, CA: SAGE Publications.

Jacobs, T.O. (1996). *A Guide to the Strategic Leader Development Inventory*. Washington, DC: National Defense University.

Jacobs, T.O. (undated). Cognitive Behavior and Information Processing under Conditions of Uncertainty. Alexandria, VA: U.S. Army Research Institute for the Behavioral and Social Sciences.

Jaques, E. (1986). The Development of Intellectual Capability: A Discussion of Stratified Systems Theory. *Journal of Applied Behavioral Science*, 22, 361–384.

Jefferies, C.L. (1992). Defense Decision Making in the Organizational-Bureaucratic Context. In J.S. Endicott and R.W. Stafford, Jr., (eds.), *American Defense Policy*. 4th ed. Baltimore MD: The Johns Hopkins University Press.

Kotter, J. P. (1978). Power, Success and Organizational Effectiveness. *Organizational Dynamics 6*(3): 27–40.

Krepinevich, A. F. (1995). *Restructuring for a New Era: Framing the Roles and Missions Debate.* Washington, DC: Defense Budget Project.

Larson, C. E., and F.M.J. LaFasto. (1989). *Teamwork: What Must Go Right, What Can Go Wrong.* Newbury Park, CA: SAGE.

Larwood, L., C. M. Falbe, M. P. Kroger, and P. Miesing. (1995). Structure and Meaning of Organizational Vision. *Academy of Management Journal, 38*(3): 740–769.

Lasswell, H. D. (1936). *Who Gets What, When, How.* New York: McGraw-Hill.

Rosenfeld, Y. and A. Warszawski. (1993). Forecasting Methodology of National Demand for Construction Labour. *Construction Management and Economics*, 11, 18–29.

Wong, J., A. Chan, and Y. Chiang. (2008). Modeling and Forecasting Construction Labor Demand: Multivariate Analysis. *Journal of Construction Engineering and Management, 134*(9): 664–672.

5
SUPPLY CHAIN ANALYTICS

This chapter describes supply chain analytics by presenting a whole gamut of analysis widely used across the various functions and sub-functions of the supply chain.

Overview

A supply chain is the series of processes within a firm that produces a service or product and that is related to the network, material, financial, and information flows across suppliers and customers. Supply chain analytics is an opportunity for excellence to reduce costs in processes such as purchasing, processing, manufacturing and physical distribution, inventory holding, and delivery of goods. The origin of supply chain analytics can be dated back to time study and motion study frameworks. Time study determines the time spent on each element of a job. Motion study originated from Franklin Gilbreth (1907–1930) whose motion study was related to the science of physics and momentum (Nelson 1992). Motion study implies dividing a given work into individual elements and identifying at each stage the tasks or jobs that are redundant and that can be replaced with a different task or eliminated.

One can find out the most systematic and scientific method of performing an operation or completing the job. It is defined as systematic observation, analysis, and measurement of the steps in the performance of a specific job line for the purpose of establishing a standard time for each job aimed at improving procedures and increasing productivity. The total time taken by all elements (stages) of a job is called standard time. Therefore, time studies can fix the standard time for completing jobs, and motion studies help eliminate movements or directions that are wasteful in terms of energy or momentum and should be dispensed with and can give standard directions for good flow. The benefits of time and flow include proper and fuller utilization of materials, help in assessing labour requirements, standardizing labour costs, standardizing equipment and machinery, determining the best method to finish the task, proper planning, and effective control. Supply chain analytics can ensure the fulfilment of plan items (e.g. transportation, materials, size, pieces, consumables used, contractual labour hours, equipment, machine hours, and utilities input volume by type).

Supply chain analytics can be segregated into operations analytics and working capital analytics, where operations analytics is supported by the analysis of volume,

TABLE 5.1 Engagement map of supply chain analytics

Analytics	Brief description	Audience
Inventory chain	Determine the optimal size of inventory	Store and warehouse staff
Order batch SKU	Optimal lot size of each SKU to be ordered and located	CFO staff
Best route	Length of routes linking to destination and alternatives or modes and best times	Purchase officer, logistics staff
Last-mile delivery	Consignments planning for hyper-local delivery and customer fulfillment	Distribution head
Energy efficiency	Use of energy in conversion of raw material to finished goods and fuel efficiency in distribution	Plant manager
Supplier scoring	Rating models for each supplier on the basis of their socio-demographic and historical performance	CPO staff
Sourcing gains	Measuring the savings due to re-aligned procurement from supplier locations and channels that realizes positive monetary gains	CSO
Working capital	The capital that is the backbone of running the business and includes financing, investing, and internal surplus	CFO
Open account	On open with a big supplier	CAO
Trade finance	Availing credit while importing or exporting a consignment to foreign destinations	CFO
Pre-payment	Making advance payments to vendors towards accurate and quality delivery	COO
Trade credit	Extending and minimizing credit while making delivery to customers for few days	CSO
Supplier advance	A term of credit with the supplier that is linked with annual average volume and also standing of the vendor and his score.	CPO
Pre-delivery and post-delivery finance	A nature of transaction where the payments are linked to delivery stages	CPO

distance, cycle time, efficiency in translation, conversion, and the mix of channel alternatives tied together to achieve overall cost reduction. Working capital analytics is the understanding of the nature of variation in fund requirements at each definite step of the supply chain. A modern tool that enables a supply chain model to understand both ideas is called *e-financial supply chain*.

The key questions around supply chain analytics include:

- How can one plan for product demand?
- How can one determine how much product to produce and by how many runs?
- How can one manage inventories?
- How much can one save on vendors and direct overheads?
- How can one manage networks?
- Are we consistently delivering high-quality services?
- Are we maximizing the productivity of our equipment in each stage?
- What is the progress on operational measures unique to our industry?
- How many defective products or services have been produced?
- How do I plan my supply chain for the least amount of time possible? What about responsiveness and agility?
- How can one manage the chain and nodes for hyper-local delivery?
- How do I justify my current supply performance and response?
- How do I rate my suppliers?
- Can I nurture my suppliers?

There is no single answer to these questions, and it involves the following anticipated metrics in totality. Further, one should not attempt to find separate answers to these questions on a standalone basis. Managers must find a reasonably standard, unified approach to solve problems within a few dimensions. A categorical answer is preferred.

However, conditional opinions are more desirable where the advantages prevail. For example, when it comes to supplier selection, it may not be worthwhile to look at quality or price alone but must be confounded with reliability, transformability, or the ability to nurture them towards business goals.

The next few sections succinctly describe a series of customer processes that could be used as significant differentiators of business delivery. A few major contributions are channel research (Alderson 1957), location and control of inventories in production–distribution networks (Hansmann 1959), and hierarchical production planning (Haz and Meal 1975). Channel research (Alderson 1957), as a field in supply chains, encouraged marketing and argued that postponing finished goods delivery could reduce market risks by having the product remain in an undifferentiated state as long as possible thus allowing better coping with unexpected market shifts. Channel research is outlined by Alderson (1957), who put forward the channel as a distribution focus in supply chains to build partnerships. Kahl (1999) shows that the modules of supply chains cover the processes of procurement, production, distribution, and sales. Supplier network redesign is

TABLE 5.2 Supply chain core excellence

Categories	Functional attributes	Pertinent matter
Acquisition	Number of procurements	Few, standard
	Number of sourcing points	Quicker and more reliable
	Supplier lead time	Long
	Supplier reliability	Product or process layout
	Even order batches	Number and size of batches
Assembly processing	Number of processes	Customs jobs, set-up time
	Number of products	Number of defects, losses
	Number of repeat operations	Set-up, wind-up time
	Costs of preventive and predictive maintenance	Number of abrupt stops
Distribution	Distribution network length	Number of stages
	Loading capacity per day	Loading time
	Sales cycle per product batch	Average sales
	Collection cycle per batch	Average collection
	Average returns per batch	Average returns
	Number of returns	No. of orders retuned, no. of batches returned
Network	Network	Complexity of network
	Globalization cross country	Web
	Number of decoupling Points	No. of countries
	Number of hubs and spokes	Shipping by air
		Shipping by ports
Congruence	Hierarchies	Number of levels
	No. of depts.	Distance between depts.
	Transfer price	Number of transfers
	Time to respond	Average time to respond

no longer an infrequent activity, but some companies have established a regular method that makes decisions for new products. The complexity, frequency, and impact of the supply network may overtax human planners. Lee, Padmanabhan, and Whang (1997) emphasize the bullwhip effect, which results in supply managers' actions, such as:

- Aggregating multiple forecasts for many partners and levels to a single point-of-sale (POS) level.
- Batch sizing orders for cutting fixed-level costs to place an order so as to use full truckloads.
- Ensuring last-mile delivery to the fourth stage of a local dealer; third-party agencies could be used by the partner who may find it economical to operate on the allow load.
- Strategizing orders by channel partners who order in larger quantities in anticipation of partial deliveries that should be avoided, which will reduce the drain on production and reduce excess inventory.

This would require a suitable logistics model for the company, and no single model is appropriate for all firms. For mid-term forecasting in consumer goods supply chains, this means dynamic forecasting of customer demand and minimum stocking levels are desirable.

During the customer life cycle, the company is on-boarding new customers by paid marketing, and in the end, the customer may migrate to a competitor. Attempts to build forecast models should reflect the anticipation of customer demand and factor in that customer decisions shape the demand. However, the principal challenge in supply chains is a model that combines the process of delivery end to end. Demand-shaping decisions could be pricing, promotions, product bundling, and new product launches. The variations in inputs from marketing are supposed to be accommodated by the supply manager from time to time, and hence the supply chain team works in tandem with the marketing team. Many times, price promotion has resulted in jumps in customer demand that the production team is unable to cope with due to capacity limitations. Consider a scenario with two products being bundled as a promotion to generate additional demand. When there is limited availability of a bundled product, the sale of main products also suffers. At times, there may be conflicting demand between two competition regions, which may hamper supply such as seasonal promotions in two parallel regions. When new products are introduced, it captures sizable volume as compared to old products given that the total capacity is limited. Strategies exist such as producing ahead of a promotion; producing in earlier periods, while increasing seasonal stocks and storing them; producing at alternate sites and bearing transport costs; with alternate modes of production (by substituting input or raw materials, procuring from vendors); working overtime to produce more; increasing the storing capacity of all warehouses; producing at alternate location with higher products; sourcing products from vendors with higher costs; or working overtime to fulfil the order.

An e-financial supply chain is defined as the process of back-end invisible support in the form of a chain of financial transactions or events linked to the associated supply chain task. A financial chain is defined as the financial flows within the supply chain related to processes that form the counter-part to the physical supply chain. E-supply finance is a tool that enables both buyers and suppliers to manage their working capital and cash conversion cycle more efficiently and to reduce costs. Receivables are another way of generating finance from sales based on distribution. In both cases, large corporate clients can rely on strong credit ratings to make liquidity available for supply chain partners in otherwise constrained credit environments. Traditionally, any extension will reduce the supplier's liquidity and margins without any benefits since the financing of receivables is costly and limited by the supplier's credit standing. This can mean an evolution away from fewer large transactions to a larger number of smaller transactions. Therefore, supplier finance aims at funding multiple transactions on an ongoing basis, which is not the same as transaction finance since it involves specific solutions. Transaction-based finance is considered to be a light version of supply chain finance. Therefore, supplier finance, inventory finance, and distributor finance are the channels of finance, which are further divided into pre-shipment and post-shipment payables financing. Further, export credit guarantees and credit insurance are all the more important, including warehouse receipts or invoices and bills of exchange, respectively. Credit guarantees are instruments to protect themselves from the risk of buyer's default.

Financial flows result from activities in the supply chain, which can be influenced by actors from both the logistics and supply chain environments. The financial supply chain deals with the flow of funds as well as the series of transactions. The financial origin starts by making the first sale, supports the inter-party (unit) exchange of goods and services, and ends with the settlement of payments. A process-oriented chain outlines a financial supply chain that deals with the flow of funds and related transactions and processes. The financial perspective incorporates the rate of return on capital employed in supply networks. Supply chain involves the nature of capital in facilities and long-term investment. Co-ordination involves use of information, process orientation, allocation, and dissemination. Aspects of e-financial chain that are important include advance payment guarantees, dealer acceptance, delivery orders, invoice payment settlement and collection, dealer financing, dealer pre-payments, and pre-shipment or post-shipment vendor financing, respectively.

Net working capital (NWC) is known as the difference between current assets and current liabilities. More conservative approaches to financing working capital attempt to avoid dependence on short-term financing of current assets. Although short-term financing is available, it could be prohibitively costly, and hence, a conservative approach uses more long-term financing and less short-term financing. Hence, long-term financing can be used for both creating fixed assets and managing working capital. However, a bigger firm may follow an aggressive approach where it can borrow less for the long term and more for the short term. More short-term financing can be risky when borrowing rates are going to rise. To improve working

TABLE 5.3 E-supply chain finance modalities

Payable	Description	Demerits	Benefits
Payment term extension	1 to 3 quarters	Cost shifting vs. cost reduction; suppliers do not compete on production and quality capabilities but rather financial access	Cash flow
Cash payment discount option	Aggressive management of discounts offered by suppliers	Can result in accounts payable reduction	Procurement costs
Business charge cards	Ad hoc expenditure co-operation with a service provider	Only applicable for ad hoc/low-spend supplies; transaction fees charged by card provider make it expensive	Convenient and transparent

TABLE 5.4 Supply chain finance components

Buyer	Seller	Banker
Supplier relationships	Alternate source	More collaborative relationships
Financials	Visibility and facilitate reconciliation	Increasing reach and profile of trade finance
Cash flow	More predictable cash flows	Economy of scale and efficiency gains
Payment processing costs	Better financing costs	Increasing profits due to lower capital
Commercial terms	Reduce invoicing costs	Top-line results are better
Working capital	Accelerated payment option	Health of buyer is maintained

capital, a promising alternative is changing information in order to plan material flows for considerable benefits. The re-employment rate is the rate which a firm can find in the market when it wants to refinance, i.e., a new loan rate with the same characteristics as the initial loan. The manager may choose to enhance the volume of production or balance finished goods and higher lead times to replenish widely clustered warehouses. Alternatively, the manager may choose to switch to minimum production runs with even balances of finished goods stock to reach the company stores in time.

The most promising solution is the nature of inventory financing solutions and a pecking order among alternatives based on the trade-off between costs, risks, and degree of control on the chain. Early payment discount programs point to rather aggressive management of discounts offered by some suppliers or for the negotiation of new payment terms that include early payment discounts. This is an option for large companies with influence over their suppliers. This may make suppliers charge higher prices to the buyer and increases costs of the supply chain as a whole.

Demanding discounts from suppliers will increase the financing costs of the supplier rather than the buyers, which may add to supply chain risk by disrupting and destabilizing them financially. The most vulnerable suppliers will accept the same. Consignment stock by vendors will imply that the inventory remains in the ownership of suppliers, which is located on the premises of the buyer. Stocks of inventory remain on the balance sheet of the supplier. As inventory that is managed by the vendor (supplier), this means the vendor determines when to replenish and how much to replenish. The borrowing rate can be reduced by factoring a pool of receivables or using factors specialized in certain industries that can consider the worthiness of the buyer. Inventory by itself can serve as an asset for a loan. When it comes to supply managers in the sector, they value inventory more than a bank does, which is obviously due to their knowledge of specific assets and its use in production processes and the market destination where the inventory can be reused or sold for gain. Banks are selective about inventory and look for liquid and finished goods rather than loose items as against unfinished or semi-finished goods. However, finished goods result in cash outflow in the form of excise and customs duties, unlike postponement tactics. Hence non-perishable and standard items are only considered as secured assets for borrowing. Warehouse receipts from warehouses that are well reputed and of public scale can be used as collateral and can also serve as a secured asset. A warehouse receipt can be pledged or on lien with a bank. Cash-pooling techniques can be applied for a single vendor or related vendors over a series of related transactions at a group-level netting of cash and liquidity. The extension of pooling has the potential to strengthen its financial performance but requires that the relevant accounts of the supply chain members must be combined to collect funds and liquidity reserves of the entire supply chain. Short-term cash surpluses and the cash needs of individual members are balanced out, and overall financing costs are reduced by avoiding forms of short-term financing with high financing costs. This can lead to reduced processing costs, especially in the bank's view, and being as lean and cost efficient as possible. Insuring goods stocked in the warehouse can improve the quality of inventory and its worthiness.

Instead of directly dealing with many suppliers, such as a two-stage suppliers' model, the first stage is an upstream supplier, a trader aggregator (bigger firm) that is backed by small and medium enterprises (SMEs). From a supply chain view, leveraging financial strength is beneficial to the supplier and is also a volume commitment from them. The financing costs of a whole supply chain can be reduced, and its performance is increased. A bigger player with more resources and cheaper access to capital could support financing activities for financially weaker SMEs. The buyer pays the upstream suppliers for the material, and the bigger suppliers make payments for their value-adding activities only.

There are two options for reducing process costs: first by using costlier technology and second by reducing financing costs in the supply chain. The focus may shift to financing current assets and reducing fixed assets through outsourcing tactics, leasing, and other modes. Hence, the e-financial chain can create value by sensible investment and financing decisions for logistics and working capital. This definitely

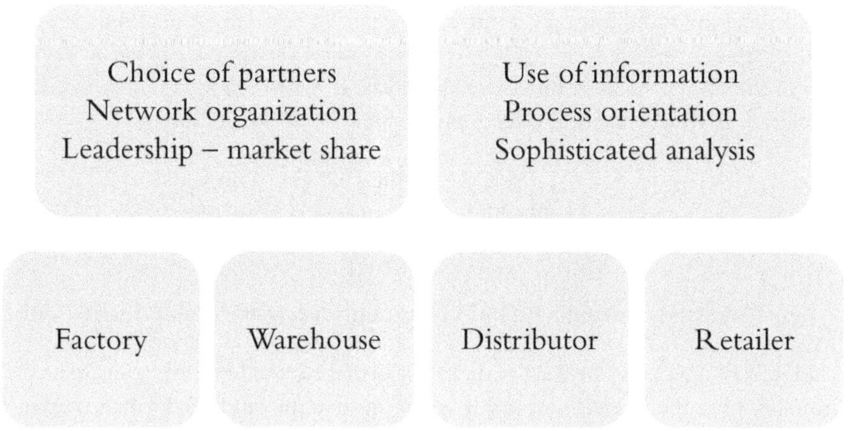

| Choice of partners
Network organization
Leadership – market share | Use of information
Process orientation
Sophisticated analysis |

| Factory | Warehouse | Distributor | Retailer |

FIGURE 5.1 Supply network strategy

requires skills of financial knowledge in the logistic field and the application of financial tools to support decision making. For example, making use of trade credit is simpler and more convenient compared to alternative sources of funds. While the terms of sales are defined in the contract, credit arrangements in long-term relationships and repetitive transactions are done via an open account or a current account with the buyer.

Working capital analytics

Working capital, cash conversion, and financing cost reductions are the key dimensions of supply chain finance. A positive net working capital arises when the current assets are higher than current liabilities. Since working capital fluctuates widely with business needs, it poses business risk, and one cannot always counter these changes. Changes to working capital are identified only when it impacts both the current account and the capital account. The chief financial officer's (CFO) staff have the dual knowledge of the sources of changes to working capital and also where to invest idle funds. One cannot split working capital analytics into component-wise analyses of the individual parts of working capital. This is because working capital is jointly determined and exhibited in business.

Working capital analytics can answer these relevant questions:

- What is the liquidity position?
- How can one optimize investment in current assets?
- How should current assets be financed?
- What is the cause of changes in working capital?
- What is the level of fixed assets required by the firm?
- How much of working capital can be met from internal surplus?
- Which is the short-run debt limit?
- How much of current assets can be held?

The decision to follow a given financing choice of working capital is dependent on the cash conversion cycle (CCC), which measures the time lag between cash to cash in the business. The cash conversion cycle is the time interval between cash collections from the sale of products and cash payments for resources.

$$CCC = DIH + DSO - DPO$$
$$\text{Days inventory held (DIH)} = \text{inventory} / \text{annual sales} / 365$$
$$\text{Days payable outstanding (DPO)} = \text{accounts payable} / \text{annual cost of goods sold} / 365$$
$$\text{Days sales outstanding (DSO)} = \text{accounts receivable} / \text{annual sales} / 365$$

Liquidity analytics is defined as the art of managing the liquidity position of the firm and gives the mix of long-term versus short-term funds to finance working capital. The firm has to invest enough funds in current assets for generating sales. Current assets are needed because the sales do not convert into cash immediately.

The operating cycle is the time duration to convert sales, which involves the acquisition of raw material, labour, power, and fuel; the conversion of raw material into a product; and the time taken to realize cash sales. Normally, the sum total of inventory conversion period, selling period, and debtors' conversion period give rise to the operating cycle. The goal is to reduce the payable period and the cash-to-cash cycle to reduce the net working capital and enhance the firm's value. When the procurement cycle is longer, more cash is held up in inventory, and when customers are B2B, they take much longer to clear their dues, which results in higher accounts payable and lower working capital. According to the DuPont formula, the proportion of sales that enters into net profit is important, because the gain in profit is offset by fall in asset turnover. Asset returns are defined as the ratio between inventory and assets. Identifying changes to fixed assets and linking this to sales can identify sources of deficiency in capacity utilization. A fund flow statement is the statement of changes to the sources and destinations of working capital. Cash flow statements summarize the causes of changes in the cash position.

The choice of the pecking order of e-financial tools for managing supply chain finance includes liquidity, payment terms, trade finance, advances to vendors, and credit extended to customers. Payment terms may be extended in every two out of three suppliers, and a trade-off may exist between the quality of procurement and the duration of extension. Extension of trade credit can play a major role in buying decisions. Firms can raise cash against a letter of credit from banks and add to the characteristics of open account arrangements that do not require documentation with suppliers. Letter-of-credit financing is a mode of trade financing only used in case of overseas suppliers. Larger firms can be expected to have wider access to financing and might indeed be willing to support their own suppliers or distributors. Large firms with considerable market power might be able to actively increase their trade credit usage and payment terms.

Alternate instruments include reverse and forward factoring, defined as the handing over of the burden of collecting bills payable at a discount to a bank. The negative impact of traditional working capital improvements on a supply chain can be disastrous, and hence, one can consider using reverse factoring to compensate for some of the disadvantages. Simple process efficiency-driven management of cash flows between parties within the supply chain is desirable to reduce the financing costs across the entire chain as needed. A business needs to develop collaterals that rely on secured transactions to avoid risk.

E-finance score

The presence of a unique score card for supply chain networks that can be construed as an e-financial supply chain score that integrates inventory, e-financial support, and channel indicators is desirable. An agile score card is enshrined by cycle time, responsiveness, quality, and costs. Responsive chains refer to development speed, faster delivery, degree of customization, variety, volume flexibility, and quality. For example, a furniture business can find suppliers providing independent

Supplier rating model

While selecting a supplier among many, the total costs of the supplier is the sum of material costs, freight costs, inventory costs, and administrative costs. Material costs equal the product of volume and the price net of discounts. Transport costs are the costs incurred depending on the location of the supplier, size of the shipment, number of shipments, mode of transport, technology used, manpower used in unloading the consignments, and regularity in receipt.

Annual inventory costs are the total of the cycle inventory and pipeline inventory, which equals $(\frac{Q}{2} + d \times L)H$.

Administrative costs include managerial time, travel, investment in technology, and other overheads associated with the supplier. This is dependent on the ownership time, size, and location of the supplier.

The total supply costs give rise to:

$$TC = p \times d + \textit{freight costs} + \frac{Q}{2} + d \times L \times H$$

According to Roylance (2008), a supplier rating system is based on the three essential dimensions of price, quality, and service. The ranking of suppliers identifies product quality as much more important than the product price. Examples of the attributes used in supplier evaluation are competitive pricing, stable prices, discounts and payment terms offered, durability, reliability, on-time delivery, complaint handling, technical documentation, emergency support, and responsiveness. The relative importance of different supplier attributes in the actual choice of suppliers is not the same as the perceived importance. Managers perceive quality to be the most important attribute, but they assign more weight to delivery performance and/or cost when they actually choose a supplier. The perceived importance of supplier selection criteria (quality, cost, delivery performance) identifies the relative weights of the attributes in actual selection of suppliers. In addition to quality, cost, delivery, and flexibility (Hayes and Wheelwright 1984), are also considered.

The multinomial logit (MNL) model of choosing a supplier is expressed as:

$$P_{ij} = exp\mu V{ij} / \sum exp^{\mu\mu Vkj},$$

where P_{ij} represents the probability of selecting alternative from the choice set containing K possible choices. V_{ij} represents the systematic utility of alternative i in choice set j.

$$V_{ij} = \beta_1 x_{ij} + \beta_2 x_{ij} + \ldots + \beta_5 x_{ij} + \varepsilon,$$

TABLE 5.5 Supplier model rating model estimates

Multinomial logit model parameter estimates

Dependent variable	Supplier rating	Number of levels = 5	
Variable	Beta	Std. Error	P-value
Intercept	1.0895	0.118	0.0010
Unit cost of components ($)	-0.5771	0.124	0.001
Quality of components (%)	0.3838	0.117	0.001
Delivery lead time (days)	-0.2871	0.115	0.0001
On-time delivery performance (%)	0.4157	0.118	0.0001
Flexibility in order (%)	0.0445	0.113	0.0001
No. of purchase orders/transactions = 928		Unique populations = 258	
Log likelihood ratio	287.61		0.003

Note: Number of levels refer to number of choices and unique populations refer to combinations.

where x_{ij} is the level of attribute *l* of alternative *i* in choice set *j* and $\beta_1 - \beta_5$ are the relative utilities associated with attribute *l*.

The MNL regression model shows that managers assign more weight to cost and on-time delivery, as compared to quality.

Assume that there are only two suppliers with two attribute levels (cost, quality). Supplier 1 has lower costs but relatively lower quality and unreliable delivery performance, while Supplier 2 has higher cost, higher quality, and reliable delivery performance.

Let the probability of selecting Supplier 1 be 39% while the probability of selecting Supplier 2 is 60%. The impact of a change in strategies can be easily calculated from the MNL model.

When Supplier 1 increases its quality level from a lower level to an above-average level and Supplier 2 retains its current delivery standard, then the probability of selection of Supplier 1 and Supplier 2 rises to 58% and 42%, respectively. Therefore, the manager need not base their choice on Supplier 2 vis-à-vis Supplier 1, due to higher likelihood.

SKU rationalization

SKU rationalization is an important technique in inventory management that helps retailers optimize their assortments by removing some of the non-productive merchandise. A SKU is defined as a specific item stored to a specific location. All units stored in the same SKU are supposed to be indistinguishable from each other. SKUs have simplified most inventory control operations. A SKU is bounded to a particular location of specific destination within the business facility. For a given product (e.g. a book identified by its ISBN barcode), a retail chain can have as many SKUs as there are fixed locations where the book can be stored; typically one SKU per store and per warehouse. Each SKU is associated with its stock on hand, which represents the number of units readily available for consumption at the SKU location. The stock on order represents the amount of inventory in transit yet to arrive at the yard. Inventory age is the average time goods are residing in stock. The transportation lot's sizing stock is held at the start and end points, while the transit inventory is the average inventory quantity and is the product of transit duration (days), the average transportation time, and the average demand. This is to meet the demand that occurs during transportation time. Seasonal stock can help reduce lost sales, costs for working overtime, or opportunity costs for unused machines and technical equipment. Seasonal stock is common for a group of items sharing the same capacity.

SKU analysis may select high-return items for the rack and reject low-margin terms. When one flavour of a brand has lower value share compared to its volume share in the display/storage rack, attempts are made to alter the SKU plan by moving towards higher-value proportions and lower volume share. When one brand in the category has a 20% dollar share with 30% of the SKUs on the shelf, it is over-spaced relative to the sales that are being delivered, and assortments should be reduced. For example, lowering the SKU share that leads to higher gains in unit sales are preferred. Conversely, if a 20% share brand has 10% of the SKUs on the shelf, the brand is highly remunerative, and it will have a relatively easy time to further grow sales. SKU-wise, sales productivity is a more accurate assessment of consumer preference for a brand or segment.

Unit velocity change compares the units per SKU (i.e. velocity) of a brand or segment to similar for an annual period. Using the same 20% brand share (Brand A) to illustrate, let's assume this brand has shown 25% growth versus last year. Introspection reveals that Brand A grew their SKU count by 50% from last year, while

TABLE 5.6 Challenges to advanced distribution planning

Challenges	Techniques	Outcome
Distribution network	Rational allocation model	Agile, responsive delivery
Capacity planning	Projecting maximum levels and safety stocks	Better customer service
Fixed costs	Internal transhipments between warehouses	Reduced costs of shipment
Capacity lower	Combining shipments for common destinations	Lower transportation costs
Safety stock	Choosing uniform source of procurement and mode of delivery	Minimization of inventory and loss
Deadlines	Efficient and rational allocation	Planned schedule and distribution

generating only 25% gain in unit sales. This means that the average velocity per item (i.e. units per SKU) actually decreased by 17% [(1.25 / 1.50) − 1], which makes it less remunerative than it was last year. This means Brand A's underlying trend is actually negative rather than strongly positive. In another scenario, Brand A generates 25% growth with only an 18% gain in SKU count. This reflects velocity growing by 6% [(1.25 / 1.18) − 1] despite an 18% gain in SKUs. Velocity was not diluted at all. The 6% growth is highly encouraging of future trends over the next 12–24 months for Brand A.

One key aspect of order fulfilment is the logistics process, which delivers the product to the customer. ABC analysis, which categorizes items into fast moving, slow moving, and relatively dormant, can be extended for demand analysis in the short term. Eventful and sporadic demand occurs for C-class items drawn from periods and intervals of stock-outs at retail outlets. The amount of lost sales causes the sales to ease the sales figures and underestimate the demand. Managers may view lost sales by considering the observed sales as a censored sample of the demand sample.

Baseline demand

Baseline sales capture the unit sales in the absence of promotions. Wittink (1988), Abraham and Lodish (1993), and Bechtel and Jayaram (1997) maintained that aggregated sales data use led to biases in forecasting and instead suggested using disaggregated data at the unit level or, if possible, at the customer level. Bechtel and Jayaram (1997) suggested a base model that can be used for market-level data.

The base model has the following equation:

$$\text{Sales}_t = \alpha_t + \beta_t \varphi_t + \gamma_t I_t + v_t,$$

where φ_t is the promotion dummy and represents another category-specific dummy such as a seasonality dummy.

From here, sales are a function of the dynamic baseline sales (α_t), the promotional activity (P_t), and explanatory variables (I_t), where:

Baseline retail sales $\alpha_t = \lambda_t \alpha_{t-1} + \omega_1 t,$
$\beta_t = \delta_t \beta_{t-1} + \omega_{2t},$
$\gamma_t = \rho_t \gamma_{t-1} + \omega_{3t},$ and
baseline lift parameter = $\alpha_t.$

The price index is an explanatory variable with a promo dummy variable φ and the lift parameter (β) and permits testing for promotional wear-out effects over time; a week without promotions shows a lower level of sales variability than promotion weeks. This baseline model also has the advantage of not being expensive in terms of data and can be extended to any retail chain with weekly point-of-sale data.

Spend analytics

Spend analytics is defined as the intensive alienation of the total spend of the entity with a goal to enhance sourcing leverage and buyer power. This also considers balance-of-trade, pricing, and procurement decisions and provides complete visibility into direct and indirect spend across the enterprise such as spend by commodity and supplier, purchase organization, cost centre, expense by employee unit, buyer unit, etc.

A few relevant questions are:

- Which suppliers provide the greatest value to the enterprise?
- How does total spend roll-up in corporate families create increased leverage to reduce supply costs?
- Which commodity and service areas represent the greatest sourcing opportunities for spend reduction?
- What is my total spend by industry classification?
- How much of a vendor's business do I represent?
- Where is the spend occurring with non-preferred suppliers?

Spend category analysis covers spend cycles, spend scores, and spend incidence. Store item analysis, value share, quantity shares, movement of items, etc. are focus areas of interest to retail chains.

Supplier performance analytics

Supplier performance analytics is a periodic evaluation done at the supplier level. This analysis enables businesses to have a picture of the performance of their suppliers, including supplier scorecards, procurement cycles, supplier price performance, delivery performance, quality, on-time payment ratings, payment activity and volume, and payments overdue. This is done at the supplier level and then is mapped to the customer level. This combines supplier performance, supplier cost intensity, supplier scores, sourcing efficiency, etc.

TABLE 5.7 Supplier performance review

Supplier ID	Number of purchase orders	Number of consignments received	Total purchase amount ($)	Number of returns	Value of returns ($)
00123	12	12	73,250	2	8,500
00124	14	12	48,365	4	4,500
00125	12	10	89,450	6	2,680
00126	13	12	88,950	1	3,500
00127	14	12	105,240	3	3,900

Inventory analytics

Inventory analytics is the analysis of inventory held by business, bills of materials (BOMs), movements of inventory in and out, manufacturing plants, distribution centres, and storage locations. This enables companies to monitor inventory-level trends in sales performance to improve cost exposure, increase turnover through inventory-level reduction and increased velocity and deployment of inventory at the right location. Customer returns need to be minimized to maintain quality levels.

The key questions around inventory analytics involve:

1. How much should be ordered?
2. When should inventory be ordered?
3. How can one minimize supplier returns?
4. How can one minimize customer returns?
5. What are the risks involved (supplier obsolescence, technological obsolescence)?
6. What is the average life of a product, inventory, supplier, customer, or process?
7. What is the replacement cost of a BOM or a supplier?

Capacity enhancement can be achieved with extended duration of operation, which, in the case of mass production, may work differently in case of parallel sequences of two intermediate outputs to two or more associated products. Scheduling of machines for parallel operations to manufacture one or more products is challenging. This is due to the fact that a particular item in the sequence may be broken or be active in operation among many machines. Distribution consists of the distribution structure, pattern of delivery, deployment of transportation facility, and possible loading options, which describes the network between the factory warehouse and the customer. In a three-stage structure, there is an additional layer between the central warehouse and regional warehouse. It is natural for fast-moving consumer goods (FMCG) businesses to have a production facility located close to customers since these goods are consumed often. In the computer goods industry, supply decisions will shift patterns because of low flexibility and the build-up of seasonal stock, and hence, dynamic forecasting in shorter periods is used. There is high risk of overstocking components because of their short life cycles. One has to take care about promotions of discounts in order to get rid of obsolete component stocks (e.g. garments, leather goods, personal care). Older components have to be replaced with their more modern substitutes.

Economic order quantity (EOQ) is the comfort level of both ordering costs and carrying costs and gives the manager the option of trading between the two. EOQ minimizes the total of ordering and carrying costs, which needs to be determined for a given category. Ordering costs are used in the case of materials and supplies that are the sum total of requisitioning, purchase ordering, transporting, receiving, inspecting, and storing costs. Ordering costs increase with number of orders, if the firm maintains a larger-size inventory, which decreases ordering costs. Carrying costs incurred for maintaining a given level of inventory are called and include storage,

50 Supply chain analytics

insurance, taxes, deterioration, and obsolescence. Storage costs comprise of cost of storage space, warehouse costs, or storage handling costs and clerical costs as here:

$$\text{Total costs} = \text{total carrying costs} \left(\frac{Q \times C}{2}\right) + \text{total order costs} \left(\frac{A \times O}{Q}\right)$$

Carrying costs (C) increase with inventory, and it is a trade-off between the two. Expected EOQ is a result of expected ordering costs and expected carrying costs, which is modelled around uncertainty. Both the inputs could be passed as parameters from demand functions available with the business. This gives rise to:

$$EOQ = \sqrt{2\frac{A \times O}{C}}$$

Since $A(.)$ is randomly distributed, one may assume a discrete probability distribution for $A(.)$, such as a Weibull, Poisson, or gamma distribution, and obtain optimal order quantity.

The optimum production run is determined by the right size of manufacturing (assembly). The total costs are set-up costs and carrying costs. Set-up costs (S) will include costs on preparing and processing, stock orders, design, tooling machines set-up, handling and re-handling of machines, equipment and materials, overtime, etc. Production costs or set-up costs will reduce with bulk production runs, while carrying costs will increase as large stocks of manufactured inventories will be held. The optimum production batch is where the total costs are at a minimum.

The economic lot size (ELS) is given as:

$$ELS = \sqrt{2\frac{A \times S}{C}}$$

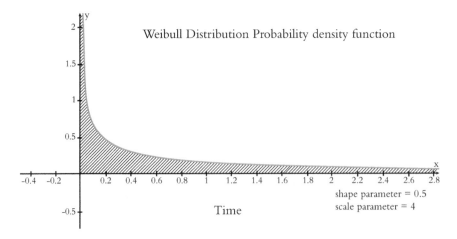

FIGURE 5.2 Weibull distribution of ordering volume $A(.)$

where $A(.)$ is the estimated production volume and S is the set-up costs and C is the carrying costs.

Therefore, $A(.)$ can be modelled using a discrete probability distribution, and the analytical parameters can be determined. S will involve scheduled data on set-up.

The firm may aggressively negotiate and bargain with suppliers on bulk purchases availing discounts. The firm will save on the purchase price per unit and procure more, which will reduce the ordering costs and increase the carrying costs. Order placing costs, transportation, receiving costs, inspecting, and storing can cut down on clerical and other staff, warehousing, and handling, insurance, and lastly deterioration and obsolescence of finished goods. This is a situation of trade-off between both kinds of costs or benefits.

Alternatively, the firm may produce more to fulfil a promotion program run by marketing where the customers are given upfront discounts to encourage repeat buying or buying in larger quantities. When the firm offers discounts, it has to ramp up large production sizes to meet the demand, which will reduce set-up costs and may increase inventory holding costs. The decision to increase the processing batch size will depend on arriving at the net expected return.

The expected demands can be obtained from the demand schedules at the product, market, unit, or customer levels, which are supplied by marketing.

These equations provide savings due to set-up costs:

$$\text{Ordering costs} = O \times \frac{A}{Q} - O \times \frac{A}{Q_2}$$

$$\text{Incremental carrying costs} = C \times \frac{Q}{2} - C \times \frac{Q_2}{2}$$

This shows a comparison between the discount rates given to our customers versus the discount rate that our suppliers can offer. Promotional campaigns can be successful when the discount gained from suppliers by increasing the order sizes and savings gained by reducing set-up costs are passed on to customers.

A reorder point is when to order next and is the inventory level at which an order should be placed to replenish the stock. The reorder point tracks the remaining inventory of a SKU.

Each time, a withdrawal decision is made to determine whether it is time to reorder. Therefore,

Inventory balance = balance on hand + scheduled receipts − back orders
Reorder point = average demand during lead time + safety stock
$= d \times L + z \times \sigma_{dLT}$,

Where d is the average demand per week and L is constant lead time in weeks and safety stock = $z \times \sigma_{dLT}$,
Where deviation of demand (σ_{dLT}) during lead time $\sigma_{Dlt} = \sigma_{d\sqrt{L}}$ and

$$\text{Time between orders} = \text{TBO}_{EOQ} = \sqrt{2\frac{EOQ}{D}} \text{ (52 weeks per year)}.$$

Sensitivity analysis is the understanding of changes to the EOQ and is important to make decisions by alternatively changing the parameters to determine the effects of a change.

$$\text{Demand} = \sqrt{2\frac{DS}{H}},$$

where an increase in lot size reduces EOQ.

$$\text{Order set-up costs} = \sqrt{2\frac{DS}{H}}$$ weeks of supply decreases and inventory turnover increases because the lot size decreases

For holding costs, larger lots are justified when holding costs decrease.

A firm that has accomplished just-in-time (JIT) delivery would have to fix the time points of orders which are much shorter. One must have lead time, average use, and EOQ where lead time is the time taken after the order is placed, which means it is the product of average use (per period) and the lead time (period of procurement). However, both parameters are not certain, and hence, it is modelled using simulations on the historical inventory consumption behaviour of the firm (e.g. in a Monte Carlo simulation). For example, if expected lead times are increasing, then the re-order point will be earlier than the previous, and if expected uses increase, so does the re-order point preceding the last re-order.

Safety stock ($z \times \sigma_{dLT}$) is when the demand for material fluctuates and so does the actual lead time. If the actual lead time increases or is delayed, the firm can face the problem of a stock-out, which can prove to be costly. A buffer inventory to safeguard against an operational risk of eventual stock-out is termed as safety stock. The distribution of stock-outs, which the business needs to accommodate, includes extreme value distribution models such as analyzing the maximum loss that the business can bear due to a stock-out. Discrete outlier models help arrive at the expected stock-out (e.g. extreme events model). One can find out the expected stock-out units per week, and the safety stock is the product of lead time and the expected stock-out units.

Safety stock model

The safety stock model involves ordering a variable quantity (Q) every fixed period of time T in order to maintain an inventory position at a pre-defined base stock level S. The base stock level S is determined by calculating the quantity needed between the time the order is placed and the time that the next period's order is received, adding a quantity of safety stock to allow for variation in the demand.

The time between the placing of the order and the receiving of the next period's order is the sum of the review period t and the replenishment lead time l.

The demand per unit of time μ is multiplied by the time between order placement and the next period's order arrival ($p + l$) to determine the expected quantity to be held. The safety stock depends upon the variability in the demand and the desired order fill rate.

Using a standard loss function, $L(z)$,

$$L(z) = \frac{(1-f) \times \mu p}{\sigma(p+1) \times \frac{1}{2}}$$

Where desired fill rate is f, the demand is μ, its standard deviation is σ, the time between orders is t, and the replenishment lead time is l.

Once $L(z)$ is known, z can be found in a normal distribution table, and the safety stock can be calculated by:

$$\text{Safety stock} = z \times \sigma \ (p+l)^{\frac{1}{2}}$$

If the review period p is reduced, the safety stock does not necessarily reduce because p is in both the numerator and denominator of the standard loss function that determines the value of z.

When several components are needed, each component having the same fill rate (r), the overall system order fill rate (multi-item fill rate) will be lower than the component fill rate.

For n items having the same component fill rate,

Order fill rate = (component fill rate) r^n.

The total safety stock required at the last-mile distribution centre can be reduced by a factor of $n^{1/2}$, where n is the number of different SKUs for which the final assembly is held up until it reaches the destination. However, this is subject to the availability of skilled personnel.

To maximize the benefits of postponement (in the form of lower levels of safety stock), the product should be designed to be localizable by distribution centre. However, postponement is a challenge in case of product quality testing for assembled products. The variable features of the product can be isolated into one or two modules that can be installed (assembled) in the distribution centre (customer delivery point).

Facility planning in logistics

Supply networks are prone to risks associated with project execution to make facilities ready for use by people associated with goods to be dispatched towards the carrier on the way to dealers or customers. The completion of the facility is broken down into activities with reasonable time estimates. Optimistic time (α) is the shortest time in which an activity can be completed, followed by most likely time (m), which is the time taken to perform the activity (normally on an average), and pessimistic time (β), which is the longest estimated time to complete the project. The mean (μ) and variance (σ^2) of each activity in the schedule and time is a random distribution, the mode of which can provide the value of most likely time (m).

Supply chain analytics

TABLE 5.8 Minimization of project overrun (time)

Activity	α	m	β	μ_t	σ_t^2
1	11	12	13	12	0.11
2	7	8	15	9	1.78
3	5	10	15	10	2.78
4	8	9	16	10	1.78
5	14	25	30	24	7.11
6	6	9	18	10	4.00

Note: $\mu_t = (\alpha + 4m + \beta) / 6$, $\sigma_t^2 = (\beta - \alpha / 6)^2$.

Six standard deviations (σ) of the estimated time would cover 99.75% of the normal distribution.

Most likely, time has four times the weight of pessimistic and optimistic time.

The mean completion time is given as $\mu_t = (\alpha + 4m + \beta) / 6$.
The variance completion time is given as $\sigma_t^2 = (\beta - \alpha / 6)^2$.

The alternatives include beta distribution.

Bill of materials (BOM) analysis

A bill of materials is a record of all components of an item, the parent–component relationships, and the usage quantity derived from the design of the products. Some products have several levels of intermediate items; the parent of one intermediate item can also be an intermediate item. Intermediates are assembled from more than one component. A component may have more than one parent. Commonality in parts is known as standardization of parts or modularity and is the degree to which a component has more than one immediate parent. The same item may appear in several places in the bill of materials for one product or in the bills of materials for several different products. For example, a seat sub-assembly is a component of a ladder-back chair, and a kitchen chair that is a part of a family of products. The usage quantity refers to a specific parent–component relationship. The usage quantity for any component can therefore change. Using the same part in many parents increases its volume and repeatability, which provides several advantages and helps minimize inventory costs. The bill of materials for every product is contained in the product.

There are various types of bills of materials used in practice, however. The time-phased bill, which is a time-phased assembly, is more practical and feasible to implement. The product registry graphically shows the lead time required to

Components and benefits of inventory control

Analysis	Control Factors	Expected Outcome
Product lot sizing stock	Frequency of set up	Lower time to set up and costs
Transportation lot sizing stock	Quantity of shipment	Lower transportation costs
Inventory in transit	Time to transport	Lower transportation costs
Seasonal stock	Peaks in demand	Reduced costs of over time
Work in progress	Lead and cycle time	Higher capacity utilization
Reserve and buffer	Uncertainty in lead and demand	Lower distress costs

FIGURE 5.3 Benefits of inventory control

purchase or manufacture an item. The metadata and the data model of a BOM is a significant input or output in the planning of BOM.

When several components are needed, if each component has the same fill rate (r), the overall system order fill rate (multi-item fill rate) will be lower than the component fill rate.

Inventory financing alternatives

To oversee the management of inventory, a decision to determine to change the level of inventory is an investment decision. One may invest in inventories by borrowing funds from the bank, which can only be fruitful when there are economic gains due to such investments. A firm that is not a market leader may not gain as much as compared to a leader in the industry. However, no business can afford to lose a purchase order from a worthy customer. The changes that are impacted to the financials of the firm are operating profit, cost of investment and rate of return. Rationalizing investments made in inventory is a challenge for managers and must be attempted continuously. Larger inventories are supported by higher working capital financing. The sharing of resources, facilities, warehousing, distribution networks, and channels; standardization of the procurements policy; or uniformity of customer requirements, etc., can go a long way in justifying such investments as unquestionably attractive.

Incremental operating profit is the simple difference between gross sales and the cost of goods sold. Incremental investment is the result of increased finished goods inventories and the corresponding increase in other net working capital to support the higher level of sales resulting from the increased level of finished goods. Return on investment is the ratio between changes to operating profit and changes to investment. Hence, a manager needs to arrive at a situation that will depend upon the required rate of return on the incremental investment into inventories. However, the business may not realize receivables, and the finished goods may become obsolete, which is a business risk that must be incorporated while calculating the rate of return.

56 Supply chain analytics

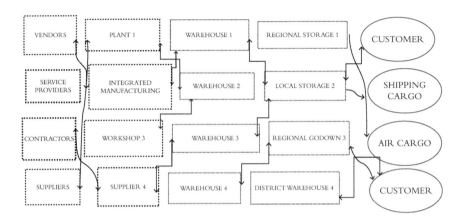

FIGURE 5.4 Rational distribution model

Distribution planning

Transport costs are a function of distance, time, and load volume where gravity is the centre of all three indicators taken together to determine the location of a facility or warehouse, whether a firm follows the hub-and-spoke model or multi-stage distribution models. Two alternatives techniques, the centre of gravity technique and the load distance technique, could be used. For a single potential location, the load distance value is calculated as:

$$LD = \sum_i l_i d_i,$$

where LD = load distance value (in tonnes/km),

L_i = load expressed as weight or number of trips (average trip per load fixed),

d_i = is the distance between the proposed site, and location I_i is the Euclidean distance between two points.

$$I_i = \sqrt{(x_i - x)^2 + (y_i - y)^2}$$

The co-ordinates of the new facility using the formula for centre of gravity are given here:

$$x = \frac{\sum xiWi}{\sum Wi} \text{ and } y = \frac{\sum yiWi}{\sum Wi}$$

A transshipment model is an extension of the transportation model in which intermediate transshipment points are added between the sources and destinations. For example, in three-stage transportation, a warehouse is located between the plant and the stores. The actual transportation may involve transport between sources, between destinations, or from the hub to a spoke or store, and vice versa (e.g. UPS parcel distribution models).

Simplifying the number of demand models is the analytical aim of a business, and the business as far as possible must model at the highest granularity, which is at the level of the customer. Load balancing is achieved against higher capacity utilization due to unified demand planning. Congruent and evenly balanced order batches are desirable for smooth functioning of the logistics unit of the business. Transport costs are reduced only with full trucks, and loads can be shared by combining unrelated goods for the same destination or sometimes from other partners aiming for the same destination. Interestingly, it is easier to handle last-mile

TABLE 5.9 Cost planning options

Order costs	Both recurring and delivery costs are reduced, with automated receiving and minimizing set-up time for subsequent runs and staging or raw materials or vendor-managed inventory.
Inventory costs	Open and flat space demarcation and utilization with one-way entry and exit layout storing more with artificial barricades.
Postponement	Partially finished product in inventory and components from vendors in real time to save on excise duty.
SKU	Equivalence of an ABC segregation to sort items into positive gross margin, zero margins, and negative margins; mingling the combination of SKUs towards higher gains.
Acquisition	Supplier lead time, transportation time, or receiving cycle time; reducing lead time variability, increasing supply reliability, and reducing safety stock inventory.
Number of aggregators/ vendors	Procure a mix of SKUs from a few suppliers to build relationships and obtain greater value from them, preferably located nearer to manufacturing hub.
Negotiation	Maximize the bulk purchase discount to be garnered by renegotiating with suppliers supported by reverse auction.
Number of storage points	A single storage location can optimize inventory better than multiple points.
Delivery shipment	Aggregating customer requirements into unified delivery order reduces delivery costs.
Transshipment	Inter-location transshipment with in-house logistics facility is cheaper to meet customers at scattered clusters.
End-of-season closing stock	Sale at season's end at a discount is the better option.
Multi-consignment	Two mini-consignments destined for the same location can be merged in transit by a collaborative arrangement with the transporter.
Vendor-managed inventory	Suppliers take the responsibility for replenishment against the indent of the buyer.
Payment	Lengthen payment period to suppliers.

58 Supply chain analytics

delivery better when the consignment is handled for the same delivery point destination rather than two different points of destination within a city. Cities are scattered when it comes to receiving consignments, and from one part of the city to another, it can take too long. The highway line delivery team must be independent from the local or hyper-local and handle only the movement of consignments on highways.

Cost planning options are exercised by the manager to balance the itemized costs of acquisition, production, storage, and delivery.

Applied questions

From the following data, calculate the net gains from sourcing through an ordinarily conducted, periodic, online reverse auction model by the procurement team of Nepta Ltd, which routinely procures agency services for delivering multi-channel digital branding. The trade-offs are against the incremental brand equity. Which vendor is the most suited for the business?

The annual quotes received for the servicing of the multi-channel branding from all the six vendors are:

- Vendor 1: $12 million
- Vendor 2: $11 million
- Vendor 3: $11 million
- Vendor 4: $15 million
- Vendor 5: $14 million
- Vendor 6: $12 million

Further, the expected impacts on market share that will be achieved at the end of the contracts are:

- Vendor 1: 1.5%
- Vendor 2: 2.00%
- Vendor 3: 3.00%
- Vendor 4: 2.5%
- Vendor 5: 1.00%
- Vendor 6: 1.5%

Using brand equity = $e^{-\alpha s}$, where $\alpha = 0.5$ and s is the increase in market share, recommend the best vendor.

Using the expression for brand equity, we find the changes to market share for vendors that are expected to cause impact to brand equity:

- Vendor 1: exp(0.5 × 1.5%)
- Vendor 2: exp(0.5 × 2.00%)
- Vendor 3: exp(0.5 × 3.00%)

- Vendor 4: exp(0.5 × 2.5%)
- Vendor 5: exp(0.5 × 1.00%)
- Vendor 6: exp(0.5 ×1.5%)

Thus, the brand equity changes are:

- Vendor 1: 100.75%
- Vendor 2: 101.01%
- Vendor 3: 101.51%
- Vendor 4: 101.26%
- Vendor 5: 100.5%
- Vendor 6: 100.75%

The procurement officer has to balance the trade-off between benefits and costs to make a decision. Vendor 3 can provide the maximum brand equity of 101.51%. Alternatively, the benefit–cost ratios (brand equity / quote) across vendors are:

- Vendor 1: 8.4
- Vendor 2: 9.18
- Vendor 3: 9.23
- Vendor 4: 6.75
- Vendor 5: 7.18
- Vendor 6: 8.4

The most suited vendor for the trade-off solution is Vendor 3 against all other vendors because choosing Vendor 3 results in the maximum net savings to the business.

References

Abraham, M. M., and L. M. Lodish. (1993). An Implemented System for Improving Promotion Productivity Using Store Scanner Data. *Marketing Science,* 12, 248–269.

Alderson, W. (1957). *Marketing Behavior and Executive Action.* Homewood, IL: Richard D. Irwin, Inc.

Bechtel, C., and J. Jayaram. (1997). Supply Chain Management: A Strategic Perspective. *The International Journal of Logistics Management,* 8(1): 15–34.

Charnes, A., and W. W. Cooper. (1961). *Management Models and Industrial Applications of Linear Programming.* New York: John Wiley & Sons.

Chavez, A., D. Dreilinger, R. Guttman, and P. Maes. (1996). A Real-Life Experiment in Creating an Agent Marketplace. In: *Proceedings of the First International Conference on the Practical Application of Intelligent Agents and Multi-Agent Technology* (PAAM'96), pp. 75–90. London, UK.

Chopra, S., and P. Meindel. (2002). *Supply Chain Management: Strategy, Planning, and Operation.* Upper Saddle River, NJ: Prentice Hall.

Dantzig, G. B. (1963). *Linear Programming and Extensions.* Princeton, NJ: Princeton University.

Davenport, T. (2000). *Mission Critical: Realizing the Promise of Enterprise Systems.* Boston, MA: Harvard Business School Press.

Gass, S. (1975). *Linear Programming.* 4th ed. New York: McGraw-Hill.

Handfield, R. B., and E. L. Nochols, Jr. (1999). *Introduction to Supply Chain Management.* Upper Saddle River, NJ: Prentice Hall.

Hansmann, F. (1959). Optimal Inventory Location and Control in Production and Distribution Networks. *Operations Research* 7, 483–498.

Hayes, R. H., and S. C. Wheelwright. (1984). *Restoring Our Competitive Edge: Competing Through Manufacturing.* New York: John Wiley.

Haz, A. C., and H. C. Meal. (1975). Hierarchical Integration of Production Planning and Scheduling. In: M. A. Geisler (ed.), *Studies in Management Science* (vol. I: Logistics, pp. 53–69). Amsterdam: Elsevier.

Hopp, W. J., and M. L. Spearman. (1996). *Factory Physics: Foundations of Manufacturing Management.* New York: McGraw-Hill.

Kahl, S. J. (1999, Fall). What's the "Value" of Supply Chain Software? *Supply Chain Management Review*, 59–67.

Lee, H. L., V. Padmanabhan, and S. Whang. (1997). The Bullwhip Effect in Supply Chains. *MIT Sloan Management Review*, 38(3): 93–102.

Levi, D. S., P. Kaminsky, and E. S. Levi. (2000). *Designing and Managing the Supply Chain: Concepts, Strategies, and Case Studies.* New York: McGraw-Hill.

Moore, L. J., S. M. Lee, and B. W. Taylor. (1993). *Management Science.* 4th ed. Needham Heights, MA: Allyn and Bacon.

Narahari, Y., and S. Biswas. (2000). *Supply Chain Management: Models and Decision Making.* Coimbatore, India: Coimbatore Institute of Technology.

Nelson, D., (ed.). (1992). *A Mental Revolution: Scientific Management since Taylor.* Columbus: Ohio State University Press.

Roylance, D. (2008). *Purchasing Performance: Measuring, Marketing and Selling the Purchasing Function.* Abingdon, UK: Ashgate.

Shapiro, J. F. (2001). *Modeling the Supply Chain.* Pacific Grove, CA: Duxbury Thomson Learning.

Taylor, B. W. (1999). *Introduction to Management Science.* 6th ed. Upper Saddle River, NJ: Prentice Hall.

Tayur, S., R. Ganeshan, and M. Magazine (eds.). (1999). *Quantitative Models for Supply Chain Management.* New York: Springer Science.

Viswanadham, N. (2000). *Analysis of Manufacturing Enterprises.* Boston, MA: Kluwer Academic Publishers.

Viswanadham, N., and Y. Narahari. (1998). *Performance Modeling of Automated Manufacturing Systems.* Englewood Cliffs, NJ: Prentice Hall.

Wagner, A.M. (1975). *Principles of Operations Research.* 2nd ed. Upper Saddle River, NJ: Prentice Hall.

Wittink, D. R. (1988). *The Application of Regression Analysis.* Needham Heights, MA: Simon & Schuster.

6
CUSTOMER ANALYTICS

Customer analytics refers to the processes that bestow businesses with the engrossing customer outlook necessary to deliver services that are accurately anticipated. It is the practice of visualizing customer transactions in order to find underlying patterns, behaviours, or anomalies. For all business-to-customer activities, customer analytics embodies methods and practices that are aimed at customer processes with the intention of making gainful investments. Customer analytics is more focused than customer intelligence, which is generic in nature. Understanding a customer implies deciphering and decoding an individual within the immediate surrounding in which he or she prospers. The origin of customer analytics goes back to individual psychology, aspiration, and motivation surrounded by sociological transformation in the form of a household, marriage, family, social interaction, and peer dynamics. Sociological studies (Jensen 2001) look at family life cycles, gender, age, occupation, income, lifestyle groups, income, and lifestyle.

Jensen (2001) provides a view of customers and argues that the biggest influences are the family, the manner of upbringing, and the culture in which individuals live. When there are two siblings in the family, one may be more influenced by the outside social ecosystem than the internal family, whereas the second sibling may be more influenced by the internal family than the external ecosystem. Social adaptation includes all those processes when species and individuals change their forms and functions in ways that respond effectively to environmental changes, among other concepts that have been mentioned by researchers. In evolutionary theory, these adaptive advantages are often ascribed to individuals but can also be applied to our understanding of species as a whole. The distinction between the broad category of psychological change and the more narrow changes that shape individuals to survive is a distinction drawn from applied psychology. The decoding of customers implies understanding of their socio-demographic, socio-economic, and self-actualization needs.

Individual differences	Processing	Decision outcomes
Abilities	Problem recognition	Change
Motives	Heuristic processing	Take action
Personality	Satisficing	Include others
Attitudes	Deliberate processing	Adaptation

FIGURE 6.1 Contextual factors

Alternatively, businesses are firms who have their own characteristics owing to idiosyncrasies of location, size, years in operation, product type, level of maturity, knowledge, network impact, and so on, which influence their ability to draw attention from customers, suppliers, or society. In *The Behavioral Theory of the Firm*, Cyert and March (1963) redefined firms as heterogeneous organizations possessing standard operating procedures as their paraphernalia. Because these procedures are frequently difficult to codify, Cyert and March argued that they are not easily imitated by others or even replicated by the firm itself. This explanation of firm heterogeneity and immutability provided an important foundation for understanding firm-level behaviour. It demonstrated that the ability of the firm to adapt to its environment is not easy and that an entrepreneurial firm has an advantage over its competitors. Customer analytics is a heterogeneous operational procedure that speaks to the uniqueness of the business.

The key questions around customer analytics include:

- Who are the customers acquired by the business today?
- How have they been acquired (channel, closure time, etc.)?
- What is the profile of new customers acquired? Which is the product by which new customers usually establish a relationship?
- Which source channel is the most effective to acquire new customers?
- What is the basic profile of existing customers by products they use and to what extent?
- What are the profitability, revenue, and earnings measures against each of the customers?
- Are there differences in customer profiles between different regions, products, or vintage?

There is no definite and single answer to all these questions. Further, one should not attempt to find separate answers to these questions on a standalone basis. Managers must find a reasonably standard, unified approach to solve problems within a few dimensions. A categorical answer is preferred. However, conditional opinions are more desirable where the advantages prevail. For example, when it comes to attrition, it may not be worthwhile to look at attrition just by products, clusters, or period of acquisitions, but attrition should be visualized against the profitability segment, the usage segment, or the financial viability segment to which the customer belongs.

The engagement map of customer analytics is presented in Table 6.2.

TABLE 6.1 Customer analytics users

Role No.	Designation	Role No.	Designation	Role No.	Designation
First-level users		*Second-level users*		*Third-level users*	
1	Campaign analyst	1	CRM analytics head	1	Cluster head
2	Telesales representatives	2	Product manager	2	Business head
3	Customer service representative	3	Senior financial analyst	3	Operations manager
4	Field sales assistant	4	Campaign manager	4	Retention manager
5	Relationship manager	5	Telesales officer	5	Group CFO
6	Channel representative	6	Customer service officer	6	Marketing head
7	Branch manager	7	Telesales manager	7	Product head
8	Operations team analyst	8	Campaign analyst	8	Cluster head
9	Assistant product manager	9	Senior marketing analyst	9	Business head
10	Telesales representatives	10	Sales manager	10	Operations manager
11	Customer service representative	11	Marketing analyst	11	Retention manager
12	Channel representative	12	Campaign analyst	12	Group CFO
13	Channel manager				

TABLE 6.2 Engagement map of customer analytics

Type of customer analytics	Description	Audience
Cross-product holding	A view of the multiple holding of product families by the customers	CMO, product manager
Product-level holding	Product-level holding by demographic dimensions to identify and explore new products and services	CMO, product manager

(Continued)

TABLE 6.2 Continued

Type of customer analytics	Description	Audience
Attrition analysis	Identifies the profiles of customers who have closed their relationships with the business as well as customers who are reducing the extent of relationship with the business	CMO, product manager
Cohort analysis	Specific and detailed view of customers from a given acquisition period	CMO, product manager
Cross-sell analysis	Emphasis on customers based on certain profile characteristics and product family holdings for cross-sell opportunities	CMO
Customer profitability analysis	Profitability of customers and gathering measures of profits and earnings	CMO
New customer analysis	A comparative profile of new customer vis-à-vis existing customers	Product manager
Customer spend analysis	Customer transaction behavior and purchase behavior to understand spend patterns and potential	CMO, product manager, operations manager
Customer risk profile analysis	Understand risk profiles of the customer base against the intersection of time, channel or other dimensions	CMO, product manager

The next few sections succinctly describe the series of customer processes that could be used as significant differentiators of a business delivery.

Cross-product holdings

Cross-product holding recognizes that there are multiple holdings of product families by the customers. This could further vary by customer profile, vintage, and geography as well as the number of products held by the customer, etc. Products of a business are grouped into *product families*, and the holdings of the entire portfolio are viewed across these product families. This shows different combinations of product families across customer demographics and over time. This tracks the acquisition history of customers against product families and identifies these product families by customers.

- How many customers hold Product Families A, B, or C?
- What is the change in the product family holding over time?
- What is the cross-sell opportunity for a particular holding and a given customer profile?
- Which product family or product family combinations elicit the maximum responses across campaigns?
- How many campaigns have been launched for the promotion of a particular product over the last 5 years? What has been the amount invested so far?
- Which customer segments should be targeted for campaigns based on responses across prospect and customer demographics?
- What are the common response types and response methods?
- Why did prospects that showed a positive response not get converted into customers?
- Which product family offering generated the maximum interest?
- What are the leads for a particular product?

Product-level holdings

This analysis of product-level holdings by demographic dimensions to identify new customer segments, as well as hidden trends, may be explored by introducing new products and services. This analytical domain also facilitates comparing one demographic feature with another, so that the entire portfolio can be analyzed against various demographic combinations.

A few relevant questions are:

- Which channel of customer booking leads to a higher level of product usage?
- How are the customers distributed across a given product family combination?
- Is there a trend between such a product acquisition history and customer vintage?
- How long does it take a customer to acquire each of the products in his portfolio? What is the sequence of such acquisitions?
- Which product is most favoured by the customers? What is the profile and source channel of such product-holding customers?
- Which is the most popular product family holding, and what is the associated customer profile?

Attrition analysis

It is believed that a business spends five times more money on acquiring new customers than on retaining existing customers. Attrition analysis of customer behaviour prior to closure can assist in reducing further attrition. This analytical domain identifies the profiles of customers who have closed their relationship with the business as well as customers who are reducing the extent of their relationship with the business. Identifying and understanding customer behaviour at the time of termination of their relationship is important because most customers decide to switch

Churn analysis

Churn analysis, the description of the percentage of customers who abandon the service mid-way, can be measured at weekly or monthly intervals. Churn is calculated in a simple and accurate manner such as the ratio of the numbers of churns during a period divided by the number of customers at the beginning and the number of customers at the end. For example, customer lifetime value (CLV) implies that we cannot focus only on profits but also on costs, and hence, the ratio between customer acquisitions costs (CAC) and customer lifetime value is very related. For customers who have closed their relationships, have not renewed, or who are reducing the extent of their relationships, the business needs to focus on the reasons for attrition and take proactive steps to control attrition in the future. Since there are no third-party scores available from external sources, the business has to develop an internal score to gauge likely inactivity and eventual termination.

Cohort analysis

Cohort analysis is a longitudinal array (as opposed to a cross-sectional array) that combines subscribers from given acquisition periods. Cross-sectional samples do not provide accuracy in projecting subscriber behaviour. The crux of subscriber behaviour lies in tracking a fixed batch of subscribers belonging to one group over a period of time and in observing them as they evolve over time. For example, new subscribers are different when it comes to their usage of the product as compared to older subscribers. This implies subscribers can be compared separately by their date of acquisition. The subscriber experience varies with their on-boarding

TABLE 6.3 Churn analysis

Month	Jan.	Feb.	Mar.	Apr.
Active users	1,200	1,200	1,200	1,200
Paying users	1,000	1,000	1,000	1,000
Newly acquired users	100	100	100	100
Total users	1,300	1,300	1,300	1,300
Lost users	300	300	300	300
Net users	1,000	1,000	1,000	1,000

TABLE 6.4 Movement and migration of segments (%)

Value based/turnover based	Gold	Silver	Bronze
Gold	15	12	18
Silver	18	16	24
Bronze	38	22	25
Total	71	50	67

Note: Migration happens on account of customer activity.

experience. Cohorts display uniformity in projecting subscriber performance and lifetime value. Since each separate group forms an independent cohort, they can be compared to other cohorts to find out whether during the life cycle they impact the outcome towards greater value creation or not.

Summarizing usage value is done by moving averages. A mere moving average across all months will not be accurate as to whether performance is getting better or worse over time. Therefore, the averages need to be broken down into months and measured over quarters to discover the trends. For example, poor receipts in early months were diluting the overall health of the usage. The first month usage was growing rapidly and dropped later.

Cross-sell analysis

It is widely known that the more products and services that a customer uses, the more difficult it is for competition to wean him/her away. Businesses therefore endeavour to cross-sell an increasing number of products to their existing customers. It is easier and cheaper to cross-sell a product to an existing customer than to sell the same product to a new prospect. Cross-sell analysis identifies the customers, based on certain profile characteristics and product family holdings. It identifies cross-sell opportunities for a given product family combination.

A few questions are:

- Could cross-selling result in either enhanced or reduced activity on the old product account?
- Similarly, what happens when we cross-sell a higher-category product (gold card) when the account is holding a lower-category product (silver card)?
- What are the effects of cannibalizing the portfolio of the existing brand or product to which a cross-sell campaign has been conducted?

Cross-sell strategies are very specific to the product to be sold. For instance, the strategy to offer a mortgage to a card base could be very different from offering either a personal loan or an instalment loan or a business product to the same card base. Similarly, cross-selling a mortgage to a card customer, versus cross-selling the same mortgage to an instalment loan customer, would also be very different. Further, the success of cross-selling is very specific to the channel or to customer touch points. This depends upon understanding product penetration within customers by volume (% overlap) and quality (% contribution).

The cross-sell score predicts the likelihood of a customer accepting an offer for a specific product. Cross-sell scores are built to satisfy organic business goals such as targeting the existing customers on our portfolio against an existing product or a new product, or assigning a cross-sell score to a new customer in a prospect database against a pre-defined cross-sell combination. Depending on the size of the business, the number of products, and applicability of cross-selling, the opportunity could differ.

Customer profitability analysis

One may conceive customer lifetime value as a profitability measure. The principal idea of customer profitability is that the lives of products are unequal. Product life may depend upon their behavioural, attitudinal aspects, which must be considered. Customer profitability is defined in many spheres and in a variety of contexts. Although it is a concept that originated from the services industry, today, with the orientation of marketing heads of manufacturing industry towards the life cycle of a customer, it can be applied in any situation. Customer profitability analysis measures the profitability of customers across their product holdings, the customers that are most profitable, the measure of profit earnings, etc. The other aspect is that of potential cross-selling which the customer is subjected to and his/her cross-sell profitability. The two determinants of lifetime value of a customer are the average life of a product and the expected usage for a given customer. Net present value (NPV) from forward-looking projections of average balances (sales) can derive the interest income and also interchange (from merchandise), other income (cross-selling, fees, etc.), and all costs (including cost of funds [COF], losses, and operating and marketing costs) during the average life of the account. Exponential smoothing or ARIMA models can help you project the monthly balance (sales or cash flows) during the period of projection, which is the average life of the account. The user will provide a base attrition rate and an adjustment factor for the projection period.

Pre-screen score

Pre-screen scores are widely used as a prospect/customer marketing tool to target prospects for a new product offer or to cross-sell to include new customers. A pre-screen score uses the existing relationship type and could be used as a proxy-dependent or target variable to target the prospect/customer for the related product. For instance, one can build a model on prospects who already hold a credit card to target them or build a model on prospects who already hold a mortgage to target them for mortgage offers. For instance, a higher average balance on cards or higher utilization on cards could mean the need for a cash loan. Propensity refers to likelihood or apparent need or affinity for a new product. In live campaigns, response status is determined based on their responses during a response window. In cases of outbound telemarketing (OBTM), inbound telemarketing (IBTM), web marketing, and e-marketing, responses are obtained instantaneously whereas in case of direct mail, responses are obtained within a span of 6–8 weeks. Channels (e.g. social media, web, OBTM, IBTM, web, etc.) are important distinguishers of the response behaviour. Business can build channel-specific response scores instead of a generic response score across all channels.

Net response scores (approval scores) are another category of response scores that are built on approved accounts. A net response score as a tool is used occasionally, since approval of an account is subject to market policy changes. A mix of both types of response score (gross and net response) can be built and used.

A response score can be used in conjunction with or without prospect segmentation. The response score, when implemented in top deciles or top demi-deciles, helps differentiate prospects with higher likelihood of response. However, for each of the segments, the mail base selection would select varying depths of the mail base so as to maximize the benefit of the campaign based on their scores.

Campaign profit score

A campaign profit score seeks to estimate the net profit from a campaign and considers income accrued by the campaign and expenses for the campaign. This analysis is done at the campaign level. Business risks arise out of acquired accounts, which can be apportioned from portfolios or which may be aggregated at the profit-centre level, can be allocated across risk types such as credit, market, operational, or other risks.

Model to compute the campaign profit score:

1. Other income
    - Fee income (including all non-price income fees other than cross-sell fees): segment and duration of fee income (in years)
    - Annual adjustment factor (forecast safety factor)
    - Output: net fee income (fee income × annual adjustment factor)
2. Expenses
    - Marketing expenses: cost per mail piece, cost per telephone call, cost per field sales visit
    - Marketing expenses: cost per bureau list processing or other costs
    - Reward costs

3. Cost of funds

- COF (%): Input from the CFO's office for the given segment and time
- Discount rate (%)

4. Credit loss (%)

- Net credit loss for segment and year
- Adjustment factors

5. Business income ($)

- Total revenue = interest income + interchange revenue + other income (cross-selling, fees)
- Open accounts = open accounts (1 − attrition rate %)
- Net receivables = total revenue − cost of funds
- Business income = net receivables − total expenses − losses
- Profit centre earnings = business income × (1 − tax rate)
- Net present value = profit centre earnings × (1 + monthly discount rate)

The redemption of rewards would be specific to a reward program by the business and also the expected redemption rate against all such reward programs:

- Reward offer type: duration (years) of reward
- Reward type: points or cash
- % of new accounts to the reward program
- % redemption rate
- Unit cost of reward
- Merchant cost of reward
- Cost of redemption
- Output: redemption cost for the segment for number of years

Lifetime value

Lifetime value is a number that represents the current discounted value of expected earnings accruing from an account during the average product life of an account. Lifetime value is an important decision tool in all marketing decisions such as acquisition, retention, and also life cycle management. The potential and expected earnings from an account are derived from the historical earnings on that account with an understanding of activity.

The granularity of profit score is the large volume of retail accounts; it would be difficult to obtain a profit score on every account, since it would be a computationally intensive exercise. Further, all profits are based on historical earnings, which means the business must have sufficient history available for each account. Therefore, it is imperative to model profit scores at the segment level rather than at the account level, which means that, within a segment, all accounts have similar earnings potential. It is assumed that the average earnings will vary by portfolio, vintage, product, offer, channel, customer segment, etc. Profitability is based on the channel of acquisition since it is presumed that potential earnings are different for different channels of acquisition.

Chapter 8 will describe the use of proxies for the operating parameters of a business as represented against the drivers of revenue or costs. Therefore, profitability at the account level could be depicted using the drivers of revenue and costs at the account level only.

The drivers of revenue include:

- Price income from

  - Interest income
  - Interchange income

- Non-price income from

  - Late fees and renewal fees
  - Cross-sell income and other income

The drivers of costs include:

- Cost per acquisition (direct or indirect selling and administration)
- Cost of funds
- Losses due to attrition
- Credit losses
- Operating, servicing, and other costs

There are four principal drivers of earnings on an account, balance (or direct sales in case of credit or debit cards, referred sales); payments or pre-payments; attrition; credit losses; etc. Depending on a retail product type, the relevance of a balance model or a sales model could differ. For example, in the case of fixed instalment products such as personal loans, home loans etc., the interest income is based on a schedule of payments, which is given at the time of loan disbursal. The stream of payments differs in fixed rate or variable rate loans. However, financial services sales are significant drivers of the resulting revenue in the form of interest income or interchange income (from merchants) or both.

Payment is an important driver of revenue for credit cards, and pre-payment could affect revenue income in other instalment products. However, in debit card products, payments happen at the point of sale, and hence only the strategic business unit (SBU) earns the interchange. In financial services, the risk capital is regulated and is charged to the business separately, which is dependent on the risk-weighted assets.

Cross-sell and other income such as commissions, fees etc. are also provided as input data. Tax rates prevailing in that country would be the earnings before interest and taxes (EBIT).

New customer analysis

New customer analysis looks at new customers who are compared against the requisite of existing customers and their performance in the company's books. New customers are on board, and they come with unique expectations about brand image and the value to be derived from your product and are completely unaware of the existing level of services with old customers. The expectations of old customers may be considered reasonable. Never ever, down the line should the marketing manager attempt to sell a bundle of products to a new customer until he is denoted as an existing customer for it may intimate him/her. The distinction between a new and old customer could be 6 months to 1 year, depending on the type of industry.

An itemized enumeration of flows of new customer analysis is presented in Table 6.5.

Cross-holding analysis

The customers distributed across a given product family combination, first and second product families are most common, couplings across product-holding combinations, which is interestingly applied for existing customers. The average customer

TABLE 6.5 Focus on new customers

Type	Description
New customers	Number of new customers
New customers	% of new customers
Revenue	Revenue per customer
Revenue from cross-selling customers	Revenue per customer for cross-selling
Service performances	% customer service performance
Customer service request resolution	Time for customer service request resolution
Global customers	% of global customers
Cost of acquiring a new customer	Unit cost of acquiring a new customer

TABLE 6.6 Cross-sell summary

Product family	Assets	Liabilities	Cards	Insurance	Investment
Assets	100	15	25	5	5
Liabilities	15	100	80	4	6
Cards	25	80	100	10	12
Insurance	5	4	10	100	80
Investment	5	6	12	80	100

Note: Overlap exists between financial services products.

does hold more than one product family, where two consecutive product families are related such that customers have proven to generate higher lifetime value than single product holders. Therefore, the volume of second product holding, the usage of second holding, the usage of second product holding, and the time period that elapses between the two are important. The exact nature of association of these two products is also important. The marketing manager can align the channels suitably to cause efficient sourcing of customers holding multiple product families. Table 6.6 provides an association analysis of product holdings.

Product offer analysis

Businesses do not sell one product to one customer who then makes multiple purchases of items that are related to one another. Accessories are purchased immediately after the main product. Assortments, which are combined with a core product, are attractive for customers when bundled appropriately in packaging style, quantity, and price. These multiple purchase patterns reveal the basis for segmentation based on needs, such as buying special aluminium rims for their cars, fire extinguishers, dashboard covers, funky horns, etc. Purchasing accessories implies a different kind of customer need. The profile of cross-sold customers is different from normal customers in terms of average lifetime, eligibility of liberal time, and degree of usage. Consumption patterns based on historical information will suggest what he/she should be offered and when. The offers are attractive when they are the lead offers as compared to competitors, and hence, the business should constantly thrive to remain ahead of the market.

Customer spend analysis

Both the sources and the destination of customer spend is insightful including spend category, spend history, spend affinity, merchandise, interchange, etc. Analyzing customer transaction behaviour gives valuable insight in positioning the right product or service to the customer, the transactional purchase behaviour of the customers, etc. The merchandise earned from categories of spend are different. Segment or category analysis can lead to targeted rewards for individual customers that are based on volume, type, and time of spending. This can further enhance the proportion of merchandise expected from the specific merchants or payment gateways.

An individual makes a purchase for rational reasons and also for emotional reasons that satisfy some functional needs. For example, gifting an item of display may not serve the functional need of the buyer but will service the functional need of the person to whom it is gifted, and the buyer derives emotional satisfaction. In a B2B market, purchases could be made for competitive strength or gaining market share and not as much as a pure operational need, and hence, they are driven by relations.

Customer risk profile analysis

Customer risk profile analysis would provide businesses with the ability to understand the risk profiles of the customer base, the risk profile of customers, and how they are distributed across various demographic indicators, and distinguishes the riskier from the less risky. It scrutinizes the customer against credit, operations, attrition, litigation, service resolution, or dormancy together. Over time, with changing socio-demographic elements, payment behaviour, exposure to larger numbers of products, and increasing ownership, the risk profile of customers may improve or deteriorate. For example, a FICO or DUNS score in the USA or a CIBIL score in India can give a pre-defined score, which can be appended to existing customers to generate the analysis. Alternatively, the business can develop an internal risk score appended to existing customers to do the analysis discussed in the use cases.

A few relevant questions are:

- What is the utilization level of various products?
- What has been the source of acquiring new customers?
- How many customers have been lost in the past month or quarter?
- How many customer complaints have been received?
- What is the degree of customer resolution or satisfaction?
- How have customers that have been acquired because of campaign fared over time?
- Which customers have been dormant across all channels for the past 2 months?
- Who are the profitable customers who also show high ATM usage? Who could be offered higher transaction limits?
- Who are my problem customers who log a large amount of complaints?
- Who falls in top 10 percentile of ATM, branch, and POS users etc.?
- Which customers have shown an increase in internet usage?
- What is the profile of customers who have closed their relationship or closed accounts during the performance period? Which products did these customers hold?
- What is the profitability of the customers who have closed, and how is the profitability of the business affected by such attrition?
- What is the risk profile of customers, and how are they distributed across various demographic indicators?

Market segments

Consumers have become extremely sophisticated with regard to their beliefs and aspirations and demand personal attention in terms of choice, product benefits offers, and levels of service given. This has comprised of smaller markets with thinner ultrafine segments. The key challenge is to offer generic products that are presented as specific values to customers. The volume of information on customers needed to extricate the purchase behaviour is huge. This has put marketers on their toes. Well-contemplated segmentation can come to their rescue.

Key questions around segmentation involve:

- Which segments are the most important in terms of sales, growth, and profit?
- Which segments are growing, declining, or static?
- Who are the major competitors in each segment, and what are their strengths and weaknesses?
- How are the turnover and migration rates in each segment?
- What are the reasons behind purchases in each segment?
- Where do customers make purchases?
- How is the merchandise displayed?
- What features and benefits rewards are demanded?
- What are the price levels and value quality of products by segment?
- What are overall expectations about service quality, delivery, and fulfilment?

TABLE 6.7 Value proposition in FMCG

Benefit segment	Demographics	Behaviour	Psychography	Favoured brands
Economy	Men	Heavy users	Value oriented	Anchor White
Medicinal	Joint	Medium	Hypochondriac	Babool
Cosmetic	Teenagers	Medium	Socially active	Colgate Total
Taste	Children	Heavy	Self-involvement	Colgate Gel

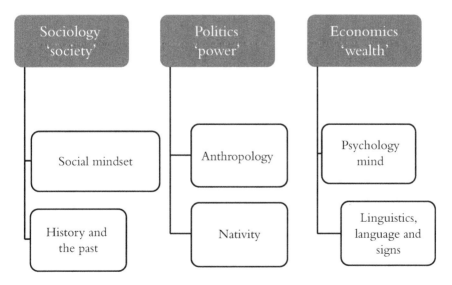

FIGURE 6.2 Social nurturing of a customer

Customer segmentation

When Coca-Cola changed its beverage products in 1985, new soft drinks were targeted at everyone, in contrast to Coke's targeting of males. There exist three choices for a marketer: first, making one product that is sold to everyone; second, making another product and selling to each segment; and third, concentrating on only one segment solely. Therefore, a segment decision is a choice from several alternatives and is a function of the value and the cost of each alternative. Perceived value from a segment depends on the size of the segment and the life of the segment because segments are not always sustainable. Natural clusters formed from the population are robust and render stable sub-populations. Unlike operationally created splits, which are subject to changing demographics and socio-psychological facts, scientifically developed segments are more stable due to rationality in the choice of variables. Customers within a segment do migrate from one segment to another (inter-segmental migration).

Psychographic segmentation is the science of using psychology and demographics to understand consumers. One of the most popular available classification systems based on psychographic measurements is the VALS1 system. Mitchell (1983) identified attitudinal and demographic questions that helped categorize adult American consumers into one of nine lifestyle types, namely survivors (4%), sustainers (7%), belongers (35%), emulators (9%), achievers (22%), I-am-me (5%), experiential (7%), societal conscious (9%), and integrated (2%). The major dimensions of the VALS framework are primary motivations called the horizontal dimension and resources (the vertical dimension). The vertical dimension segments people based on the degree to which they are innovative and have resources such as income, education, self-confidence, intelligence, leadership skills, and energy. Motivation explains consumer attitudes and anticipates behaviour. VALS includes three primary motivations that matter for understanding consumer behaviour: ideology, achievement, and self-expression. Consumers motivated by ideology are guided by knowledge and principles. Consumers motivated by achievement look for products and services that demonstrate success to their peers. Consumers who are primarily motivated by self-expression desire social or physical activity, variety, and risk taking. A person's tendency to consume goods and services extends beyond age, income, and education and includes his or her levels of energy, self-confidence, intellectualism, novelty seeking, innovativeness, impulsiveness, and leadership.

A business does a good replica with only five segments because, with too many segments, the number of sub-populations per group falls, which leads to problems in the confidence level of sub-population estimates. Similarly, when the segments are more the proportion of inter-segmental movement is higher, which can lead to unstable sub-populations. The choice and design of variables in segmentation are selected appropriately so that they are less interactive among themselves and more representative of basic demographic traits, endowments, and entitlements.

Segment optimization

The objective of the segment optimization report is to help the user select segments for the purpose of targeting and dealing with them. A decision to retain or reject segments would be based on a total cost (inclusive of marketing and other costs) or total revenue or profit across the segments. Selecting the size of the mail base, choosing customers for an OBTM offer, stamping customers for special discount offers in an IBTM offer, launching an exchange offer for existing customers, identifying suppliers for nurturing and rewarding incentives for employee retention are examples of situations where segment optimization is applied, which makes the problem of selection rational.

Let the optimization objective be:

Minimize total cost $Z = \Sigma_i\ C_i \times X_i$

or

Maximize total revenue $Z = \Sigma_i\ R_j \times X_j$

Where,

C_i = cost per account,
X_i = size of the segment i,
R_j = revenue per segment j,
RR_i = response rate for segment i,
A_i = average approval rate for segment i, and
CPA_i = unit cost of acquisition per segment i.

For deciding on the cumulative size of mail base, one should minimize total mailing costs or maximize total revenue as long as the mailing size is less than or equal to ($\leq$) the mail base (MB).

Optimization steps follow a segment creation model(s) using supervised learning techniques as described later.

TABLE 6.8 Segment optimization report

Test	Segment	Size	Cumulative size	Total cost of segment ($)	Cumulative cost of segments ($)
	Segment 1	20,000	20,000	40,000	40,000
	Segment 2	16,000	36,000	32,000	72,000
	Segment 3	11,000	47,000	22,000	94,000
	Segment 4	29,000	76,000	58,000	152,000
	Total	76,000	76,000	152,000	
Control		35,000	35,000		70,000

Note: Test and Control are drawn separately for the campaign.

Decision tree model

When a decision tree method is used to create segment nodes, the individual nodes adjacent to each other can be merged together to create segments. The modeller must take care not to mix these nodes, and each segment should be mutually exclusive. The number of segments could be summarized in the form of a lift chart to figure out the stopping criterion (B) of the test mailers. The stopping criterion (B) is the sum total of individual segments that gives exactly B number of mail pieces. The average expected response rate (or approval rate) of each segment should be at least double or more the reference (random) response rate (or approval rate). The control group of mailers can be chosen by drawing a random sample from the population. Therefore, to create a sub-population of test mailers, the campaign manager has to draw stratified random samples from two or more segments to match a given number. Later on, the control group and test group can be launched in practice. The ratio between the size of the control and test groups will depend upon the size of the original population base and also on the accuracy desired in reading the operational results of the campaign. One limitation of the decision tree model is that it results in discrete sizes of nodes and is not flexible enough to arrive at a pre-planned mailer size.

Logistic regression targeting

Unlike the earlier clustering technique or the decision tree model, which creates definite segments, a logistic regression results in each prospect (observations) being assigned a score or a probability called look-alike score. The parameter estimates of a logistic regression model could be arrived at by fitting the model to a campaign results dataset and building a campaign score. The choice of variables for the campaign includes socio-demographic, locational, work–life, and behavioural elements of the prospects or customers.

For example, one could create 20 demi-deciles of the prospect database by sorting by descending score and grouping them as given in the Applied Question section for offer targeting. This targeting methodology intends to offer low-return (higher return to business) offers to highly responsive demi-deciles because they are more likely to respond. When the lower demi-deciles' look-alike scores are lower, the business would need a better offer (lower return to business) than the upper demi-deciles. The scoring of each observation in the sub-population gives enough room and flexibility to the campaign manager to create target test mailers of any size. Further, the control group is created by drawing a random sample from the given population. Here, the manager can choose two or more groups as one control group (base offer) and multiple test groups (low-return or high-return offers), which depends on the size of the original population base and also on the accuracy desired in reading the operational results of the campaign. This strategy is also known as offer alignment, and the consideration involved is offer analysis. A second-level look at confounding attributes (elements that could not be used in the model) that can better explain the demi-decile profiles should be used to diagnose affinity.

Social media analytics

Social media analytics is the evaluation of a business's digital presence and positioning with data to achieve effective branding. This includes tracking the number of followers, number of comments, number of tweets, responses against a "post" etc., which engages the users in a media website.

The purposes are to:

- Deal with followers on a one-to-one or one-to-many basis
- Enhance social collaboration for areas such as customer service, marketing, tech support, etc.
- Fulfil the customer experience
- Generate traffic to web portals and foot traffic to brick-and-mortar locations
- Convert anonymous web traffic into leads
- Derive live responses from campaigns
- Serve as a medium of escalation for customer support

Therefore, it is a medium to understand real-time consumer preferences and the network effect of customer referrals. One good part of social media campaigns is the direct impact on online traffic and sales.

Monitoring attributes in social media include information gathered from the top few social networks and those that matter the most to the business.

Applied question

A proposed cross-sell strategy for customers intends to target customers and requires teaser offers to make the customers migrate to a higher-value proposition. The higher value premium product yields higher returns to the business. The retail stores business offers two kinds of reward coupons: $100 and $500 coupons to be redeemed to two groups of customers. These first-time users of the premium

TABLE 6.9 Focus on social media

Number of users	Number of users by community and reach
Followers	Number of followers
Activity per user	Number of likes, number of dislikes, number of referrals customers against a given routine promotion or ad hoc message board/posts over time
Number of relationships the user has in other communities	Multiple presence (Twitter, Facebook, Orkut, LinkedIn, and others); referrals; comments

product will get the redemption benefit. Using the following data on the strategy, find out if it is worthwhile to conduct the reward program.

The response rates for $100 and $500 coupons are given as 2.5% and 4.5% against 850 and 1,630 new customers, respectively. The conversion rates for the $100 and $500 coupons offered to customers are 1.5% and 2.5%, respectively. Mailing costs are negligible.

The decision is based on a trade-off, which starts with calculating the number of new customers from the $100 coupon (0.015 × 850 = 13) and from the $500 coupon (0.025 × 1,630 = 41) only. The upfront reward costs to the business are $13 × 100 + $41 × 500 = 1,300 + 20,500 = $21,800. For every 100 customers who were offered $100 coupons, 60 converted, and of those that were offered $500 coupons, only 55 converted. This means that, by offering $100 coupons to all 200 customers, the business can save on reward costs.

Therefore, from the total of 850 + 1,630 = 2,480 mailers, the business, by making $100 offers to all 2,480, will incur reward costs of only $100 × 2,480 × 0.015 = $3,750.

Note

1 Developed in 1978 by social scientist and consumer futurist Arnold Mitchell (1983).

References

Blattberg, R. C., G. Getz, and J. S. Thomas. (2001). *Customer Equity: Building and Managing Relationships as Valuable Assets*. Boston, MA: Harvard Business School Press.

Bonacchi, M., and P. Perego. (2012, Fall). Measuring and Managing Customer Lifetime Value: A CLV Scorecard and Cohort Analysis in a Subscription-Based Enterprise. *Management Accounting Quarterly*, 27–39.

Brewton, J., and W. Schiemann. (2003, January/February). Measurement: The Missing Ingredient in Today's Customer Relationship Management Strategies. *Journal of Cost Management*, 5–14.

Brown, S. A. (1996). *What Customers Value Most: How to Achieve Business Transformation by Focusing on Processes That Touch Your Customers: Satisfied Customers, Increased Revenue, Improved Profitability*. Toronto, Canada: John Wiley & Sons.

Brown, S. A. (1999). *Strategic Customer Care: An Evolutionary Approach to Increasing Customer Value and Profitability*. Toronto, Canada: John Wiley & Sons.

Cardinaels, E., and D. Van Ierland. (2007, May/June). Smart Ways to Assess Customer Profit. *Cost Management*, 26–34.

Cardinaels, E., F. Roodhooft, and L. Warlop. (2004). Customer Profitability Analysis Reports for Resource Allocation: The Role of Complex Marketing Environments. *Abacus*, 40(2): 238–258.

Cokins, G. (2015, February). Measuring and Managing Customer Profitability. *Strategic Finance*, 22–29.

Connell, R. (1995). *Measuring Customer and Service Profitability in the Finance Sector*. London, UK: Chapman & Hall.

Crafton, T. W. (2002). Do You Really Know Your Customers? *Strategic Finance* (October): 55–57.

Cravens, K., and S. C. Guilding. (1999). Examining Brand Valuation from a Management Accounting Perspective. *Advances in Management Accounting*, 8, 113–137.

Cyert, R., and J. G. March. (1992). *A Behavioral Theory of the Firm*. New York: Wiley-Blackwell.

Dalci, I., V. Tanis, and L. Kosan. (2010). Customer Profitability Analysis with Time-Driven Activity-Based Costing: A Case Study in a Hotel. *International Journal of Contemporary Hospitality Management, 22*(5): 609–637.

Davenport, T. H., J. G. Harris, and A. K. Kohli. (2001, Winter). How Do They Know Their Customers So Well? *MIT Sloan Management Review*, 63–73.

Davenport, T. H., J. G. Harris, G. L. Jones, K. N. Lemon, and D. Norton. (2007, May). The Dark Side of Customer Analytics. *Harvard Business Review*, 37–48.

Hammond, K. A. (1995). Grocery Store Patronage. *International Review of Retail, Distribution and Consumer Research, 5*(3), 287–302.

Jensen, D. T., L. Carlson, and C. Tripp. (1989). The Dimensionality of Involvement: An Empirical Test. *Advances in Consumer Research*, 16, 680–689.

Mitchell, A. (1983). *The Nine American Lifestyles*. New York: Warner.

Sinha, A. (2000). Understanding Supermarket Competition Using Choice Maps. *Marketing Letters, 11*(1): 21–35.

Timmermans, H.J.P. (1997). Store Switching Behavior. *Marketing Letters, 8*(2): 193–204.

Vilcassim, N. J., and D. C. Jain. (1991, February). A Semi-Markov Model of Purchase Timing and Brand Switching Incorporating Explanatory Variables and Unobserved Heterogeneity. *Journal of Marketing Research*, 28, 29–41.

7
BUSINESS PROCESS ANALYTICS

Business process analytics provides process champions and decision makers with knowledge about the efficiency and effectiveness of business processes. The search for rational information can be motivated by performance improvement or regulatory compliance considerations. From a performance perspective, the intent of process analytics is to shorten the reaction time of decision makers to events that may affect changes in process performance and to allow a more immediate evaluation of the impact of process management decisions on process metrics. From a compliance perspective, the goal of process analytics is to establish the adherence of process execution with governing rules and regulations and to ensure that contractual obligations and quality-of-service agreements are met. The origin of business process analytics can be dated back to motion study. This also includes application of mass flow rate, the measure of heat transfer in a process, which is common to processing industries (e.g. chemical plants, refineries, fertilizer manufacturers, gas transfers, etc.). Typical major functions in business process analytics could be process oriented, where the activities are repetitive in nature and are performed at periodic intervals. The volume of matter handled is larger, such as a batch, and the granularity of the analysis can be translated to individuals. It is in the interest of the business to gather its strength in processing efficiency by improving accuracy, reducing cycle time, and increasing volume. These processes include acquisition, delivery, fulfilment, operations, marketing, production, processing, collection, credit risk, fraud control, campaigns, customer service resolution, etc.

Key questions around business process analytics include:

- What is the process cycle of the business?
- What is the profile of new business?
- How are the new businesses doing by revenue and earnings against the plan?
- How are the business promotions and campaigns doing?
- What is the best that can be achieved in marketing analytics?

- What is the performance on collections by delinquency buckets?
- What is the performance on fraud with a fraud interception strategy?
- How can one ensure maximum achievements in customer service resolution?
- What are the vendor- and quality-dependent processes to be monitored?
- What is sales cycle effectiveness?
- What is the sales force effectiveness?

Table 7.1 presents the engagement map of business process analytics by describing individual components and audiences.

TABLE 7.1 Engagement map of business process analytics

Type of business process analytics	Description	Audience
New business analysis	The general performance of new businesses and attempts to conceive them. One can introduce a new bonus program for sales force (employees), which should be made effective to result in more new businesses.	CPO
Collections analytics	Collection will need to measure the full customer-to-cash process to ensure that both efficiency and effectiveness are tracked, monitored, pursued, and realized.	CSO
Fraud analytics	Fraud analytics detects fraudulent patterns of transactions in the form of a fraud score and determines the fraudulent nature of a transaction on the fly.	COO
Marketing analytics	Marketing analytics helps design the most optimal campaigns and measures their effectiveness and profitability over time.	COO
Campaign performance analysis	The campaign could be a campaign for acquiring new customers on a prospect database or a cross-sell campaign on existing customers.	CPO, CMO
Yield management	Also known as revenue management where revenue or profits are maximized by adopting dynamic pricing demand into tariff groups and single-order quantities.	CMO, product managers
Service resolution analysis	Service levels define customer satisfaction to a great extent. This would help the business analyze the service levels within a department and take corrective action. The business can analyze the effectiveness of its various service centres, and the quality of and time duration of service.	CMO, COO
New operations analytics	The operations champion's role in a business refers to the process functions of the business by organizing and controlling entire operations. In bigger businesses, involvement includes environment, people, and health interfaces for compliance with applicable laws, ordinances, codes, and policies.	Business head

The focus of business process analytics is on a product and its evolution, which could be a result of B2B strengths. B2B analytics locates partnership opportunities to influence and exceed the target of performance by constantly engaging partners to whom non-core activities could be outsourced. For example, an automobile company may hire design firms for elegant and superior designs, may engage agencies for product promotion, and may also outsource part of the components development to suppliers. The strategic control and monitoring of such activities are within the scope of business process analytics. Partnerships are desirable in each stage of product marketing, which starts with the product roadmap and product development, product manufacturing and prospecting, targeting, selecting and serving the key challenges to prioritize in a given channel, recruiting the right dealers, and incentivizing and retaining the sales force. Analytics can help find the trade-off between the costs of incentives and the benefits of continued relationships.

For example, in the dealer channel, the original equipment manufacturer (OEM) constantly strives to track the real-time sales details for all items in stock. Nowadays with enterprise resource planning (ERP) applications, it is possible to obtain real-time stock lying with the dealer. Depending on the partnerships and working practices, business delivery activities are standardized so that variations are kept to a minimum. The challenge for marketing processes is to find out which of these re-engineering choices, namely product design, product management, or product launching, can be made to add value for the customer. Knowledge on processes can be used in re-engineering to influence buyers and may guide buyers towards making direct purchases and eventually satisfy the customer. Competitive mapping is a routine process that can deliver significant impact to thinking about the product.

The next few sections succinctly describe business processes that could be used as significant differentiators of a business delivery.

New business analysis

Businesses incur substantial expenditures in acquiring new customers. Acquiring, bringing in new customers, is not an end in itself and a lot more is desired. An analysis of new customers answers questions such as: what is the emerging profile of new customers? What products are attracting them? Through which channel were they acquired? What was the general performance of the business and how did it attempt to acquire them? One can introduce a new bonus program for the sales force (employees), which should be made effective to result in more new business.

This analysis answers the following strategic questions:

- Who are the customers acquired today, over the last week, over the last 2 weeks, or over the last month?

- What are the profitability, revenue, and earnings measures against each customer?
- How have they been acquired (channel, deal closure time, etc.)?
- What is the profile of new customers acquired? Which is the product by which new customers usually establish a relationship?
- Which source channel is the most effective in acquiring new customers? Is there a relationship pattern between source channels and the profile of new customers acquired?
- How are the daily/weekly/bi-weekly tallies of new businesses doing in terms of revenue and earnings against the planned tallies?

TABLE 7.2 New business branch outlook

New business – branch aggregate
Branch name: Branch code:

Product name	New accounts	%	New customers	%	Balances Debit	Credit	Fees collected	Accounts from existing customers (%)
Auto	459	2.0	21	1.5				2.0
Cash credit	200	2.0	9	1.5				2.0
Current account	230	2.0	20	1.5				2.0
Total	889	2.0	50	1.5	$250	1.0%	$245	2.0

TABLE 7.3 New business product outlook

Product code: 0502

Branch name	New accounts	%	New customers	%	Balances	Fees collected	Accounts from existing customers (%)
High Street Branch	100	2.0	100	1.5	$2,000	200	2.0
Downtown Branch	143	2.0	51	1.5	$5,800	85	2.0
Total	243	2.0	151	1.5	$25,800	285	2.0

Collections analytics

Accounts receivables represent outstanding revenues from trade debtors. B2B customers take much longer to clear their dues, which results in higher accounts payable and lower working capital to a business. Collection will need to measure the full customer-to-cash process to ensure that both efficiency and effectiveness are tracked, monitored, pursued, and realized. The collections team measures the relationship between volume (calls, invoices, credit memos, etc.) and the staff required to run the transactions.

A few questions that are asked with collection analytics are:

- What is the trend and source of delinquency at the portfolio level?
- What are the roll rates by products or segments?
- What is the success of various stages in delinquency?
- What is the associated level of recovery by stages?
- What is the delinquency rate by price points and vintages?
- How can one contain delinquency and improve recovery?
- What are the recovery costs?

The measures shown in Table 7.4 are appropriate to diagnose collection processes.

TABLE 7.4 Engagement in the collection process

Collection efficiency	Indicators
Days sales outstanding (DSO)	The average time in days for when receivables are outstanding
Number of days credit sales	Number of days from invoice date to reporting date
Average days delinquent	Average time from the invoice due date to the paid date
Past due	Past due collected
Bad debt	Bad debt to sales
Active customer accounts per credit representative or collector	Active customer accounts per credit representative or collector
Operating cost per employee	Total dollars spent per employee
Cost of collections write-offs	Cost per sales dollar; write-offs as a percentage of outstanding loans
Operating efficiency	Operating cost per employee
	Cost of bad debt collection
	Number of accounts / no. of agents
	Number of calls / no. of agents
	Roll rates
	Charge-offs
High-risk accounts	Minimum $2,000 over 60 days and a total due of $5,000

Fraud analytics

Fraud analytics is contained within the operational risk function of the business. Fraud by nature could be application and transaction fraud, and the application fraud can be a source of identity theft. The sophistication of text mining or neural network algorithms can make deployment of fraud solutions a big challenge. Businesses can attempt to detect fraudulent patterns of transactions in the form of a fraud score. Customer behaviours can be associated with a transaction fraud score, which determines the fraudulent nature of transaction on the fly. The challenge is to reduce false positives to eliminate customer dissatisfaction. For example, a decline of a customer transaction at a point of sale (POS) can lead to immediate attrition and dissatisfaction. Transactions such as, late nights, being out of the city, unusual merchants, repeat transactions, and large withdrawals or transfers can be fraudulent in nature. Name fraud occurs when the applicant has only a "first name," or the "first name" is equal to the "last name" or "incomplete address," etc. Therefore, the ability to intercept fraud is based on *Bayesian* weights on occurrence, timing, location, manner, nature, product, customer segment, loss value, etc. The degree of loss recovery from fraud varies by employee, customer, supplier, or another party or by types of fraud. Fraud by employees or vendors is not easy to intercept and requires different techniques. Standard neural network tools can generate a fraud score by developing a fraud tree on a training sample to be tested on a validation sample. Fraud rates that are actually low in businesses (< 0.5%) can be challenging to fit models, which need to be scientifically enhanced to > 1% by bootstrapping or biased sampling or by rejecting inference methods. The number of weights and associated nodes in fraud engines (sets of rules) are many, and hence deployment in real-time environments is difficult. For greater accuracy, qualitative attributes (or a call back with the customer or merchant) need to be combined with the fraud score that eliminates Type II errors, which occur when customer transactions are mistakenly viewed as fraud. Table 7.5 shows a swap set to arrive

TABLE 7.5 Swap set analysis

Sub-population	Swap in		Swap out		Difference (%)	
	Actual	Projected	Actual	Projected	Actual	Projected
	No. of accounts (%)	No. of accounts (%)	No. of accounts (%)	No. of accounts (%)	(%)	(%)
Fraud Score ≥ 500	950 4.75%	1,300 6.5%	700 3.5%	1,100 5.5%	1.25%	1.0%
Fraud Score ≤ 500	1,050 5.25%	1,700 8.5%	1,500 7.5%	1,400 7.0%	−2.25%	1.5%
Total	2,000 10.0%	3,000 15%	2,200 11%	2,500 12.5%	−1.0%	2.5%

88 Business process analytics

at a cut-off limit for the ex-ante detection of fraud. The incoming set is compared against the outgoing set.

Marketing analytics

The most recent CMO Survey in 2015 reported that companies currently spend 6.7% of their marketing budgets on analytics and expect to spend 11.1% over the next 3 years. Brands plan to increase their spending on the category by a whopping 73% over the next 3 years, according to a recent *Venture Beat* report (2015).

The focus of marketing analytics is to help design the most optimal campaigns and measure their effectiveness and profitability over time. Marketing processes include the analysis required for designing campaigns, identifying campaign affinity, and generating campaign lists. Therefore, an important output of the marketing analytics will be customer and prospect target lists, which can be used as inputs to different operational customer relationship management (CRM) systems, for the purposes of defining and executing campaigns. This will embody append scores, which will be

TABLE 7.6 Engagement in marketing process

Type	Description
% gross margin for all channels	Gross margin for all channels
% revenue from emerging markets and new markets	Revenue from emerging markets and new markets
% revenue from lead channels	Revenue from lead channels
% revenue from alternate channels	Revenue from alternate channels
% revenues from new services/products to total revenue	Revenues from new services/products to total revenue
% revenue from products in each line to total products	Revenue from products in each line to total products
Months to new product launch	Months to new product launch
% costs of launching new product	Costs of launching new product
% cost of sales and marketing	Cost of sales and marketing
% Channel migration across all channels	Channel migration across all channels
% gross margin on cost of goods sold	Gross margin on cost of goods sold
% sales and marketing expenses in emerging markets	Sales and marketing expenses in emerging markets
No. of new followers in social media channels (Twitter, Facebook, What's Up, Orkut)	No. of new followers in social media channels (Twitter, Facebook, What's Up, Orkut)
No. of referrals in social media channels	No. of referrals in social media channels
No. of likes/comments in social media channels over a period of time	No. of likes/comments in social media channels over a period of time
% market share	% market share
% gross margin for all channels	% gross margin for all channels

computed using advanced predictive models, so that campaigns are designed with greater insight into the prospect population to whom the campaign is to be targeted.

Campaign performance analysis

Net present value (NPV) is effectively used when the NPV measures campaign performance. The campaign could be a campaign for acquiring new customers from a prospect database or a cross-sell campaign to existing customers. Campaign performance analysis is evaluated using campaign profitability.

The results of prospect segmentation could be used to map or populate the base curves (historical measures to be used in the model) in the case of a campaign on a prospect database.

The essential inputs in the case of campaign profitability would be:

- Campaign response rate
- Campaign approval rate
- Campaign acquisition rate

A campaign design process will start with the following steps:

1. Setting the campaign expectations

    i. Response rates
    ii. Lead rates
    iii. Win rates

2. Identifying the campaign objectives

    i. Maximize revenue
    ii. Minimize costs
    iii. Maximize returns

3. Campaign metrics

    i. How many records
    ii. How many leads
    iii. How many wins
    iv. How much revenue

Nevertheless, a model would specify the campaign metrics for a given product, segment, offer, and channel combination, since the expectation would vary by all these combinations. Realistic campaign planning must also consider competition and the economy while planning for these metrics.

The following information needs to be provided for the campaign design process:

- Name and description of the offer
- Name of the campaign segment
- Method of contact and/or channel

- Number of mail base
- Response rate (%)
- Approval rate (%)
- Acquisition rate (%)
- Number of acquired accounts
- Cost per acquisition ($ per account)

Campaign affinity

Campaign affinity is defined as the likelihood of a prospect or customer being responsive to a particular promotional offer. All promo offers need to be aligned (customized) for each segment for a given campaign. A model would have suites of offers on hand to target more than one segment during the campaign. However, sometimes it so happens that the prospects are looking for a different suite of products or offers. The accurate alignment of offers to different segments is challenging to model accurately in the absence of adequate test results and data about the market and about competition. Hence, offer alignment seeks to match the value needs of a prospect segment identified with one or more offers so as to maximize the response for a given campaign. There exists no deterministic way of understanding the offer needs of a segment, and therefore, the profiles of each of the segments need to be studied. For instance, a Value Seeker could be willing to pay a higher fee for a better value proposition whereas a Reward Seeker would be looking for more reward points. Testing of random segments with varied product offers could help understand the sensitivity of prospect segments periodically. For instance, if there is a fee product with reward points, a low-interest product with option for balance transfer, and an instalment loan product, the sensitivity of the prospect segments to each of these products will not be the same and needs to be determined so that the targeting could be accurate.

Hence, the top-ranking response scores with high offer affinity are located, and the output is the offer alignment report.

Campaign performance analysis

Promotional activities like campaigns help to expand and also exploit an existing customer base. This helps businesses analyze the effectiveness of campaigns against the costs incurred and number of new customers/new accounts acquired. This looks at the cross-section of the population to whom a campaign was targeted and the patterns of responses. It helps in innovating the customer clusters to which campaigns could be targeted by incorporating the lessons from the previous campaign. The success of campaigns is gauged from the analysis described hereafter.

Sales analysis

The success of a sales cycle is built upon the fundamental foundation of direct marketing. Direct marketing is defined as a two-way process of targeted communication

TABLE 7.7 Focus area in the sales process

Type	Description
% growth in sales	Growth in sales
Days to sales cycle close	Days to sales cycle close
% sales accounts receivables	Sales accounts receivables
% sales account receivables from new accounts	Sales account receivables from new accounts
% deal conversion to all prospects	Deal conversion to all prospects
% cost of deal conversion to total number of deals	Cost of deal conversion to total number of deals
% back order sales to total sales	Back order sales to total sales
% renewal sales accounts	Renewal sales accounts
% sales price to MRP	Sales price to MRP
% sales returns	Sales returns
% growth in sales	Growth in sales
Days to sales cycle close	Days to sales cycle close

that uses one or more media channels to reach the target. Direct marketing is incomplete when the receiver fails to acknowledge or comprehend the piece of "matter" reached out to him or her.

Table 7.7 shows how successful sales are gauged.

Yield management

Yield management is known as revenue management where revenue or profits are maximized by adopting dynamic pricing. It is applicable to hotels, airlines, or telecommunications, which are perishable services accompanied by uncertain demand. The nature of problems includes overbooking, partitioning demand into tariff groups, and single-order quantities. When there are assorted products along with the main producer revenue, management becomes challenging. Hotel and airlines with reservation policies lose money when there are no-shows or cancellations half an hour before the actual check-in or departure. This results in airlines and hotels overbooking their systems where turned-out customers will be compensated. Similarly, depending on the level of overbooking or each segment, the business may charge differential fares from customers. Table 7.8 shows some examples of dynamic and differential pricing.

The useful life of objects such as newspapers, flowers, baked goods, and seasonal items is shorter, and hence only single-order delivery takes place. The overestimation of demand must be balanced with the cost of underestimating the demand.

A few questions that are answered by yield management:

1   For how long does a customer book a stay at a hotel when there is variable pricing?

2 What causes the involuntary cancellation of bookings?
3 How do airlines price tickets for different flight legs?
4 How do hotels deal with guests staying over multiple nights?
5 How do hotels deal with low-demand stays through several high-demand days?
6 How do assortments like restaurants, convention space, and other services affect pricing and contribute to a hotel's profitability?
7 How can one price peak-hour video on demand against an off-peak download request from a mobile internet user?

These questions are answered with a uniform approach to modelling traffic where the functional form would vary with the nature of subscribers (customer or guests).

Let Co = cost of overestimating demand or no-shows,
Cu = cost of underestimating demand or no-shows,
$P(N < X)$ = probability of overestimating demand or no shows,
$P(N \geq X)$ = probability of underestimating demand or no shows,
N = number of units demanded or no shows, and
X = number of units ordered or overbooked.

Introduce some protection level for a fare, which is the number of rooms reserved for that fare or higher, and denote it with M. Set some booking limit for low-fare rooms. The booking limit is the limit on the number of reservations allowed at that fare or lower:

Protection level for M fares = capacity − booking limit of L fares

Table 7.8 describes a situation to determine the maximum percentage of overbookings that should be allowed. The column shows the joint probability of overbooking when differential prices are charged.

The optimal no-shows falls between 0.4 and 0.7, and since the manager is concerned with no-shows less than or equal to 0.517, we choose the next lowest value (0.4), which points to 3% overbooking rate. On the other hand, extreme shortages are important costs.

TABLE 7.8 Forms of dynamic pricing and differential pricing

Dynamic pricing	Differential pricing
Discounts during off-season	Bulk discount (group pricing, size based)
Periodic sales (customers reservation price)	Channel pricing (different channels)
	Geographic (regional)
Adjusting period to period aggregate demand	Time-based differentiation (different rates for different delivery times)
Periodic discounts during off-season	Product version (offer variants)
	Loyalty pricing
	Payment mode (pre-paid, online, cash, credit)

Service resolution analysis

Service levels define customer satisfaction to a great extent. This would help the business analyze service levels within the department and take corrective action. The business can analyze the effectiveness of its various service centres. The quality of and time duration of service resolution are critical. In businesses, service levels define customer satisfaction to a great extent. Service resolution analysis helps managers analyze the service levels within the organization and take corrective action. The manager can analyze the effectiveness of its various service centres.

This analysis leads to answers to the following questions:

- What are the rates of delays in processing service requests?
- Are there any patterns in these slippages?
- What is the inquiry channel commonly used by customers?
- Which product accounts for most number of service calls?
- Which types of customers log a large chunk of service requests?
- Which types of service requests do customers frequently make? This can throw light on the way the calls are attended to or the sufficiency of the information provided to customers.
- What is the time lag in closing the service requests?
- How are service requests closed: normally or by paying a penalty?

Process re-engineering

Re-engineering is the fundamental rethinking and radical redesign of processes to improve dramatically in terms of cost, quality, service, and speed. Process re-engineering is about reinvention rather than incremental improvement. Process improvement is the systematic study of the activities and flows of each process to improve them. The purpose is to learn the cycle, understand the process, and dig out the details using process tools such as the *fishbone diagram* and process charting. The steps, which are performed in cycles, could be segregated into basic operations, such undertakings as delivery, fixing, mending, bending, handing over, changing the shape of an object, creating a new design, etc. The second activity is transportation from one point to another point by a machine or an object using a man, machine, or device. Delays are the time lags between any two subsequent operations because of a capacity mismatch or a processing time mismatch. Staging, stowing, storing, or stocking are examples of storage operations that are essential to fulfilling customer orders. Pareto charts are tools to make decisions on focusing on critical and important activities that matter to the business the most.

Table 7.10 uses the example of a leading, multi-cuisine restaurant trying to use process re-engineering to maintain overall customer satisfaction at a fixed level.

TABLE 7.9 Service resolution report

| Request types | Complaint report – monthly outlook ||||||||||||
| | Month 1 |||| Month 2 |||| Month 3 ||||
	Number of requests	Status	Average resolution times	Average customer feedback rating (1–10)	Number of requests		Average customer feedback rating	Average resolution time	Number of requests		Average resolution time	Average customer feedback rating
New account welcome kit	81	Closed	1.5	5.5	89		1.5	5.5	84		1.5	5.5
	20	Open	2.5	6.5	22		2.5	6.5	21		2.5	6.5
Change of address	75	Closed	1.5	5.5	74		1.5	5.5	70		1.5	5.5
	11	Open	2.5	6.5	14		2.5	6.5	10		2.5	6.5
Total	187		2.25	6.25	199		2.25	6.25	185		2.25	6.25

Business process analytics 95

TABLE 7.10 Restaurant Pareto analysis

Complaint	Frequency	Percentages	Cumulative percentages
Poor ambience	5	4%	4%
Poor welcome	10	8%	13%
Mistakes in billing	12	10%	18%
Delay in order taking and service	20	17%	27%
Delay in billing	22	18%	35%
Unclean tables	24	20%	39%
Crampy toilets	26	22%	42%
Total	119	100%	122%

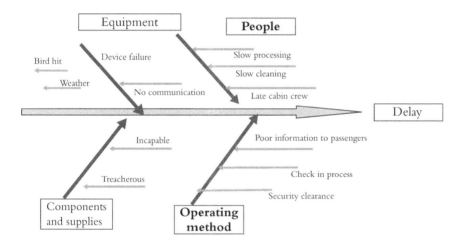

FIGURE 7.1 Fishbone diagram – customer delay in logistics

Fishbone diagrams (also called cause-and-effect diagrams) are another tool that can relate performance issues to their potential causes, which could be caused by humans or machines in operation. In a fishbone diagram, the main performance gaps are found at the fish's head, which is the target to be measured and controlled. The fish is made up of bones and ribs, where the bones are the major cause groups and the ribs are the attributes that relate to the major groups. Figures 7.1 and 7.2 use a fishbone diagram and a Pareto analysis, respectively, to explain the reasons for flight delays at major airports.

The Pareto chart indicates the causes that account for more than 75% of the delay or defect. The Pareto chart also provides a comparison between two causes against a given incremental contribution to the accumulated frequency. Managers should concentrate on the most critical cause and also the cause that contributes to the maximum incremental defects.

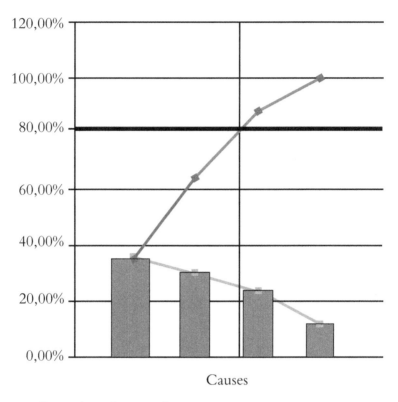

FIGURE 7.2 Pareto chart of cause attributes

Simulation

Simulation is useful for businesses in many situations and is recommended to understand behaviour, outcomes, results, and phenomenon where it is impossible to conduct real tests without dismantling or disturbing the components of the system, such as people, machines, materials, or environments. Simulation can also be used in situations where no or very little data is available. Simulation itself is an experiment where the scenario of a revised or changed layout of producing the product is realized. Simulation can be used to obtain operating characteristics (estimates) in much less time than is required when gathering the same operating data from real systems. For example, a simulation of airport delays can generate data on arrivals, data on landing time, entry gate, etc. The analysis of simulation results can be done fairly quickly, and faster decisions can be made.

The following two examples describe applications of simulations in business situations.

The first case is that of a small bank branch where customers enter into one of three lines served by three tellers and leave the branch only after their requests are served. Currently, the branch has three tellers working from 10:00AM to 4:30PM with a 30-minute break any time between 1:00PM to 3:00PM. There are often customer complaints regarding the waiting time, which varies a lot not only during the day but also around weekends. Further, there are government receipts at every quarter end and salary disbursals at the beginning of every month.

Management is discussing two options, adding one more counter with a fixed cost of US$9,000 and variable costs of US$10,000 per annum or rationalizing the work allocation across the three counters so as to maximize the productivity. The second option is favourable only when the three principal transactions – cash receipts, cash disbursals, and issues/cancellations of demand drafts – are divided across the three. However, the alternative is to make all the three counters multi-purpose so that all three types of transactions can be handled. Every batch of customers in units of ten could be alternatively aligned to any of the three multi-purpose counters. For each counter, there is a waiting time (minutes) and processing time (minutes), and customers may not jump or skip a queue. Three types of information are required for determining the optimal combination that works for the manager in the best way. This case explains the three counters, which can be extended to any situation, and the multiple numbers of counters in real life. By asking, when customers enter the queue, how long it takes to serve them, the maximum length of the queue can be determined for rationalizing manpower.

Each of the alternatives planned by the manager can be run separately for 50 or 100 trials from 10:00AM to 2:00PM and from 2:00PM to 4:30PM. The random simulation provides data on how many customers could be accommodated at what time of the day and also the tolerance limits of processing time. Managers can report the distribution of these data and obtain estimates of median, mode, and mean of the processing time and length of the queue for all the three counters separately. Table 7.11 shows the results of the simulation cases of thirteen trials conducted on the three teller counters separately, and the results are summarized by combining the three counters together in Table 7.12.

In the second case, traffic analytics examines the traffic of online customers to a web portal, which is random and discrete, by look at waiting lines and arrivals using Littles's law. The number of customers in a waiting line is related to the arrival rate and the waiting time of customers, which is expressed as $L = \lambda$, where λ = number of visitors / hour:

The average time spend by a visitor = no. of visitors / λ

When the time spent by a visitor at a portal without any activity is unreasonable, the web administrator can focus on adding the capacity of the website to accept requests or can improve the processing speed of servers to improve the user experience. Simulation studies using runner tools can be used to generate scenarios of traffic and its management. Assuming that more than one server exists in the back-end to serve burgeoning traffic, a visitor unaware of the facility could be automatically directed to one of the other servers.

98 Business process analytics

TABLE 7.11 Simulation trials of branch banking tellers

Trial no.	Teller							
Case	Tellers			Teller 1		Teller 2		Teller 3	
	Start time	Random no.	Waiting time	Processing time	Waiting time	Processing time	Waiting time	Processing time
1	10:00AM	87	4	7	2	9	8	5
2	10:30AM	91	3	8	3	8	3	3
3	11:00AM	56	3	8	1	6	3	7
4	11:30AM	9	5	9	2	8	6	4
5	12:00AM	89	2	9	3	7	4	6
6	12:30PM	82	1	6	3	7	4	6
7	1:00PM	89	1	9	3	6	5	3
8	1:30PM	15	2	8	3	7	5	3
9	2:00PM	83	1	8	2	8	4	6
10	2:30PM	2	4	9	3	8	6	6
11	3:00PM	68	1	7	4	6	9	5
12	3:30PM	6	3	7	2	8	4	7
13	4:30PM	7	2	7	5	7	2	2
Mean		2.46	7.85	2.77	7.31	4.95	4.86	4.86
Median		2	8	3	7	4	5	5
Mode		1	7	3	8	4	6	6
Std. Deviation		1.25	0.95	0.99	0.80	1.7	1.8	1.83
Minimum		1	6	1	6	2	2	2
Maximum		5	9	5	9	9	7	7

Source: Krajewski, Lee J.; Ritzman, Larry P.; Malhotra, Manoj K., *OPERATIONS MANAGEMENT*, 9th Ed., ©2012, pp. 251–252. ISBN 0136065767 Reprinted by permission of Pearson Education, Inc., New York.

TABLE 7.12 Simulation summary of branch banking tellers

Waiting time	Frequency	% cumulative	Waiting time	Frequency	% cumulative
0–1	5	12.82%	0–2		2.56%
1–3	18	58.97%	2–6	1	33.33%
3–5	12	89.74%	6–9	12	77.12%
> 5	4	100.00%	> 9	26	100.00%

When there are m identical servers, the service distribution of each server is exponential with a mean service time of $\frac{1}{\mu}$.

Let rho = average utilization of the system,
P_0 = probability that zero visitors are hitting the portal, and
P_n = probability that n visitors are hitting the portal.

The arrival distribution of visitors is a Poisson distribution for n customers in T time periods:

$(l_m T)^T / n! \, e^{-\lambda T}$ for $n = 0, 1, 2, \ldots$

where $P(t \leq T)$ is the probability that the surviving time of a visitor will be no more than T time periods.

The probability can be calculated by $1 - e^{-\mu T}$ where μ = average number visiting and exiting the portal where,

t = servicing time spent by the visitors,
T = target servicing time,
L_q = average number of visitors in the waiting line,
W_q = average waiting time of visitors in line = $\frac{L_q}{\mu}$,
W = average total time spent in the system including browsing, clicking, and exiting = $W_q + \frac{1}{\mu}$, and
L = average number of visitors in the service system = $\lambda \times W$.

Using exemplary numbers, the web administrator can plan resources and deploy web services.

This can be applied to the most visited cases in modern-day call centre operations to please the customers while profiting. A call centre has ten seats that are full-time equivalents (FTEs), serving calls that discretely arrive inbound when the time taken per call is 2 minutes and the calls arrive at an average of 81 per hour. Calls need to wait in a queue before they are assigned to seats, and waiting times exceeding 5 minutes are monitored.

The following example calculates the utilization time of handling and routing incoming calls in an inbound call centre.

Let the utilization ρ derived using λ as the number of calls per unit time and μ as the time spent per call.

$\rho(\text{rho}) = \frac{\lambda}{\mu} = \frac{81}{60/2} = 0.9$, which means the agents are occupied 90% of the time.

Average time spent in the system $W = W_q = \frac{1}{\mu}$

Hence,

$$P_0 = \frac{1}{1 + \frac{81/30}{1} + \frac{2.7^2}{2} + \left[\frac{2.7^3}{26} \times \left(\frac{1}{1-0.9}\right)\right]} = 0.0249$$

$$L_q = \frac{0.0249(81/30)^3(0.9)}{3!(1-0.9)^2} = 7.352 \text{ visitors}$$

$$W_q = \frac{Lq}{\lambda} = \frac{L7.352}{81} = 0.0908 \text{ hour}$$

$$W = W_q + \frac{1}{\mu} = 0.0908 + \frac{1}{30} \text{ hour} = 0.1241 \times 60 = 7.45 \text{ minutes}$$

Therefore, the average time of servicing is 7.45 minutes against a capacity utilization of 7.352 calls.

Learning (η) in production (conversion)

A production process involves the iterative feeding of batches or volumes of a combination of inputs, such as labour, capital, raw material, energy, and overheads, to produce finished goods. The sum total of all such inputs together defines the technology to produce output. The specific technology in question is the result of output from inputs and is not a constant parameter that changes over time with increasing number of iterations. The effect of changes to the churning of output from a fixed set of inputs is known as learning efficiency or conversion efficiency. Improvement occurs because workers learn by repeating as they work on the job, which is more directly felt and observed in service sector units. The learning effect can be measured in the form of reduced conversion time, higher quality of output, or reduced length of engagement with the task assigned to the agent. The benefit of learning curves is the planning of factors in order to optimize scheduling of jobs and also manpower or resources.

A simple way to gauge the learning curve is by assuming the time required to produce the nth unit, given as:

$$t_n = t_1 L n^b$$

Where t_n = time required to produce the nth unit,
t_1 = time required to produce the first unit,
n = cumulative number of units, and
$b = \dfrac{Lr}{Ln2}$ where r is the learning curve coefficient.

In the case of multiple products/segments and customers, r_i would reflect the learning coefficients, which would be modelled when products or segments could be substituted. However, when services are substitutable, the lessons from one product could be applied to other products and also other segments. The factor r is adjusted for both the number of products of a given type and the total number of products across all segments and types produced. The point of inflexion of the learning curve is the saturation level of r for an optimum volume of output. The coefficient r varies from sector to sector, but it can be derived using a likelihood maximization model.

New operations analytics

The operations champion's role in a business refers to the process functions of the business by organizing and controlling entire operations. In bigger businesses, involvement includes environment, people, and health interfaces for compliance with applicable laws, ordinances, codes, and policies. Therefore, setting up a new branch, facility, installation, customer care centre, production centre, manufacturing centre, or processing centre is an important area contributed by new operations.

The metrics shown in Table 7.13 reflect the interest of managers in new operations analysis.

TABLE 7.13 Focus in new operations

Type	Description
% new employees in operations	New employees in operations
% operating expenses	Operating expenses
% asset utilization to revenue	Asset utilization to revenue
% employees in research and development	Employees in research and development
% employees in sales and marketing to total employees	Employees in sales and marketing to total employees
% cost of research and development to total operating expenses	Cost of research and development to total operating expenses
No. of new % employees in operations	No. of new employees in operations
% operating expenses	Operating expenses

To summarize, there exists fundamental difference between B2C and B2B processes when it comes to deciding analytics delivery forms purely on account of the distinctive consumers (managers). For example, managers who handle business customers have longer cycles, lower responses, larger ticket sizes, and gigantic collection efforts with the risks of reputation or credit loss. The relationships are based on legal service agreements and need the consent of the onsite engineering team. Supplier dependency for a given new customer is much higher. Specificity in value propositions is the key to success in B2B transactions. A reverse supply chain is also highly desirable.

B2C analytics is aimed at meeting the routine demand for the periodic consumption of brand-specific analytical outputs by retail managers. Short-cycle, low-ticket seasonal, and mass-selling products make the nature of B2C analytics speedier, more standardized, and penetrative. A well-designed array of distribution networks can help tap into the B2C market, which creates the need for tracking lower average life cycle products. Lost sales and back orders are acceptable in B2B but not so much in B2C.

Applied questions

From the following data, calculate the sample size for a promotional campaign for a business that results in the maximum performance for the business. How would you align offers to customers that achieve the intended mail base and minimize the total mailing costs?

The expected response rate from the two segments is 2.5% and 3.5% against a uniform approval rate of 60% for both. The fulfilment costs per account are $2 against mailing costs of $1 per piece. These two segments will be offered two different terms for the offer. The campaign manager intends to achieve a net income of $160 per account, which is possible by choosing an appropriate sample size. Each account can deliver a lifetime value of $220.

Using the formulae of minimum sample size $n = \dfrac{z^2 \times p \times (1-p)}{e^2}$, we find

$$n_1 = \dfrac{1.96^2 \times 0.025 \times (0.975)}{0.03^2} = 104, \text{ and } n_2 = \dfrac{1.96^2 \times 0.035 \times (0.965)}{0.03^2} = 144. \text{ This is}$$

when the campaign manager wants to be 95% confident that the response rates have been estimated to be within ± 3% (*e*) (for *p* = 0.025 or 0.03) of the true value. With a 60% approval rate, this results in 1.5% and 2.3% of conversation rates from each segment, respectively. Let *MB* be the total mail base where $MB = n_1 + n_2$, which results in $0.015 \times n_1 + 0.023 \times n_2$, the number of approved accounts expected to make a gain of $230 × (0.015 × n_1 + 0.023 × n_2) of income.

The total costs of mailing and fulfilment equals $20 × ($n_1$ + n_2) − $100 × (0.015 × n_1 + 0.023 × n_2), which puts the total net income as *NI* = [$220 × (0.015 × n_1 + 0.023 × n_2) − $20 × ($n_1$ + n_2) − $100 × (0.015 × n_1 + 0.023 × n_2)], and *NI*/account = *NI* / (0.015 × n_1 + 0.023 × n_2) = $167.00 ≥ $160. The multiples of the ratio of a segment-based mailing proportion, $n_1 : n_2$ = 104 : 144, can be maintained to achieve the average net income of $167.00 per account.

References

Apostolou, D., G. Mentzas, L. Stojanovic, B. Thoenssen, & T. P. Lobo. (2010). A Collaborative Decision Framework for Managing Changes in E-Government Services *Government Information Quarterly, 28*(1): 101–116.

Beck, T., A. Demirguc-Kunt, and M.S.M. Peria. (2007). Reaching Out: Access to and Use of Banking Services across Countries. *Journal of Financial Economics, 85*, 234–266.

Brown, I., Z. Cajee, D. Davies, and S. Stroebel. (2003). Cell Phone Banking: Predictors of Adoption in South Africa – An Exploratory Study. *International Journal of Information Management*, 23, 381–394.

Chen, L.-d. (2008). A Model of Consumer Acceptance of Mobile Payment. *International Journal of Mobile Communications, 6*(1), 32–52.

CMO Survey. (2015). *Strong Economic Outlook Spurs Marketing Spending, – Highlights and Insights Report, February 17th, 2015.* New York: CMO.

Donner, J., and C.A. Tellez. (2008). Mobile Banking and Economic Development: Linking Adoption, Impact, and Use. *Asian Journal of Communication, 18*(4), 318–332.

Dumas, M., M. La Rosa, J. Mendling, and H. A. Reijers. (2013). *Fundamentals of Business Process Management.* Heidelberg, Germany: Springer.

Galbraith, J. R. (2005). *Designing the Customer-Centric Organization: A Guide to Strategy, Structure and Process.* London: John Wiley & Sons.

Gillot, J.-N. (2008). *The Complete Guide to Business Process Management.* New York: Joel-Noel Gillot.

Gong, Y., and M. Janssen. (2011). From Policy Implementation to Business Process Management: Principles for Creating Flexibility and Agility. *Government Information Quarterly, 29*(Supplement 1): S61–S71.

Harmon, P. (2007). *Business Process Change: A Guide for Business Managers and BPM and Six Sigma Professionals.* New York: Morgan Kaufmann Publishers.

Kim, C., M. Mirusmonov, and I. Lee. (2010). An Empirical Examination of Factors Influencing the Intention to Use Mobile Payment. *Computers in Human Behavior, 26*, 310–322.

Ko, R.K.L. (2009). A Computer Scientist's Introductory Guide to Business Process Management (BPM). *ACM Crossroads, 15*(4): 11–18.

Krajewski, L. J., L. P. Ritzman, Malhotra, and K. Manoj. (2012). *Operations Management.* 9th ed. New York: Pearson. Reprinted by permission of Pearson Education, Inc., New York, New York.

Laforet, S., and X. Li. (2005). Consumers' Attitudes towards Online and Mobile Banking in China. *International Journal of Bank Marketing, 23*(5), 362–380.

Laukkanen, T., and M. Pasanen. (2007). Mobile Banking Innovators and Early Adopters: How They Differ from Other Online Users? *Journal of Financial Services Marketing, 13*(2), 86–94.

Ould, M. (2005). *Business Process Management: A Rigorous Approach.* London: The British Computer Society.

Panagacos, T. (2012, September 25). *The Ultimate Guide to Business Process Management: Everything You Need to Know and How to Apply It to Your Organization.* Create Space Independent Publishing Platform.

Smith, H., and P. Fingar. (2003). *Business Process Management: The Third Wave.* Tampa, FL: Meghan-Kiffer.

Spanyi, A. (2003). *Business Process Management Is a Team Sport: Play It to Win!* Tampa, FL: Anclote Press, an imprint of Meghan-Kiffer Press, 2003.

Thiault, D. (2012). *Managing Performance through Business Processes: From BPM to the Practice of Process Management.* CreateSpace Independent Publishing Platform.

Venture Beat. (2015, December 16). The State of Marketing Analytics: Insights in the Age of Customer. *Venture Beat*

8
FINANCIAL ANALYTICS

This chapter deals with financial analytics, an explicit part of business analytics, and provides nuances to understanding, reckoning, and interpretation to demonstrate subtleties of financial analytics.

Defining financial analytics

Financial analytics is defined as the elicit derivation of the financial impact of business analytics, which is an essential facet of business analytics and is represented in the form of a profit and loss (P&L) statement and thus can provide the overall material burden on a balance sheet. Financial analytics has evolved as a discipline as it actually provides a common language for analytical communication to all the stakeholders of a business organization for them to understand and appreciate the discipline of business analytics. In fact, financial analytics has made business analytics easier to contemplate and apply across various cross-functional units within the business. The origin of financial analytics is rooted to applied finance and asymmetric information, namely Brealey and Myers (2002); Brigham and Weston (1993); Ross, Westerfield, and Jaffe (1995); etc. Therefore, any mention of business analytics in the context of strategic initiatives is incomplete without financial analytics. This argument of commonality in expression can render the regulatory compliance or soundness of business operations. The facets of compliance obligations are multi-dimensional. with which the business needs to comply generally as an enterprise.

Key questions around financial analytics include:

- What is the level and degree of financial impact?
- What are the measures of financial impact?
- What are the drivers of financial impact?

- How much did the firm grow in net interest margin (NIM), return on investment (ROI), return on equity (ROE), net contribution margin (NCM), and return on total assets (ROTA)?
- What are the financial performances relative to sales and total assets?
- What is the economic capital charge?
- What is the regulatory capital charge?
- How much does it pay to implement a new marketing campaign?
- How much does it pay to introduce a new customer segmentation schema?
- Should sales force deployment require incentive pre-planning?
- Why should pricing be dynamically determined?
- How can one calculate the economic value of assets (EVA) and shareholder value added (SVA)?
- How can one balance the rewards to offer a given customer?

A simpler look at financial analysis can be found in Table 8.1, which provides an enumeration of simple financial measures.

The most unique aspect of financial analytics is the inherence of working with net (final) turnout, which is derived only when taxes, duties, levies and penalties, or capital obligations are charged to the business. Similarly, financial analytics encompasses the versatility of the risks of doing business and also translates such risks into net turnout. For example, the factors that are measured in value terms and denoted in a currency include annual transportation costs, taxes, inbound and outbound transport, labour wages, utilities, and separate revenue sources (sales, stock or bond issues, interest income). These financial components can be aggregated to a single measure of financial merit such as total costs, return on investment, and many others. Therefore, financial analytics deals with refined numbers rather than raw figures of activity.

TABLE 8.1 Simple financial measures

Ratio	Indication
No. of days in cash-to-cash cycle time	Cash conversion
% profit after tax	Net income
Price to earnings ratio	Worthiness
% transfer price	Intermediation
% cost of capital	Cost of funds
% working capital cost	Incremental cost of funds
% accounts payable turnover	Creditors
% accounts receivable turnover	Debtors
% net operating margin	Value added
Days of maturity of debt	Borrowing cycle
Leverage	Leverage
Cash conversion cycle	Cash cycle
Collection period	Debtors' cycle
Economic value added (EVA)	Value added

TABLE 8.2 Engagement map of financial analytics

Type of financial analytics	Description	Audience
Profitability analytics	A detailed view of the synthesis of profitability in alternate forms	CFO, SBU head
Cash flow analytics	Determines free cash flows and forecasts cash flow	CFO
Interest rate analytics	The dynamics of interest rate as against asset and liability structure	CFO, fund managers
Liquidity analytics	The drivers of liquidity problems in the short-term both in terms of shortfall/ excess liquidity	ALM managers, CCO, SBU head
Incremental capital	The burden of buffering more capital against expected business risks that arises in every new transaction	CFO
Regulatory capital	The need to maintain minimum Basel II capital for the risk weighted assets and the changes thereupon	CRO, CCO
Maturity and behavior	Insight into the pattern of maturity and timeliness of assets and liabilities to make fund allocation decisions and also the need to raise incremental debt against equity	CFO
Merger and de-merger analytics	Different ways of measuring the success of M&A, the rationale for value maximization, distinguishing between short-run and long-run performance and value creation, payment, and financing methods	CSO

TABLE 8.3 Ratio analysis

	Category	High	Low
A	Liquidity ratios		
	Current ratio	High level of inventory High level of book debts Prompt payment to creditors	Slow moving Faster realization of debtors Unable to pay creditors
	Acid test ratio	Idle funds	Strain on liquidity
B	Solvency ratio		
	Debt: equity ratio	Low stake Over-trading Aggressive	Low reliance on credit High capital gearing Conservative management

C	Activity ratios		
	Inventory turnover ratio	Faster sales	Obsolete stock
		Manufacturing unit diverted to trading activity	Marketing problem
			Poor demand
	Debtors velocity ratio	Slow collection	Weak management
		Highly competitive	Cautious trading
		Poor quality of goods	Only net sales taken
	Creditors velocity ratio	Poor servicing	Fall in reputation
		Quality of goods received is poor	Product in great demand
D	Profitability ratios		
	Return on investment	Efficient utilization of assets	Idle/underutilized assets
			Heavy capital investment
	Gross profit ratio	Some manufacturing expenses not accounted	Increase in cost of production
		Sales value	Selling raw materials
		Stocks overvalued	Stocks undervalued
	Operating profit ratio	High turnover	Low turnover
E	Financial stability ratio		
	Financial stability	Sustainability index	Financial goals in the short and long term; sources of income mix; fixed costs and expenses management; income generation
		Net stable funding ratio (NSFR)	Stable funding from long-term sources. More equity and less debt (in particular less short-term debt), lower loan-to-deposit ratios, and more diversified funding structures improve stability

The sustainability index refers to financial goals in the short and long term, sources of income mix, fixed costs and expenses management, and income generation.

The presence of more shorter-term debt harms stability. Higher reliance on short-term debt is associated with an increase in distress. Higher reliance on wholesale funding (a higher loan-to-deposit ratio) is linked to higher distress. This funding ratio seeks to calculate the proportion of long-term assets, which are funded by long-term, stable funding. The three forms of stable funding include customer deposits, long-term wholesale funding, and equity. For a financial services business, long-term assets are a combination of all (100%) loans longer than 1 year, a portion (85%) of loans to retail investors with a remaining life shorter than 1 year, half (50%) of loans to corporate investors with a remaining life shorter than 1 year, and a small part (20%) of business investments in government and corporate bonds, which also include off-balance sheet exposures.

Measuring financial impact

The next few sections succinctly describe a series of financial processes that could be used as significant differentiators of a finance function.

Product profitability analysis

Product profitability is defined as the difference between the revenues earned from, and the total costs associated with, a product over a specified period of time. Product profitability analysis requires that all relevant costs be traced to products and then matched to their corresponding revenues. Such analysis can induce a wide range of management decisions, such as product pricing and product portfolio analysis, across acquisition, retention, and life cycle management.

The benefits of product profitability include a deeper view of which products and product mixes are cost effective for refining product pricing strategies. Real-time analytic capability of what discounts can be given to customers while accurately assessing the impact on margins to ensure margin protection; identifying pockets of growth in margins, not just in revenue; and accurately forecasting the profitability of new products and proposed product mixes.

Product profitability is a result of expected earnings from a product and is derived from the historical earnings on that account. Further, profits are based on historical earnings; profitability at the account level could be gauged using the drivers of revenue and costs at the product level. Costs that cannot be allocated to individual accounts are arrived at the unit level. Therefore, expected profits are defined as the stream of net earnings that accrue to the business when each identified earning amount is associated with a probability of occurrence. The drivers of profit include the drivers of revenue and the drivers of costs of doing business.

The drivers of revenue include:

- Price income from sales
- Interest income from investments
- Interchange income from brokerages
- Non-price income from other sources
- Late fees and renewal fees
- Cross-sell income and other income

The drivers of costs include:

- Cost per acquisition
- Cost of funds
- Losses due to attrition
- Credit or fraud losses
- Operating and other costs

Hence, there are four principal drivers of earnings on an account:

- Balance (or sales revenue)
- Payments (or pre-payments in financial services, trade credit periods)
- Attrition (likelihood of voluntary or involuntary departures)
- Credit or fraud losses (likelihood of delinquency)

Cash flow analysis

Cash flow analysis is defined as the technique of apprehending cash flow that varies in duration (maturity) with a goal to manage cash or cash equivalent and deploying surplus cash. It aims to equip the decision making towards cash estimation, timing of inflows and outflows, maintaining optimal levels, and generating incremental returns from investments. Cash flow analytics evaluates the availability of funds and revolves around the principal and interest of each payment, collateralization and interest coverage, re-investment of proceeds, early amortization, and the spread of a firm. The inflows are financing and investing, whereas the outflows could happen across all three sources. Achieving the right mix and maturity of inflows is the principal challenge.

A few questions to be answered are:

- What are the future cash inflows and outflows in different time buckets?
- What are the resultant gaps for the institution?
- Which regions/branches have a fair balance between cash inflows and outflows?

TABLE 8.4 Product sales data of garden furniture products

Year 1 estimated unit sales	100
Year 1 unit price	400.00
Unit price compound annual growth rate (Years 2–5)	5.00%
Year 1 market size ($)	50,000,000
Market size (Years 2–5)	10.00%
Year 1 variable cost per unit	250.00
Variable cost per unit (Years 2–5)	5.00%
Year 1 fixed costs	250,000
Fixed cost (Years 2–5)	3.00%
Target operating income (Year 5)	100,000
Target market share (Year 5)	2.00%

TABLE 8.5 Cash flow ratios

Type	Description
Operating cash flow	Operating cash flow / sales
Free cash flow	Free cash flow / operating cash flow ratio
Cash flow coverage ratios	Short-term debt coverage
	Ratio of operating cash flow and cash dividends
	Sum total of capex and cash dividend coverage ratio
Dividend pay-out ratio	Ratio of the dividends per common share and earnings per share

The pure liquidity health of a firm is better understood with cash flow analysis. The cash flow ratios are given in Table 8.5.

Cash flow forecasting

The sources of cash include that from operating, non-operating, and financing sources of cash, which are derived from sales forecast. The value of cash is adjusted for sales returns, bad debt, discounts and commissions on sales, etc. Non-operating cash includes sale and disposal of old assets, dividends, or interest income, and lastly, short-term borrowing from external sources can also be included. Forecasting uses two principal methods known as the receipts and disbursement method and the adjusted net income method where the former is used for short-term forecasting (1 week or more) and the latter for longer-term forecast. Businesses that run on a cash basis are suited for the receipts and disbursement method of forecasting where certainty around cash inflow and cash outflow events is higher. For example, small businesses, retail services, fuel gas dealerships, and many more businesses adopt cash-based accounting. Forecasting the cash outflows in the short run includes cash purchases of supplies and materials, account payables, advances to suppliers, wages and salaries, and other operating expenses such as contractual payments, repayment of loans, interest on loans, and tax payments.

The adjusted net income method utilizes the tracing of working capital flows. It is also known as the mapping of sources to destination method, where the company can generate funds internally to satisfy its needs for a future date. The adjusted cash balance is obtained from the net income by adding depreciation, taxes, and dividends or subtracting forecast items such as the pre-payment of supplies or the foreclosure of loans. Alternatively, the receipts and disbursement method divulges the timing and magnitude of expected cash receipts and disbursements over the forecast period. Cash flow analysis leads to more accurate estimation of net working capital.

Economic capital

Economic capital is a buffer capital to counteract economic risk, which is the combined risk due to credit (default), market (asset price changes), and operation (e.g. fraud and catastrophe) including business risks. Economic capital is used to measure the relative performance of various business lines and support decisions about what transactions to pursue. The focus is on allocating against those portfolios that give the best return on the firm's limited economic capital. There are four types of economic capital, which are purely differentiated by the source: credit risk, operation risk, market risk, and lastly, enterprise risk, which combines the former three types of risk. Enterprise risk economic capital is the most formidable and judicious evaluation of risk capital in business. Economic capital is arrived at by simulating and arrived at Monte Carlo simulation of interest rates.

Interest rate risk analytics

Interest rate analytics (IRA) is defined as the technique of gauging the impact of duration or intensity changes in the interest costs of financing to a balance sheet. Interest rate analytics includes the gap in re-pricing, earnings at risk for asset liability management. Changes in interest rates affect earnings and also affect the underlying value of the assets because the present value of future cash outflows changes when interest rates change. The benefit of IRA is the deeper interpretation of the term structure of a business portfolio it gives to the managers in the components of repricing gaps and sensitivity analysis. The intention is to assess the impact of changing rates on earnings and capital to provide senior management a complete and comparative description of the institution's interest rate risk (IRR) exposure.

$$\text{Duration gap (DUR}_{gap}) = \text{DUR}_a - (MV_L \times \text{DUR}_l) / MV_A,$$

where DUR_{gap} = duration of the gap,
DUR_a = duration of the assets,
DUR_l = duration of the liabilities,
MA_A = market value of assets,
MV_L = market value of liabilities, and
$\Delta NW/A = -\text{DUR}_{gap} \times \Delta i / (1 + I)$.

Interest rate risk uses liquidity, zero coupon rate, and maturity and gives cash flow. Rate-sensitive and higher-cost deposits, such as brokered and Internet deposits, would reflect higher decay rates than other types of deposits since $\Delta i / (1 + I)$ changes with i.

Economic value added (EVA) and the economic value equity (EVE)

The economic value of equity (EVE) could also be used to capture all future cash flows expected from existing assets and liabilities, by including changes in rates of greater magnitude (e.g. up and down 50 and 100 basis points) across different durations to reflect changing slopes and twists of the yield curve. The economic value of equity (EVE) is a numeric proxy for the future earnings capacity that resides within the financial positions existing in the balance sheet. The EVE is defined as the net present value of a balance sheet's cash flow. EVE is calculated by discounting the anticipated principal and interest cash flows under the prevailing interest rate environment.

The economic value of assets (EVA) is analogous to the book value of equity, where the economic value incorporates market discount rates with sources from on-balance sheet positions and derivatives contracts (e.g. forward rate agreements [FRAs], swaps, futures, and option contracts). For EVA to equal the balance sheet's market value, every account position would need to be precisely tuned to prices observed in established and recognized markets. EVA is derived from market-derived factors and is the best estimate of capital's fair value. EVA is viewed as a proxy of the balance sheet's earning-producing capacity.

EVE is related to earnings of the business, which is determined by measuring the changes to EVE due to changes in interest rates and the economic value of the investment portfolio on the overall value of the balance sheet.

Three direct methods to arrive at EVE are:

EVE = EV (economic value) of assets − EV of liabilities
EVE = present value (asset principal cash flows − liability principal cash flows) + present value (asset interest cash flows − liability interest cash flows)
EVE = present value of carrying equity + present value of net interest income

The difference in the economic values of the assets and liabilities is the residual value of future cash flows ultimate due to shareholders. The larger the residual value, the more earnings can potentially be pulled from the balance sheet in future reporting periods. Because cash flow has principal and interest components, EVE contains two components to represent the financial condition and future margin effect.

Earning at risk (EAR) analysis

An asset or a liability with an interest rate subject to change within a year is considered *rate sensitive*. One whose interest rate cannot change for more than a year is considered *fixed*. The margins and earnings are a reflection of the assets created and investments made years ago. The margins also depend upon the liabilities that were priced months ago. The pricing loans and liabilities or securities selected for purchase today have an impact on the income statement in the future. Margins and earnings performance are the dynamics of re-pricing assets and liabilities over time.

The impact of change in the rate of interest on the business's earning due to changes in the net interest income (NII) and net interest margin (NIM) is known as earnings at risk (EAR). The analysis on NII facilitates visualizing the impact of movement in interest rates resulting in repricing of assets and liabilities. It shows the change in NII for any change in yield or cost across the maturity bucket (e.g. 1–6 months, > 6 months). There are two ways: first, by changing yield and/or cost curves, i.e. if a positive change of 50 basis points in the yield in the first maturity bucket and/or 25 basis points in the cost in the second maturity bucket is envisaged. Scenarios 1 to 6 given in Table 8.5 provide the inputs of the interest change, which will be different in different maturity bucket of the asset or liability. Second, another method is by changing the specified portion of rate-sensitive assets (RSA) and/or rate-sensitive liability (RSL) (the re-priced portion of the asset and/or liability) for a change in market rate.

Interest rate movement can be set in terms of percentage of yield change and cost change or in terms of basis points of yield change. Earnings are also at risk due to pre-payment on assets of longer maturity. Pre-payment rate can be projected on the portfolio. Previous data on pre-payment rate, as a dependent variable, and refinancing incentive rate, pre-payment penalty rate, house price inflation rate, age on book, rise in per capita income, as independent variables, are used to project payment rates. Pre-payment rate is the percentage of loan amount pre-paid in a month in the pool of retail mortgage loans.

The pre-payment rate is the dependent variable in the regression model.

The refinancing incentive rate is defined as the difference of contract rate over current rate $= \frac{c}{m} - 1$, where c is the contract rate and m is the current rate.

For a pool of loans, c and m will be the weighted average rates where the weight is the ratio of loan amount outstanding for a particular borrower to the total loan outstanding in the pool.

The higher the refinancing incentive rate, the higher the pre-payment rate. The pre-payment penalty rate is the pre-payment penalty charged to the borrowers who pre-pay the loan. The pre-payment penalty rate for a pool of loans is also the weighted average rate where weight is the ratio of loan amount outstanding for a particular borrower to the total loan outstanding in the pool. When the pre-payment penalty rate is higher, the pre-payment rate is lower. The house price inflation rate is the rising inflation rate, which induces the borrowers to sell the house and pre-pay the loan. Age on book is expressed in years. Higher age on book leads to higher chances of pre-payment and increased pre-payment rate. Similarly, a rise in per capita income (%) will make the borrowers pre-pay the loan.

The linear censored regression equation for estimating the pre-payment rate is represented as:

Pre-payment rate $(P_t) = \alpha + \beta_1 \times$ age on book $+ \beta_2 \times$ house price inflation $+ \beta_3 \times$ delinquency $+ \beta_4 \times$ drawl rate $+ \beta_5 \times$ pre-payment penalty $+ \varepsilon$

This censored model is simple enough to be estimated using regression, and the parameter estimates can be arrived at for asset types separately.

Next, we will calculate the changes in interest income and interest expenses. First, the weighted average is calculated interest rate of each product in each time bucket by the following formula:

Weighted $I_{(P1,1)}$ = weighted average interest rate for product in a particular bucket or $\sum \frac{I_1 V_1}{\sum V}$, where I_1 is the rate and V_1 is the principal amount in time bucket 1.

Similarly, the weighted rate of interest can be calculated for all assets and liabilities for all the time buckets.

Therefore, weighted average yield (WAY) on assets in the 1–6 month bucket will be:

$$\text{Weighted average yield (WAY)} = \frac{\sum R_{11} \times EOP_1 + R_{21} \times EOP_{21} + R_{31} \times EOP_{31}}{\sum EOP_1 + EOP_2 + EOP_3}$$

Similarly, the weighted average cost of liabilities can be derived for all the liabilities taken together.

The average spread is the difference between average yield and average cost distributed across maturity buckets.

In the short run, the marginal cost of funds (MCF) is also an appropriate measure for computing the cost of funds. The marginal cost should be arrived at by taking into consideration all sources of funds. Cost of deposits (liabilities or fixed deposits received from public or inter-corporate deposits) should be calculated using the latest interest rate payable on current and savings deposits and the term deposits against their respective maturity. The cost of borrowing is arrived at using the average rates at which funds were raised in the last month preceding the date of review. Each of these rates should be weighted by the proportionate balance outstanding on the date of review.

Liquidity analytics

This is reflection of the changes to the short term of shortfall/excess in liquidity. Liquidity measurement involves assessing the cash flows of a company to identify the potential for any shortfalls/excesses at a point in time. This also includes cash flows relating to all commitments including off-balance sheet commitments. Liquidity is the ability to use available cash specifically when it is needed. This requires fixing tolerance limits for liquidity gaps and monitoring them.

Maturity gap calculations of cash flows are based on contractual maturity. Suitable adjustment factors can be applied on the basis of the behavioural pattern to get a refined view. Cash inflows and outflows can be calculated with certainty. The cash outflow risks arising out of off-balance sheet (OBS) commitments are treated as operational risks since there are no credit relationships involved. Therefore, such obligations can be translated into expected burden on cash as fixed percentage of total outstanding OBS commitments. For example, the exposure against an outstanding letter of credit could be 50% of the guaranteed amount against the counter-party.

Liquidity is demystified as structural liquidity, contingency liquidity, and market liquidity. Mismatch refers to the degree of imbalance in balance sheet due to gap in maturity or in the cash flows due to individual commitments. Contingent liabilities are the result of unexpected need of funds, which all businesses are subject to. Unexpected obligations arise due to unusual deviations in the timing of cash flows. Market liquidity refers to the inability to sell assets or conduct distress sales of assets at or near the fair value. It can arise when a market disruption impairs the firm's ability to sell large or lower-quality positions.

Key questions include:

- What are the future cash inflows and outflows in different time buckets and the degree of resulting gaps for the institution?
- What are the impending liquidity problems facing the short term both in terms of shortfall/excess liquidity?
- Can rational limits be set for liquidity gaps and the same monitored in terms of percentage of outflows?
- Which regions/branches are functioning at the optimum level and have a fair balance between cash inflows and outflows?
- What is the liquidity mismatch for each currency and its impact on the overall liquidity position?
- Is the institution capable of examining the potential cash flows from its off-balance sheet activities?
- What proportion of maturing assets will be renewed?
- What is the expected level of new business?
- What is the pre-payment rate?
- What is the rational limit to be set for liquidity gaps in terms of percentage of outflows?

The liquidity gaps in the various time buckets which are arrived at from the cash flow data could be regrouped into four time buckets, i.e. liquidity gap up to 1 year, over 1 year and up to 3 years, between 3 and 5 years, and over 5 years.

The 1-, 3-, 5-, and 10-year zero coupon rates will be used to compute the net present value (NPV) of C_1, C_2, C_3, and C_4 respectively. The 10-year zero rate is taken as discount rate for gaps beyond the 5-year time bucket. The present value of the gap for each bucket i is given as:

$$NPV = \sum_{i=1}^{4} C_i e^{-r_i t_i}$$

Where C_i = liquidity gap in the respective time bucket and r = zero coupon rate.

The interest risk model can be used where m number of interest rate scenarios will be generated for each of the four time buckets from the historical daily zero-coupon rate for 1, 3, 5, and 10 years, respectively.

For each time bucket, m is the number of interest rate scenarios pertaining to a particular time bucket and will be used as input to compute m number of NPV of the gap.

$$NPV^1 = C_i e^{-\eta_i t_i}$$

The distribution of increase or decrease in NPV of the gap in a particular time bucket is arrived at by subtracting the current NPV of the gap determined in the previous step. Using the NPV of gap values under each of the scenarios in that time bucket:

$$\Delta \text{ (increase/decrease)} = NPV_1 - NPV_1 m = 1, 2, 3, \ldots 1000 \text{ (1,000 simulations)}$$

For a confidence level, the 99th percentile value is calculated as value at risk (VaR). The 99th percentile VaR values in each of the four time buckets are added to arrive at the aggregate VaR for the division. The aggregate VaR is known as the "economic capital" to be required for interest rate risk. If the value is positive, then it implies that the market value of the equity will decrease at a given confidence level and, therefore, additional capital is required. If the value is negative, then it implies the market value of the equity will increase and, therefore, there is no need for additional capital. Alternatively, conditional VaR (cVaR) is calculated as the expected value of all simulated data points that exceed the VaR. The values exceeding 99th value in a particular time bucket will be considered for the computation of cVaR and will indicate economic capital required beyond the 99% confidence level.

Spread analysis

Gross margin reflects total revenue minus the cost of goods sold (COGS). Gross margin is a company's profit before operating expenses, interest payments, and taxes. Higher gross profit margins are a result of higher prices for goods/services or lower costs of goods sold. For financial firms, spread is the difference between the borrowing rate and the lending rate. The re-employment rate is the rate at which the firm can borrow to refinance, i.e. the rate of a new loan with the same properties as the initial loan. Spread is also the difference between cash sell and cash buy rates. Spread varies over time, maturity, relationships, covenants, and credit ratings. Alternatively, there are changes happening outside the business, such as policy rate changes to repurchase or market changes to LIBOR, that can impact spread:

Absolute spread = initial loan rate − re-employment rate
Running spread = (initial borrowing rate − current refinance rate) / initial loan rate
Relative spread = (initial loan rate − re-employment rate) / initial loan rate

When spread remains high, it leads to degradation in capital and reserves. The shift in timing of borrowing can help reduce the spread. This is because, irrespective of the volume of borrowed funds, the borrowing rates in the market are dependent on the timing of the borrowing for given maturity.

TABLE 8.6 Component ALM computation

ALM ratio	Relationship
Short-term borrowing to total assets	All borrowings with residual maturity of ($\leq$ 1 month) / Total assets
Short-term borrowing to total deposits	All borrowings with residual maturity ($\leq$ 1 month) / Total deposits
Purchased funds to total assets	The sum of total high value DRI deposits and certificates of deposits (CDs) / total deposits
Net loans to total assets	(Net of total loans [bills, CC, OD, term loans, etc.] − provisions) / total assets
Core deposits to net advances	Term deposits − (deposits + plus current and saving deposits) with residual maturity of ($\geq$ 1 year) / sum of total loans (bills, CC, OD, term loan etc.) − provisions
Investment in short-term assets (maturing within 1 year) to purchased funds	All investments of residual maturity of less than one year / sum of total high-value deposits and certificates of deposits (CDs)
Cash in hand to deposits	Cash / total deposits

Risk adjusted return on capital (RAROC)

Risk adjusted return on capital (RAROC) is the proportion of net income to economic capital allocated (economic net income / economic capital). At the firm level, the increase in capital costs and revenue expenses does impact the spread. This is the profitability and is comparable to minimum risk-adjusted benchmarks or hurdle rates. RAROC is therefore used as a criterion for investments. It is used as an internal benchmark to compare across strategic business units (SBUs) or profit centre entities (PCEs).

The return hurdle is calculated by:

$$EBT = (\text{net interest} + (\text{preferred dividends} + \text{minority interest})) / (1 - \text{tax rate})$$
$$EBIT = EBT + \text{net interest expense}$$
$$EBITDA = EBIT + \text{depreciation} + \text{amortization}$$

Therefore,

$$RAROC = \text{net income} / \text{economic capital} = (\text{revenue} - \text{cost} - \text{expected loss}) / \text{economic capital},$$

where revenue is equal to the sum of interest income and non-interest income or the sum of sales and other income during a period.

Non-interest income (other income) includes fee income, commissions, etc. Economic capital is different from deployed capital funds in the business. Deployed capital is equivalent to net owned funds, whereas economic capital is a measure of the economic value of capital, defined earlier.

Shareholder value added (SVA)

The amount of economic capital is compared against the size of the business. The shareholder value added (SVA) is the value added by the business for shareholders. Economic value added (EVA) is defined as the net income at the hurdle rate. This is the value that combines both profitability and the size of transactions to find whether a transaction or a sub-portfolio creates or destroys value for shareholders. It is calculated for a unit or line of business or by geography.

$$SVA = \text{economic net income} - (\text{economic capital allocated} \times \text{hurdle rate}),$$

where economic net income = revenue − cost − expected loss + transfer income.

Payment is an important driver of revenue and pre-payment, which could affect revenue income and which includes both recurring or instalment products and B2B sales. In B2C, payments are assumed to have been collected upfront and in real time except when a special purpose entity (SPE) exists to finance the transaction by the customer. Receiving payments before due dates is a healthy sign in manufacturing, retailing, and others. However, when a customer makes unscheduled payments, it is a surprise for the business. It is customary to have financing entities within the group or holding company to finance the purchase of goods or services by the customer from the parent. The financing of such assets by the SPV (SPE or subsidiary) may be unsecured and should be insured and preferably refinanced by an external bank that is unrelated to the parent.

Incremental capital analytics

Incremental capital is the change in capital due to the addition of a new exposure or a customer. The economic capital against the new exposure is defined as the change in economic capital due to addition of the customer and can be used as a valid basis for pricing analysis. This is also referred to as incremental economic capital requirement and is generally calculated at an account level.

Capital requirement = total (annual net receivables) anr$ × capital ratio (r%)
Capital requirement impact = (total capital requirement − total cap requirement present month) / no. of accounts
Total revenue = interest income + interchange revenue + other income (cross-selling, fees)
Open accounts = open accounts (1 − attrition rate (%))

Net receivables = total revenue − cost of funds
Business income = net receivables − total expenses − losses
Profit centre earnings = business income × (1 − tax rate)
Net present value = profit centre earnings × (1 + monthly discount rate)

Regulatory capital

The prudential capital rates are calculated against the total assets or total risk weighted assets. The simple Cooke's ratio is calculated against total assets (TA) whereas the CRAR is calculated against risk-weighted assets (RWA). It is the prudential capital under Basel norms. Total risk-weighted assets are determined by multiplying the capital requirements for credit risk by (K = 12.5) and summating calculated figures to arrive at the total risk-weighted assets for credit risk.

The derivation of risk-weighted assets is dependent on estimates of the probability of default (PD), loss given default (LGD), exposure at default (EAD) and, in few asset classes, the effective maturity (M) for each exposure.

Correlation (R) = 0.12 × (1 − exp$^{(-50 \times PD)}$) / (1 − exp$^{(-50)}$) + 0.24 × [1 − (1 − exp$^{(-50 \times PD)}$) / (1 − exp$^{(-50)}$)]
Maturity adjustment (B) = (0.11852 − 0.05478 × ln (PD))^2
Capital requirement (K) = [LGD × N[(1 − R)$^{-0.5}$ × G(PD) + (R / (1 − R))$^{0.5}$ × G(0.999)] − PD × LGD] × (1 − 1.5 × b)$^{-1}$ × (1 + (M − 2 × B)

where M = effective maturity and risk-weighted assets (RWA) = K × 12.5 × EAD. The capital requirement (K) for a defaulted exposure is equal to the greater of zero and the difference between its LGD and the best estimate of expected loss. The risk-weighted asset amount for the defaulted exposure is the product of (K = 12.5) and the EAD (exposure at default).

Pricing analytics

Pricing analytics is defined as the domain of determining fair and agile prices for products. Beyond cost plus pricing, the domain (realm) of pricing analytics intends to arrive at prices for transactions where the incremental costs of selling are completely recovered, including the after-sale expenses. Future margin income or future expected loans are also accounted for in pricing.

Pricing analytics enables businesses in all industries to dramatically improve their understanding of what drives a product's gross margin to optimize profits.

There are two major pricing thoughts, namely future margin income (FMI) and warranty-based pricing; the first one is used in financial services, and the second one in manufacturing.

TABLE 8.7 Example for calculation of risk weight

Probability of default	PD	Portfolio, segment, asset class, exposure	0.05
Loss given default	LGD	Portfolio, segment, asset class, exposure, collateral	0.56
Maturity	M	Portfolio, segment, asset class, exposure, collateral	2.5
Correlation	R	$0.12 \times (1 - \exp^{(-50 \times PD)}) / (1 - \exp^{(-50)}) + 0.24 \times [1 - (1 - \exp^{(-50 \times PD)}) / (1 - \exp^{(-50)})]$	0.129
Maturity adjustment	B	$(0.11852 - 0.05478 \times \mathrm{Ln}(PD))^2$	0.0798
Capital charge	K (%)	$\left[LGD \times N\left\{ \dfrac{N^{-1}(PD) + \sqrt{R} \times N^{-1}(0.999)}{\sqrt{1-R}} \right\} - (LGD \times PD) \right] \times \left\{ \dfrac{1 + (M - 2.5) \times b}{1 - 1.5 \times b} \right\}$	14.91%
Risk weight	RW (%)	K × 12.5	197.67%
Correlation	R	$0.12 \times (1 - \exp^{(-35 \times PD)}) / (1 - \exp^{(-35)}) + 0.16 \times [1 - (1 - \exp^{(-35 \times PD)}) / (1 - \exp^{(-35)})]$	0.15
Residential mortgage QRRE Other retail			0.04
Capital charge	K (%)	$\left[LGD \times N\left\{ \dfrac{N^{-1}(PD) + \sqrt{R} \times N^{-1}(0.999)}{\sqrt{1-R}} \right\} - (LGD \times PD) \right]$	
Risk weight	RW (%)	K × 12.5	

Source: Bank for International Settlements 2006.

Future margin income (FMI)

Future margin income (FMI) is the amount of income anticipated to be generated over the next period available to cover potential credit losses on the exposures (i.e. after covering normal business expenses). FMI is measured as the net of reserve expenses (provisions) since there is a separate offset available for such reserves:

Let N_i be the number of customers in a pool or portfolio (segment).

Let all borrowers in a pool have the same probability of default p (= 3.00%).

Using a single-factor model (Perli and Nayda, 2004), let x be a random variable that indicates the fraction of defaulted accounts.

When x increases, the number of accounts that will be recovered also increases. Default events reduce the accruals from borrower accounts.

The probability distribution of the fraction of loss due to defaulted accounts is given as:

$$F(X) = \Phi\left(\frac{1}{\sqrt{\rho}}\left(\sqrt{1-\rho}\,\Phi^{-1}(x) - \Phi^{-1}(p)\right)\right)$$

Where ρ is the correlation factor and p is the probability of default.

For the purpose of calculating FMI, we proceed as follows:

Let B_i be the total outstanding balance amount against all borrowers in pool i.

Therefore, the total outstanding balances (B') is the sum of outstanding balances for pool i where $B = \Sigma B_{ij}$ and where B_{ij} is the outstanding amount against each borrower.

For recovery rate γ_i for a given pool i, then the loss amount at time T (net of recovered amount) implied by a fraction x of borrowers defaulting is:

$$L_i = (1 - \gamma_i)\,B_i\,x$$

Suppose an amount of B_{0i} dollars is assigned to a pool i at the beginning of the time horizon.

The borrowers would not have been offered the same interest rate on their balances; however assuming the rate to be fixed, and is r, and collected interest income by I_i, we have:

$$I_i = r\,B_{0i} - rL_i = r\,(B_{0i} - (1 - \gamma_i)B_{0i}\,x) = r\,(1 - x(1 - \gamma_i))B_{0i}$$

One denotes the constant fraction of non-interest income by λ_i:

$$NI_i = \lambda_i\,B_{0i} - \lambda_i\,L_i = \lambda_i\,(B_0 - (1 - \gamma_i)B_0 x) = \lambda_i\,(1 - x(1 - \gamma_i))B_{0i}$$
$$\text{Total revenue} = R_i = I_i + N_i = (r_i + \lambda_i) \times [1 - x(1 - \gamma_i)]B_{0i}$$

If *cof* is the average cost of funds, interest expense IE*i* will therefore be:

$$IE_i = cof \times B_{0i} - cof \times C = cof \times (B_{0i} - C)$$

122 Financial analytics

One assumes that non-interest expenses are incurred on a per-account basis and, therefore, are a constant percentage, denoted as ψ, of outstanding balances. Again, recoveries and losses are not assumed to affect ψ.

Non-interest expenses are therefore $NE_i = \psi B_{0i}$, and total expenses are $E_i = IE_i + NE_i = cof (B_{0i} - C) + \psi B_{0i}$

Hence,

$$B_{Ti} = B_{0i} - L_i + R_i - S_i$$
$$= B_{0i} - x(1 - \gamma_i) B_{0i} + (r + \lambda_i)(1 - x(1 - \gamma_i)) B_{0i} - cof\, x\, (B_{0i} - C) - \psi \times B_{0i}$$
$$= B_{0i}[(1 + r + \lambda_i) \times (1 - x(1 - \gamma_i)) - cof - \psi] + cof\, C$$

Hence, the profit ratio is

$$\pi_i = (B_{Ti} / B_{0i} - 1),$$

where π_i is assumed to follow normal distribution $G(F(x),c)$ and $G(F(x),c)$ is the probability distribution of π and $c = C/B_0$.

The capital charge will be given by the left tail of $G(F(x), c)$ at an appropriate percentile. It follows that the capital ratio c for each segment is:

$$c = \text{minimum}\, [(r + \lambda_{i+}\, cof + \psi)(1 + r + \lambda_i)(1 + \gamma_i)\, x_a, 0) / (1 - cof)]$$

TABLE 8.8 Parameters of PD computation

r	Average interest rate over balance	34%
λ_i	Average fraction of non-interest income over opening balance	2%
γ_i	Portfolio recovery rate	50%
cof	Cost of funds (interest expenses)	15%
ψ	Average fraction of non-interest expenses over opening balance	15%
c	One-factor model capital ratio factor	$(r + \lambda_i - cof - \psi) - (1 + r + \lambda_i)(1 - \gamma_i)x_a /(1 - cof)$

TABLE 8.9 FMI computation

Pools	Probability of default (PD)	LGD for the pool	FMI factor	FMI capital charge	Premium on base price
1	1.91%	0.50	6.87%	0.00%	0.00%
2	2.02%	0.50	5.18%	5.18%	5.18%
3	2.23%	0.50	5.56%	0.00%	0.00%
4	3.57%	0.50	7.76%	37.76%	37.76%

Here, c is the α (99.99%) revenue distribution. The incremental capital charge c is added to the base price to be recovered.

The FMI factor is incorporated to determine the premium over the base price. This demonstrates a case of risk-based pricing in financial services.

Contingent pricing in manufacturing

Contingent pricing is defined as the determination of the expected price of a product dependent on its failure over time. It is applied in manufacturing that drives taking into account post-sales customer issues with product defects or product warranties and vouchers for recovering a portion of the costs incurred toward product rework or replacement with extended warranties. The greater the probability that the customer subscribes to the extension, the greater the impact of the extension on the expected gain.

The reliability of the product is the probability for the product to malfunction at a given date and is defined with a Weibull distribution. The main parameter of such a

TABLE 8.10 Acceptance rates of warranty

Extended warranty price (% of sale price)	Acceptance ratio (%)
0%	100%
5%	50%
10%	30%
15%	15%
20%	10%
30%	5%

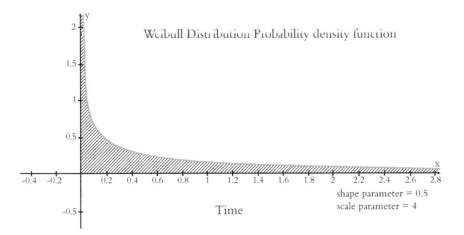

FIGURE 8.1 Weibull distribution of contingent pricing

distribution is the mean time to failure (MTTF), which is the length of time a device or other product is expected to last in operation. A lower MTTF impacts the average repair costs for the company, which is the cost incurred when a product is returned during the warranty period. The customer may want his product to be fixed outside the warranty period. The risk goes up with increased period of warranty.

The basic warranty period is to 1 year and can be extended 1 to 3 years. The customer may pay for the extended warranty, which is optional.

The ratio of subscribing customers at different price levels for warranty extensions is known. The acceptance rates of warranty extensions for a fixed period at price levels of 5%, 10%, and 15% of the product's price are key inputs for contingent pricing.

The average repair cost for the company for a product (fixed proportion) can be assumed across any degree of defect that may appear in the product. To measure the impact of the repair cost, one can run simulations for a cost equal to ($k = 10\%$) and ($k = 20\%$) of the product's price.

Hence, the product reliability is characterized by a Weibull distribution whose failure rate is constant. This distribution displays the failure rate over time.

The Weibull distribution translates to an exponential distribution with a single parameter *MTTF* (mean time to failure).

The probability density function of an exponential distribution is given by the following formula:

$$f(t) = \frac{e^{-t/MTTF}}{MTTF}$$

To measure the impact of the MTTF in this example, one can run simulations for MTTFs of 3 years and 5 years.

Retail credit risk analytics

Retail assets are defined as homogeneous portfolios comprising a large number of small, low-value loans where the incremental credit risk of any single exposure is small. These types of loans include loans to individuals such as credit cards, residential mortgages and home equity loans, student loans, or auto loans. Small business loans could also be included as long as these facilities are handled the same way as other retail credits are treated. Table 8.11 describes the retail credit risk analytics (RCRA).

Due to the homogenous nature of riskiness, the credit assessment is done by using retail credit risk. The most commonly used technique is the multiple discriminate (MDA) credit scoring analysis pioneered by Altman (1968). Mester (1997) presents the use of credit scoring techniques using four principal forms of multivariate credit scoring models, namely the linear probability model, the logit model, the probit model, and the multiple discriminate analysis model. All of these techniques identify variables that have explanatory power in differentiating defaulting borrowers from non-defaulting borrowers. Once the model's parameters are estimated, loan applicants are assigned a Z-score assessing their classification as good or bad. The Z-score itself can be converted into the probability of default (PD) and a cut-off score (fixed probability number), which can be used to sort the bad from the good in the sample.

The population stability report denotes changes happening to the incoming sample of applicants when the fixed parameters of a scoring model are applied over and over again down the line and over time. It is the measure of shift in share of applicants in each score range for the current population compared to those in the training sample against a business-wide base line. Since the purpose is to detect any shift in the population of incoming observations, a bigger shift implies characteristic changes (e.g. socio-demographic or behavioural).

TABLE 8.11 Retail credit risk analysis

Product type	Delinquency bands	Residual maturity	Gross exposure value before provisions ($)
Auto loans	0–30 days	< 1 year	12,580
	30–60 days	1–3 years	14,569
	60–90 days	3–5 years	27,560
	> 90 days (past due)	> 5 years	3,890
Home equity loans	0–30 days	< 1 year	955
	30–60 days	1–3 years	1,255
	60–90 days	3–5 years	1,685
	> 90 days (past due)	> 5 years	1,400

Note: Auto loans have an increasing tendency towards delinquency bands at medium maturity.

TABLE 8.12 Estimates of a retail credit risk delinquency model

Dependent variable	Delinquency			
Technique	Logistic regression			
Variable	Estimate	Standard error	Wald Chi-square	Probability
Intercept	0.181	0.084	2.15	0.032
Age 18–29				
Age 30–47	+0.14	0.08	3.0	0.08
Age 48+	+0.47	0.10	20.5	< 0.001
Number of credit cards	+0.05	0.03	2.4	0.12
Self-employed	−0.47	0.07	44.0	< 0.001
Months in current residence	+0.009	0.004	4.3	0.04
Income (log)	−0.0164	0.0100	1.64	0.10
Tenant	−0.155	0.039	3.97	< 0.001
Lives with parents	+0.256	0.045	5.69	< 0.001
Months in current job	+0.00210	0.00025	8.40	< 0.001
N (Total Observation)	885			
MSE	0.06			
R-Square	0.66			

Note: Significant at 99.99%.

TABLE 8.13 Population stability view

Score range	Development records (#)	Current sample records (#)	Development records (%)	Current records (%)	Difference between current to development	Ratio of the current to development	Log (ratio of current to development)	Difference between current to development XLog (ratio of current to development)
0–100	112	52	11%	10%	−0.8%	0.93	−0.03	0.0003
100–200	87	47	9%	9%	0.7%	1.08	0.03	0.0002
200–300	106	50	11%	10%	−0.6%	0.94	−0.03	0.0002
300–400	125	59	13%	12%	−0.7%	0.94	−0.03	0.0002
400–500	122	61	12%	12%	0.0%	1.00	0.00	0.0000
500–600	82	40	8%	8%	−0.2%	0.98	−0.01	0.0000
600–700	115	62	12%	12%	0.9%	1.08	0.03	0.0003
700–800	100	51	10%	10%	0.2%	1.02	0.01	0.0000
800–900	71	38	7%	8%	0.5%	1.07	0.03	0.0001
900–1,000	80	40	8%	8%	0.0%	1.00	0.00	0.0000
Total	1,000	500	100	100				0.0013

Note: A value of Δ ≤ 0.001 implies stable population.

TABLE 8.14 Characteristics analysis report

Score range	Development records (#)	Current sample records (#)	Development records (%)	Current records (%)	Difference between current to development	Ratio of the current to development	Difference between current to development X Log (ratio of current to development)
0–100	112	52	11%	10%	−0.8%	10	−0.08
100–200	87	47	9%	9%	0.7%	13	0.091
200–300	106	50	11%	10%	−0.6%	17	−0.102
300–400	125	59	13%	12%	−0.7%	21	−0.147
400–500	122	61	12%	12%	0.0%	27	0
500–600	82	40	8%	8%	−0.2%	33	−0.066
600–700	115	62	12%	12%	0.9%	18	0.162
700–800	100	51	10%	10%	0.2%	19	0.038
800–900	71	38	7%	8%	0.5%	25	0.125
900–1,000	80	40	8%	8%	0.0%	22	0
TOTAL	1,000	500	100	100			0.021

A population stability index of 0.1 or less indicates that there is no difference between the benchmark and the current sample. Higher values would imply that the Z-score needs to be revisited or maybe a revision in the cut-off score is needed. Similarly, the characteristics analysis report of Z-score attributes can be used to identify the main causes of any shift in the applicant population from the benchmark. It finds out which characteristics used in the model (out of five or six) are scoring differently than the attribute level. A deviation against a given characteristic would obviate the need to re-visit the Z-score.

Mortgage analytics

A mortgage is a relationship-based, secured product that could be securitized by the originator. There are a few important considerations in mortgage analytics. They comprise of premature payment or foreclosure, restructuring risk, default risk, refinance risk, recovery risk, collateral risk, etc. Mortgage analytics is defined as the analysis of mortgage applicants, mortgage markets and products, and the pricing of the property business, which is a part of housing markets. The primary types of analysis include premature closure of loans, default risk, refinance risks, fraud and pre-payment risks, etc. The approach to credit risk mitigation allows a wider range of credit risk litigants to be recognized for regulatory capital purposes provided these techniques meet the requirements for legal certainty. A credit risk mitigation approach is applicable to the credit sales (or lending book) exposures. Therefore, the degree of mitigation benefits available against the collaterals and its adjustment are also tested from time to time to accurately determine the recovery or impairment. The following analytical components have gained extreme importance in mortgage analytics:

- Origination and lending analytics
- Borrower profiles
- Property assessment views
- Assessing loan and property characteristics
- Mortgage fraud analysis
- Portfolio behaviour forecast
- Collateral revaluation

The types of scenarios that are evaluated in mortgage analytics may include:

1. Change in interest base rate
2. Change in interest margin rate
3. Product switch
4. Product roll-over
5. Exchange rate
6. New home buyers

Merger and demerger analytics

Mergers and demergers being common in today's marketplace, businesses devote much time to acquire companies, delist companies, and spin-off entities all over the globe. The definition of performance measures and of pre- and post-merger assessment periods does vary, since accounting treatments can distort the manner in which performance is measured. There is a need to look beyond pure economic or strategic arguments for value creation in mergers and to understand how deals are made and what impact deal characteristics have on post-acquisition performance. Characteristics of deals include whether it is a hostile bid or a friendly bid; modes of acquisition, tender, or merger; the size of the target; whether the buyer commanded premiums in the market before the deal; and the method of purchase (all cash, stock, or loans). Some embodiments of analytical interest in merger analysis, comprised of leverage buyouts (LBOs), paying for acquisitions, preparing for the M&A transaction, the pricing of takeovers, post-deal success or failure, target scanning and selecting, valuation, tax benefits for assets, financing and payment choice, have drawn the attention of merger analytics specialists.

Merger and demerger analytics answers the following questions:

1. What are the different ways of measuring the success of M&As?
2. What is the rationale for shareholder maximization?
3. What is the benchmark for assessing shareholder value?
4. How does one distinguish between short-run and long-run performance?
5. Is there any distinction between value creation by size, geography, sector methods, regulation etc.?
6. How does maturity impact mergers and for which sectors?
7. How can one contain and groom network externality?
8. What are the sources of loss of value or earning dilution in mergers?
9. How can we optimize the loss in value due to mergers?
10. Which equilibrium condition should exist between post-merger EPS and the bidder's EPS to choose the price and exchange ratio to avoid dilution?
11. What is the trade-off between exchange ratio and the price to earnings (PE) ratio for the bidder and the target?

For example, a decision on mergers and acquisitions (M&A) in the telecom space is interesting for telecom companies. Merger decisions cannot be taken by the (rat race) greed of management for market power and territorial control but are done by choosing the right target initial public offering (IPO), based on valuation of the target over the life of the deal.

Deal valuation

Valuation is the core determinant of return for investors, which increases with the market value of shares in exchange of their capital stake, and is the most contentious

TABLE 8.15 Examples of acquisitions in biotechnology

Aggregate purchase price as a multiple of LTM   *Implied firm value as a multiple of LTM*

Buyer/target	Description	% vote acquire.	Agg. purch. price	Implied mkt. cap	Implied firm value	Prem. over mkt.	LTMNI	Bookvalue	Sales	LTGrowthrate
Pioneer/Mycogen	Cash; private; 3 million primary shares @ $10; $21 million for R&D funding	13.4	30.0	257.3	196.9	(13.0)		1.8	1.7	17.5
DowElanco/Mycogen	Purchase of $9.5 million shares, from Lubrizol	36.6	126.0	444.7	358.1	(6.9)		2.3	2.9	18.0
DowElanco/Mycogen	Purchase of 1 million shares from Co. to DE stake over 50%	3.3	16.8	587.9	556.7	0.0		3.4	3.5	20.0
Monsanto/Calgene	30.2 million primary shares (49.9%) in exchange for $30.0 million in cash	49.9	144.2	299.8	268.0	(30.5)		6.5	4.8	20.0
Monsanto/Calgene	Cash; $6.25 million primary shares @ $48.00, board control with 54.6%	4.7	50.0	573.1	620.5	80.3		6.1	6.5	20.0
Monsanto/Calgene	Cash offer for last 45% stake; original offer of $7.25 negotiated with final offer @ $8.00	45.4	242.6	573.4	615.3	64.1		7.2	4.0	20.0
Bionova (ELM)/DNA Plant Tech.	Stock swap, ELM as 70% owner, $39 million deal based on last DNA Plant closing price of $7 per share	70.0	38.6	63.4	67.9	(25.3)		NM	4.5	50.0

TABLE 8.16 Operating performance after merger

Financials	Impact comparison
Cash flow	Matched against stand alone firms
Operating income	Market share, merger of equals, non-acquisition growth, extraordinary reports
Operating income (before interest and extra-ordinary items)	Market share, merger of equals, non-acquisition growth, accounting rules
Return on equity	Pre-acquisition performance
Pre-tax operating income	Industry median performance, controls for accounting method
Pre-tax operating cash flow (to market value of assets)	Pre-bid performance and size
Operating cash to total market value of firm	Industry and profitability erosion due to competition
Average net income/net assets (3–5 years)	Performance of same industry pre-merger performance
Return on assets, return on equity, return on sales	Matched non-merging firms
Non-operating cash flows (from disposal of non-core businesses)	Pre-bid performance and size

part of negotiations and can make the entrepreneur–investor relationship get off on the wrong foot.

Valuation involves the following questions:

1 What is the purchase price of the target?
2 What is the value driver in the target?
3 What is the real option and which model to use when?
4 How can one rank targets and choose between them?
5 What are the cautions when valuing private companies?

There are a number of models employed by firms to evaluate targets, which are based on earnings and cash flows. Conditional investments in multiple stages impact the value of the firm. Further, the kinds of covenants and the degrees of control over exercising covenants also determine the value. Operating characteristics could be in multiples of an identified base measure and may look at an initial level of productivity and deterioration in relative performance in the years prior to acquisition. Value from acquisitions is derived from savings due to productivity increase, efficiency, revenue enhancement, and real options. The traditional models take into account the selection of a proxy and use multiples of the proxy of the operating parameter in the form of number of times. Most common multiples are equity multiples, P/E (Price / EPS_{LTM}, Price / $EPS_{\text{1-year forward}}$).

The earnings need to be determined after preferred dividends so that they are earnings that are available to common shareholders using price to book (price / book value of equity per share). Enterprise value (EV) multiples include EV / revenues, EV / EBITDA, and EV / EBIT. (Note that revenues, EBITDA, and EBIT multiples could be computed for LTM and 1-year forward projected numbers).

These multiples are single-number valuation tools but can be derived to lead to earnings and asset multiples. The choice of a multiple depends upon the sector and also the size or kind of the firm. More than the sector, it depends on the transparency and the robustness of the multiple because the growth of business depends upon multiple stages of investments and the cash flow and earnings may not reflect the real potential of the business for today. In advertising and media, average billing rates are used. In many consulting industries, the hourly billing rates and the number and composition of clientele could be used as well as price to sales, the size of footprint for web businesses, room rates in the case of hotels, the number of customers at a restaurant, occupancy rates at a movie theatre, and so on. These multiples are correlated with profit or revenue. Mobile service providers are valued by the number of subscribers per month. The cost of building cell phone towers and retaining subscribers are not low when it comes to mobile companies.

The cash flow model is the equity residual model since free cash flow equity (FCFE) is the residual cash flow after meeting the claims of debt holders, e.g. interest. The numerator of the asset value can be expressed in terms of the free cash flow to the firm (FCFF), i.e. to both equity and debt holders. Since EBIT, EBITDA, and sales are not affected by the company's choice of capital structure (unlike cash

TABLE 8.17 Target selection scale

Factors	Description	Weight
a. Management	Promoter/founder experience	0–30
	Experience in business sector	
	Experience as a CEO	
	Experience as a product manager	
	Willing to step aside as a CEO	
	Coachable founder/promoter	
b. Target size	Size specific market for the company service	0–20
c. Competition	Status of intangible assets	20–20
	Strength of competitors	
	How large are entry barriers	
	Robust sales channels	
d. Business stage	Ranking of evolved and matured product	0–20
	Funding size	
Total		100

Note: The weights against individual dimensions are realistic for the sector.

TABLE 8.18 Projection of financials

	Growth		Margins					Returns		Credit			Interest coverage	
	Sales	Earnings	EBIT		Earnings		ROE		ROC		Leverage			
	3 years	3 years	3 years	10 years	3 years	10 years	3 years	3 years	Book	Market	3 years	10 years
Company 1	15.5	14.5	15.5	14.5	15.5	14.5	25.5	24.5	0.14	0.11	140	250
Company 2	16.5	13.5	16.5	13.5	16.5	13.5	26.5	23.5	0.16	0.11	135	255
Company 3	17.5	15.5	17.5	15.5	17.5	15.5	27.5	25.5	0.15	0.13	130	240
Company 4	18.5	15.5	18.5	15.5	18.5	15.5	28.5	25.5	0.15	0.11	135	245
Company 5	19.5	17.5	19.5	17.5	19.5	17.5	29.5	27.5	0.16	0.12	139	249
Mean	17.0	15.0	17.0	15.0	17.0	15.0	27.0	25.0	0.16	0.12	146	256
Median	16.0	14.5	16.0	14.5	16.0	14.5	26.0	24.5	0.15	0.13	144	251

Note: The sample number of companies should be large to determine benchmark numbers.

TABLE 8.19 Matched non-merging firm fundamentals (long term)

Company	Growth rates			Margin		Leverage	
	Sales	Cash flow	Five-year EPS	EBIT margin	EBITDA margin	Book	Market
	(%)	(%)	(%)	(%)	(%)	(%)	(%)
Company 1	11.2	7.2	22.0	15.5	16.6	0.14	0.11
Company 2	11.3	7.3	20.0	14.5	15.9	0.16	0.11
Company 3	10.5	6.5	19.5	13.9	14.9	0.15	0.13
Company 4	9.9	5.4	21.5	13.8	15.1	0.15	0.11
Company 5	12.0	8.0	20.0	14.6	15.9	0.16	0.12
Mean	11.0	7.0	20.5	14.8	15.5	0.16	0.12
Median	10.5	6.5	21.0	14.2	15.0	0.15	0.13

Note: The comparison indicators are best conceived by judicious choice of companies.

TABLE 8.20 Scenarios of growth on firm value

Factor	Change (%)	Likelihood of change (%)	Expected change in equity value (%)
Sales growth	1.2	0.1	4.4
Operating margin	1.1	0.1	126.0
Fixed assets investment	1.2	0.1	−5.2
Discount rate	1.5	0.1	−41.9

flow, earnings, EPS, and book value), they are the appropriate multiples to use that can be total capital and not just equity capital.

Rappaport (1986) suggested seven drivers within a business that can be managed to create value, namely a growth in sales, an increase in the operating profit margin, a reduction in the cash tax rate, a reduction in the working capital investment, a reduction in the fixed asset investment, a reduction in the weighted average cost of capital, and an increase in the competitive advantage period. Mere computation of the discounted cash flow (DCF) values of terminal values are not complete, and one must take into account the sensitivity of DCF with respect to a few parameters.

Assumptions of the DCF model are applied, such as:

1. The terminal value of the target at the forecast horizon (10 years).
2. The cost of capital appropriate for the target, given its post-period risks and capital structure.
3. Cash flows from disposals or divestments, sales of assets and pension funds, or sunk costs.

4 Debt and other expenses, such as taxes on gains from disposals and acquisitions costs, to give a value for the equity.
5 Calculations of the exchange ratio and control premium by comparing the estimated equity value for the target with its pre-acquisition standalone value and added value from the acquisition.
6 Revenue drivers are those key revenue, cost, or investment variables that determine the level of a firm's cash flows and hence its value to the shareholders (over 10 years).
7 Competitive position will get decayed due to replicability, substitute products, and a decline in market share.
8 Higher sales growth may be achieved only by increasing expenditure on marketing, advertising, or product development or by additional investment in fixed and current assets.
9 Operating cash inflows arising from the operations of the firm are post-tax flows before interest to finance the target (assuming debt-based acquisition). Cash outflows are due to additional fixed capital and working capital investments. After tax flows, the net of investment cash flows are called free cash flows.
10 The level of cash flows is capitalized by the cost of capital to yield the terminal value, where the weighted average cost of capital (WACC) is determined from the target's pre-buy costs of equity and debt.

The WACC is given as:

$$K = K_E \frac{E}{V} + (1-T) K_D \frac{D}{V} + K_P \frac{P}{V}$$

Where $V = E + D + P$,
K_E = cost of equity,
K_D = cost of debt,
K_P = cost of preference shares,
E = equity,
D = debt, and
E = market value of preference equity.

The post-buy WACC differs from the pre-buy WACC, and hence the discounting must happen on the post-buy yield.

Using the capital asset pricing model (CAPM), $K_E = R_F + \beta (R_M - R_F)$, or alternatively ($K_E$) (cost of equity) using β (beta), is the historical beta, which is expected to remain unchanged after the buy. One can use the beta value of a similar public company available in the listed firm's data. Beta values are estimated using historical prices of a matching or similar public company. The adjustment to changes in beta underlying the target due to the buy is factored in, which is logically derived from an adjustment factor (e.g. result of a simulation to the correlation) that can be applied to the formulae of:

$$\beta = \frac{COV(Ri, Rm)}{VARIANCE\ (Rm)}$$

as $\beta_{POST\ =\ FACTOR} \times \beta_{PRE}$,

where factor varies between (0,1).

The changes to beta happen on account of changes in the nature of business when the earnings fluctuate on account of business cycles. Higher operating leverage, which is the change in earnings (EBIT) due to changes in sales, causes higher beta. Similarly, financial leverage, which is the change in PAT due to changes in EBIT, increases beta. For a levered target, the proportion of equity beta is:

$$\beta_E = \beta_A\ (1 + debt/equity)$$

Since equity beta increases with debt, it is higher than asset beta. The asset beta is given as:

$$\beta_A = \beta_E \times equity\ /\ (equity + debt) + \beta_D \times debt\ /\ (equity + debt)$$

Cost of debt (K_D)

Cost of debt is not easy to estimate, since debt is not traded where the actual interest paid can be accounted for. The ability to borrow will change after the acquisition and so will the costs. The fixed rate debt does not reflect the actual cost. Similar problems may arise in case of preferred stock. This needs investment demand models to determine the post-buy effective cost of debt.

Or alternatively, for a manufacturing entity, terminal value is the value of the target at $t = T$. It is quite important and must be chosen based on the horizon and competitive situation in three stages – high growth, declining growth, and stable growth – over the years. The purchase price is the terminal discounted value (TV) which begins with the estimate of free cash flow (FCF):

> Free cash flow (unlevered) = net income (excluding extraordinary items and before preferred dividends, equity income and minority interest) + after-tax interest expense (net interest expense) + depreciation & amortization & deferred taxes & other non-cash charges − capital expenditures − difference between beginning and ending net working investment (NWI),

or

$$TV = \Sigma\ FCF_T\ /\ (1 + WACC)^t + V_T\ /\ (1 + WACC)^t$$

where TV is the target value or price to be paid for the buy,
FCF_t is the free cash flow in period t,
V_T = is the terminal value of the target at $t = T$, and
T = terminal period of 10 years.

Real options model

Corporate investments happen in a discrete fashion and in increments (stages), not a continuous process, because managers take time to translate capital infused into ready physical facilities that can deliver and realize the dollars generated with a lag of time. It is logical to make investments in steps (discretely) and exercise the option of such choices. Contingent events (e.g. falling market price of crude, exchange rates, technological changes, policy shifts, environmental activism, etc.) may alter plans to make subsequent investments and therefore impact the strike price.

The Black–Scholes (BS) real option pricing model is given as:

$$C = S \times N(d_1) - E \times \exp^n \times N(d_2),$$

where $d_1 = \dfrac{Ln(S/E) + (r + 0.5 \times \sigma^2) \cdot t}{\sqrt{t \times \sigma^2}}$,

$d_2 = d_1 - \sqrt{t \times \sigma^2}$,
C = call option value ($),
S = current price ($),
E = exercise price ($),
r = risk free rate ($),
σ^2 = variance in value ($), and
t = time to expiry (years).

Real options include opportunities to invest in real tangible assets such as capital equipment rather than financial instruments. The Black–Scholes (BS) model applied to real options is described as:

C = first stage investment ($);
S = present value of second stage investment ($);
T = time taken to make the second stage investment which is for how long the second stage can be deferred;
X = cost of the second stage investment ($);
Dividend = intermediate commitment costs to keep the second stage investment opportunity open (e.g. costs, rents, fees); and
σ = volatility in the market price of the asset.

The adjustments to the real options includes exercise price (E), which is variable because of the nature of follow-on (second stage) investments.

We present here the model for a gas reserves company that has debt of $10 billion and market value of equity at $80 per share (outstanding shares = $200.5 million). The price of oil was $30 per barrel, and the production cost, taxes, and royalties are projected at $10 per barrel.

Let the value of estimated reserve = 4000 TU (tera units):

Value of underlying asset = estimated reserves discounted for period of development (2 years)
$$= 4{,}000 \times \$\frac{30.00 - 10.00}{1.02^2} = \$76{,}893.5$$
Exercise price (E) = estimated development cost of reserves = 4,000 × $10 = $40,000 million
Time to expiration = average length of relinquishment option = 12 years
Variance in value of asset (σ^2) = variance in oil prices = 0.03
Risk-free interest rate (r) = 9%
$$\text{Dividend yield} = \frac{\text{net production revenue}}{\text{value of developed reserves}} = 2\%$$

Based upon these inputs, the Black–Scholes model provides the following value for the call:

$$d_1 = 1.6548$$
$$N(d_1) = 0.9510$$
$$d_2 = 1.0548$$
$$N(d_2) = 0.8542$$
Call value = 76,893 exp$^{(-0.02)(12)}$ (0.9510) − 40,000 (exp$^{(-0.09)(12)}$ (0.8542)
= $54,704 million − $ 9,912 million = $ 44,792 million

The gas reserves company had free cash flow (FCF) of $1,000 million from already developed reserves that will be maintained for 10 years.

The present value of developed reserves, discounted at the weighted average cost of capital (@ WACC = 10.5%) yields:

$$\text{Value of already developed reserves} = 1{,}000 \times \frac{1 - 1.105^{-10}}{.105} = \$6{,}014.77 \text{ million}$$

The total value comprises of the following components:

Value of undeveloped reserves = $44,792 million
Value of production in place = $ 6,014.77 million
Total value of firm = $44,792 million + $ 6,014.77 million = $50,806.77 million
(Less) outstanding debt = $ 10,000 million
Net value of the firm = $40,806.77 million

Value per share = $40,806.77 / 200.5 = $ 203.50
Value of equity = $80 × 200.5 = $16,040 million

The option price crosses the hurdle of investing in a real project with the hope of making similar project investments in the future.

Since the value per share arrived at using the BS model is $203.50, which is higher than $80.00, the investor must exercise this option and go for it.

Dilution in earnings

The enhanced volume of shares post-merger can lead to a decline in EPS in the year of acquisition. Earnings dilution, which is due to the exchange of shares by a premium, in contrast to loan stock or levered buy, imposes its own cost. Diluted earnings are different from dilution in earnings. Diluted earnings are the division of net income (net of preferred stock dividends) and average of shares outstanding

TABLE 8.21 Loss and gain to each player

Player	Gain/loss
B (Buyer)	$N_B / N_{BT} \times (V_{BT} - V_B)$
T (Target)	$[N_T / ER / N_{BT}] \times (V_{BT} - V_T)$

Note: N_B and N_T are pre-bid numbers of shares in B and T, and V_B and V_T are their pre-bid market values. N_{BT} and V_{BT} are corresponding figures for the post-acquisition from BT. V_{BT} = post-acquisition PER of B_T's combined earnings.

TABLE 8.22 Earnings dilution after acquisition

Year	1	2	3	4	5
EPS_B	10.00	12.00	14.40	17.28	20.74	24.88
NI_B	2.00	2.40	2.88	3.46	4.15	4.98
NI_T	2.00	2.20	2.42	2.66	2.93	3.22
NI_{BT}	4.00	4.60	5.30	.12	7.08	8.2
EPS_{BT}	10.00	11.5	13.25	15.30	17.70	20.50
DILUTION	0	4.2	7.99	11.49	14.68	17.63
NO.OF SHARES$_{MAX}$	20	18.33	16.81	15.41	14.31	12.95
EPS_{BT}	13.33	15.33	17.67	20.39	23.59	27.33
ACCRETION	33.33	27.75	22.71	18.00	13.74	9.85
NI_{BT}	4	4.8	5.76	6.91	8.3	9.95
EPS_{BT}	10	12	14.4	17.28	20.74	24.88

Note: Projection of EPS and PE ratio can fix the ER to prevent dilution. Optimal ER is when the current market price of the target is higher than the projected market price of the target. Dilution can be prevented by choosing the optimal ER.

which is adjusted for dilutive shares, whereas dilution in earnings are due to fall in exchange value.

Earnings dilution does not happen in 1 year, but it happens over several years. The gain or loss to each player is illustrated in Table 8.21.

Table 8.22 shows that, for a given level of expected earnings growth of the buyer and target, the premium paid determines whether the buy is earning-dilutive or accretive.

The maximum number of shares to be tendered is given by:

$$\text{(Exchange ratio) ER} = \frac{NI_{BT}}{EPS_B \; N_{BPRE\text{-}MERGER}}$$

While determining the ER, the buyer (B) therefore needs to take into account the expected growth in B's earnings as well as in the target's (T) earnings after the buy. If T is expected to grow at a slower rate than the buyer, the exchange ratio (ER) will be excessive and lead to significant earnings dilution. B and T's combined earnings may experience accretion rather than dilution when B avoids paying a premium.

The higher the premium, the larger the ER and the higher the rate of earning dilution. The choice of merger accounting versus acquisition accounting also matters because numbers such as return on assets (ROA) and tax/total assets (tax rate) or return on equity (ROE) will be higher under acquisition accounting *compared to the pooled method*. This is because acquisition accounting inflates the asset or equity base and reduces profits through amortization. Acquisition accounting requires revaluation of the target and also the impact on risk measures such as debt to total assets. This is advantageous due to higher total assets. Manipulation of asset revaluation in acquisitions accounting does exist.

The choice of a pooled versus acquisition treatment would depend on the choice of the payment method.

Optimizing deal financing

Although the nature of business impacts the financing choice, buyer's current liquidity, current stock price, and the leverage of buyer and target impacts the buyer's choice to make a cash offer in preference to exchanging stock offer for a few reasons. Cash offers are more certain and do not depend upon post-buy performance. One need not look at derivatives to reduce the asymmetry in post-buy stock price changes today. The cash offer can be made from sources of internal cash, from an underwritten offer, from a pre-bid loan stock issue, or from bank loans.

Levered cash financing is the bidder's ability to service the debt by periodic interest payments and capital repayment. There are few types of debt with varying degrees of risks and costs, which need prioritization with the expected purchase costs of a target.

TABLE 8.23 Ranking of financing options

Indicator/period	Year 1	Year 2
New business premium growth rate (%)		
Participating life	3.4	3.0
Participating pension	3.5	4.0
Non-participating	8.4	3.2
Linked	5.47	102.54
Net retention ratio	0.99	0.98
Expense of management to gross direct premium ratio	0.18	0.24
Commission ratio (gross commission paid to gross premium)	0.07	0.06
Ratio of policy holder's liabilities to shareholder's funds	8.99	4.18
Change in net worth	0.16	1.26
Profit after tax / total income	0.16	1.26
Total investments / (capital + surplus)	9.16	4.84
Conservation ratio (CR)	0.78	0.93
Persistency ratio (PR)		
12 months	0.85	0.92
24 months	0.71	0.82
36 months	0.65	0.78
48 months	0.60	0.70
60 months	0.55	0.65
NPA ratio		
Gross NPA ratio	–	–
Net NPA ratio	–	–

For example, resorts secure bank debt against the collaterals and covenants over a period of 5 years in the form of revolving credit at relatively low rates. The mezzanine debt is subject to restrictive covenants, which is a floating rate for a period of 10 years, and is costlier than secured debt. Bonds with longer maturities at fixed rates are costlier than bank debts with larger issue amounts and a lot of disclosure requirements. Bridge loans, which are short-term bank loans to be replaced by bond or equity, convertible bonds, or hybrid instruments are cheaper than normal bonds and are aimed at riskier investors who are diversified. The risk level of kinds of debt to be raised depends on the type of funding that replaces the first mode of high-yield bridge financing. With the latter two, the credit quality of senior debt is further strengthened, permitting a higher level of lending. Senior and mezzanine debt is also subject to covenants that constrain managerial freedom. The choice of a post-merger capital structure will involve securitization options and the taxation treatment of future assets.

Other than in a situation with a highly levered buyer, share exchange is preferred in most situations.

Choice of payment

Choice of payment is influenced by target bidder or deal characteristics from which the manager can use to make a choice.

The impact of bidder variables on the mode of payment is represented by multinomial logit as:

$$\text{Prob (choice} = K) = \alpha + \beta_1 \text{OWNER} + \beta_2 \text{FCF} + \beta_3 \text{Size} + \beta_4 \text{FIXED} + \beta_4 \text{LEV} + \beta_5 \frac{MV}{BV} + \beta_6 \text{BOARD} + \beta_7 \text{ROE} + \varepsilon$$

The impact of target variables on the mode of payment is represented by multinomial logit as:

$$\text{Prob (choice} = K) = \alpha + \beta_1 \text{SIZE} + \beta_2 \text{PAT} + \beta_3 \text{BV} + \beta_4 \text{GROUP} + \varepsilon$$

The impact of deal variables on the mode of payment is represented by multinomial logit as:

$$\text{Prob (choice} = K) = \alpha + \beta_1 \text{TV} + \beta_2 \text{HOST} + \beta_3 \text{CGT} + \beta_4 \text{TRNFEE} + \beta_4 \text{PREM} + \varepsilon$$

Where OWNER = ownership measured as the percentage share (%) held by a bidder directors,

    FCF = free cash flow,
    Size = size of bidder,
    FIXED = fixed assets,
    LEV = leverage,
    MV/BV = growth opportunity,
    BOARD = board size,
    ROE = return on equity,
    PAT = profitability,
    BV = book value,
    GROUP = group company related indicator,
    TV = transaction value,
    HOST = hostile deal indicator,
    CGT = capital gains tax charged,
    TRNFEE = transaction fees paid, and
    PREM = premium paid.

These three equations can give rise to three probabilities to find the trade-offs across bidder-, target-, and deal-level variables.

Spin-offs

A spin-off is when a portion is carved out for sale. The market perceives the sell-off as a value-creating decision, but in a large minority of cases, the reaction may be negative when the size of sell-off matters. Where the sell-off increases the focus of the residual business, the valuation impact is generally positive. The immediate financials of divestors are also important.

The common drivers of spin-off decisions that are considered important are tax avoidance, risk minimization, fund allocation, investor attraction, focusing on new markets, debt reallocation and production savings, whether the parent and the spin-off operate in the same industry, the financial position of the parent company, and the business strategy of parent.

The structure of spin-offs involves pro-rata (proportionate) distribution of shares (spin-off ratio) in the new company to parent shareholders, when the parent distributes less than 100% of their holdings in the divested unit. The ratio of shares between the two companies reflects the ratio of assets and values of the companies. The ownership structure of the parent will influence the same decision. When much of debt is offloaded upon the offspring, it becomes riskier, and the value falls. Spin-offs are also used to manipulate dividends. Spin-offs are the allocation of

TABLE 8.24 Impact after spin-off

Return on assets (ROA)	Not effectively managing its assets in order to produce net income
Operating profit margin ratio	Increase in direct cost of revenues and operating expenses (especially selling, general, and administrative)
Activity ratios	Inventory turnover and inventory turnaround days ratios, total asset turnover ratio, accounts receivables and average collection period
Total factor productivity	Spin offs lead to an increase in overall efficiency. Increase in productivity, managerial discipline, incentive contracting, more focus, and improved capital allocation.
Total employment	Downsizing labour
Total wage	Wage rationalization, decrease in workers' wages
Materials cost	Negotiating better terms with suppliers for lowered materials costs by better managerial incentives to reduce inefficient expenditures, aligned vendors
Sales	None for off-spring may be lower
New capital expenditure	None for off-spring and more for parent
Rental and administrative expenses	Increase in rental and administrative expenses due to decoupling of franchisee or facilities or parental guarantee

assets and liabilities between the parent company and the spun-off entity. High-risk businesses cannot bear as much debt as more mature business. A tax-free spin-off is where the distribution of shares is not subjected to corporate taxes by the parent company. Target valuation is not simple and is contingent upon the many similar factors, such as whether the spin-off is successful or not. After the spin-off, the offspring is no longer accounted by the parent. If the spun-off entity is profitable, then de-consolidation reduces the post-spin-off profit of the residual parent group.

Post-merger impact

It is not easy or practical to field test the holistic expectations of a merger and critically evaluate the organization's ability to effectively complete the integration and to create a new, more profitable entity. Given the risky and challenging nature of mergers, the burden of proof should be on demonstrating how a potential merger is the best strategic option facing the company. Both operating and financial parameters exist to evaluate after the purchase, such as senior most debt / EBITDA, senior debt / EBITDA, total debt / EBITDA, EBITDA / interest, (EBITDA − capital expenditure) / interest). Lenders can contribute to different layers of a debt package.

TABLE 8.25 Post-merger impact

Cause	Impact
Growth oriented	New products, service offerings, markets, customer segments, distribution channels
	Enhanced market presence, market capture
	Enhanced product development efficiency (shared R&D, internal best practices)
	Combined technologies or capabilities
	Leveraged sales force
	Increased capture of the value chain
Efficiency oriented	Common headquarters
	Integrated supply chain
	Leverage procurement volume
	Production footprint optimization
	Facility optimization
	Vertical integration, de-integration
	Distribution channel optimization
	Sales force optimization
	Consolidation
Co-ordination	Financial value (balance sheet items, taxes, etc.)
	Optimized programs and policies (e.g. benefits programs)
	Rationalization and/or elimination of special programs, projects, etc.
	Additional alliances or relationships

The debt capacity of the buyer for different layers of debt is determined by forecasting the EBITDA of the merged firms (size of debt / EBITDA). Benchmarks on the maximum level of debt based on the forecast exist. However, the manager must determine internal thresholds using internal tools rather than relying on regulatory benchmarks.

Insurance analytics

Insurance analytics focuses on business growth, claim rates, renewal rates, insolvency analysis, and yield on investment. The long-term nature of the insurance business exposes its amenability to catastrophic and non-catastrophic risks. The problem of moral hazard between the insurer and insuree does prevail with methods of identifying signals for fair pricing that should always reflect the true underwriting risks. The pricing of policies is done at a business line or segment level with no individual level differentiation. An insurer's insolvency and protection for policyholders relies on the insurer's financial ability to indemnify a covered loss. At the firm level, a less diversified business; levels of cash flow, return on equity, and leverage; and insolvency risk are important goals of an insurance business. Indicators that reflect the key aspects of an insurer's business can be categorized as follows.

TABLE 8.26 Engagement in insurance

Type	*Description*
Loss reserve deficiency	1 year reserve development / surplus or current reserve deficiency / surplus
Reserve development ratio	Reserve development / surplus or one year reserve development / prior year surplus
Operating profitability	Overall operating ratio, returns on equity, and return on revenue
Loss experience	Loss ratio
Asset mix	Bonds, stocks, mortgages, mortgage loans, real estate, cash equivalent, and the percentage of the non-classified assets
Investment performance	Investment yield
Capitalization	Gross premium to surplus ratio, net premium written to surplus ratio
Leverage	Liability to asset ratio
Business growth	Change in net written sum assured
Liquidity	Liquid assets ratio, overall liquidity, and operating cash flow to net premium written ratio
Credit risk	Surplus reinsurers aid to surplus, balance outstanding with agents (brokers) to surplus
Size	Total assets
Business concentration	Herfindahl index of premiums written among business lines

TABLE 8.27 General insurance analytics

Indicator period	Quarter 4	Quarter 3	Quarter 2
Gross direct premium growth rate (%)	7.96	9.96	13.97
Gross direct premium / net worth	1.47	2.98	1.5
Net worth growth (%)	10.18	22.4	24.24
Net retention ratio	90.63	88.7	89.75
Net commission / gross premium	5.52	5.44	5.95
Total overhead / gross premium	29.29	33.37	28.27
Total overhead / net premium	31.6	36.24	30.7
Net incurred claims to net earned premium	88.42	77.54	85.67
Gross NPA ratio	1.26	1.26	1.3
Net NPA ratio	0.14	0.15	0.16
Return on net worth	4.91	25.59	14.4
Net earnings ratio	3.61	9.34	10.45
Liquid assets to liabilities ratio	0.17	0.17	0.15
Operating profit (%)	4.21	6.42	6.8
Solvency margin / capital ratio	25	26	28

Source: Insurance Regulatory Development Authority (2010).

TABLE 8.28 Life insurance analytics

Indicator/period	Year 1	Year 2
New business premium growth rate (%)		
Participating life	3.4	3.0
Participating pension	3.5	4.0
Non-participating	8.4	3.2
Linked	5.47	102.54
Net retention ratio	0.99	0.98
Expense of management to gross direct premium ratio	0.18	0.24
Commission ratio(gross commission paid to gross premium)	0.07	0.06
Ratio of policy holder's liabilities to shareholder's funds	8.99	4.18
Change in net worth	0.16	1.26
Profit after tax / total income	0.16	1.26
Total investments / (capital + surplus)	9.16	4.84
Conservation ratio (CR)	0.78	0.93
Persistency ratio (PR)		
12 months	0.85	0.92
24 months	0.71	0.82
36 months	0.65	0.78
48 months	0.60	0.70
60 months	0.55	0.65
NPA ratio		
Gross NPA ratio	–	–
Net NPA ratio	–	–

Highly concentrated insurers exhibit higher insolvency risk. Generally, higher stock market returns lead to over-valuations (of public limited companies) and weaken an insurer's financial position and increases the chance of insolvency. A more practical method of monitoring exposure limits by geography and by lines of business is important. Re-insurers pose a challenge on underwriting prices and also credit risk. Earned premiums are lower than written premiums, which are known as net premiums. Rising claims and reducing premium growth impacts operating ratios.

Applied question

A given financial leasing company has details about the short-term and long-term deposits raised from its customers. It also has the option to borrow from other players. Calculate the marginal cost of funds using the information. Deposits from the public include short-term borrowing for 6 months (40%) and long-term borrowing for more than 6 months (60%), at the rate of 7.00% and 9.00%, respectively. Commercial papers can be raised at 6.00% now for terms of less than 6 months.

Commercial papers give the flexibility of raising funds in the short term, although are subject to market risks. The marginal cost of funds is calculated in the following way.

The cost of deposits should be calculated using the average rates at which funds were raised in the last month. Each of these rates should be weighted by the proportionate balance outstanding to date. Hence, the marginal cost of funds (MCF) is given as $0.4 \times 7.00 + 0.6 \times 9.00 = 2.8 + 5.4 = 8.2$.

The leasing company can access the commercial paper market to raise new funds at 6.00%, which is lower than the current MCF of 8.2%.

References

Altman, E. (1968). Financial Ratios, Discriminant Analysis and the Prediction of Corporate Bankruptcy. *Journal of Finance*, 23(4): 589–609.

Ambrose, J.M., and A. Seward. (1988). Best's Rating, Financial Ratios and Prior Probabilities in Insolvency Prediction. *Journal of Risk and Insurance*, 55(2): 229–244.

Bank for International Settlements. (2006). *International Convergence of Capital Measurement and Capital Standards: A Revised Framework Comprehensive Version*. Basel, Switzerland: Bank for International Settlements, Basel Committee on Banking Supervision.

Baranoff, E.G., T.W. Sager, and R.C. Witt. (1999). Industry Segmentation and Predictor Motifs for Solvency Analysis of the Life/Health Insurance Industry. *Journal of Risk and Insurance*, 66(1): 99–123.

BarNiv, R., and J. Hathorn. (1997). The Merger or Insolvency Alternative in the Insurance Industry. *Journal of Risk and Insurance*, 64(1): 89–113.

Brealey, R.A., and S.C. Myers. (2002). *Brealey & Myers on Corporate Finance: Capital Investment and Valuation*. New York: McGraw-Hill.

Brigham, E.F., and J.F. Weston. (1993). *Essentials of Managerial Finance*. New York: Dresden.

Calem, P.S., and M. LaCour-Little. (2001). Risk-Based Capital Requirements for Mortgage Loans. *Journal of Banking and Finance*, 28(2): 647–672.

Crouhy, M., D. Galai, and R. Mark. (2000). A Comparative Analysis of Current Credit Risk Models. *Journal of Banking and Finance*, 24, 59–117.

Crouhy, M., D. Galai, and R. Mark. (2001a). Prototype Risk Rating System. *Journal of Banking & Finance*, 25, 47–95.

Crouhy, M., D. Galai, and R. Mark. (2001b). A Comparative Analysis of Current Credit Risk Models. *Journal of Banking & Finance*, 24, 59–117.

Elizalde, A. (2005). Do We Need to Worry about Credit Risk Correlation? *Journal of Fixed Income*, 15(3): 42–59.

Gordy, M.B. (1998, December). *A Comparative Anatomy of Credit Risk Models*. Washington, DC: Board of Governors of the Federal Reserve System.

Gordy, M.B. (2002). A Risk-Factor Model Foundation for Ratings-Based Bank Capital Rules. *Journal of Financial Intermediation*, 12(3): 199–232.

Hamilton, J.D. (1994). *Time Series Analysis*. Princeton, NJ: Princeton University Press.

Hull, J.C. (1997). *Options, Futures, and Other Derivatives*. New York: Prentice Hall.

Hull, J.C., and A. White. (1990). Pricing Interest Rate Derivative Securities. *Review of Financial Studies*, 3, 573–592.

Insurance Regulatory Development Authority. (2010). *Public Disclosures by Insurers*. Circular No. IRDA/F&I/CIR/F&A/012/01/2010. India.

Kelly, S, Federal Reserve Bank of Philadelphia. (2003). Using Cluster Analysis for Retail Portfolio Segmentation in an Economic Capital Model: Homogeneity by Common Default Behavior over Time. NESUG03, SAS, September 2003.

Kupiec, P.H. (2001). The New Basel Capital Accord: The Devil Is in the (Calibration) Details. IMF Working Paper, Retrieved from www.imf.org.

Mester, L.J. (1997). What Is the Point of Credit Scoring? *Federal Reserve Bank of Philadelphia Business Review*, pp. 3–16.

Rappaport, A. (1986). *Creating Shareholder Value*. New York: The Free Press.

Roberto, P., and W. Nayda. (2004). Economic and Regulatory Capital Allocation for Revolving Retail Exposures. *Journal of Banking & Finance*, 28(4): 789–809.

Ross, S.A., R.W. Westerfield, and J.F. Jaffe. (1995). *Corporate Finance*. Toronto: Mason, Thomson/Nelson, Irwin.

9
IMPLEMENTING BUSINESS ANALYTICS

This chapter introduces the reader to the challenges of implementing business analytics with a practitioner's view of a real-life business situation. The on-the-floor challenges are many but not insurmountable and can be handled with better planning. This chapter is intended to explain to business managers the challenges involved in implementing business analytics solutions and methods of overcoming issues preventing successful implementation. Businesses are challenged by the commotion and confusion that analytics can create when initiated in an unorganized fashion. Teams can reach deadlocks that lead to nowhere when they attempt directionless approaches, instead of having a clear focus to discover real business opportunities or to explore important outcomes for their customers, stakeholders, and employees. This chapter shows the flow for organizing an implementation and discusses sector-specific aspects of analytics projects implementation.

Further, it also provides specific strategies for implementation across various industry sectors.

The key questions to be asked by stakeholders during implementation are:

- Should we implement in the first place?
- Is it a strategic or a tactical project?
- How can one budget the expenses and whom to account for?
- How can one uncover the value creation impact?
- What are the metrics of monitoring and reporting or choosing the investment?
- What is the distinction of business analytics projects compared to other alternatives of similar nature (e.g. IT projects or investments)?
- How can one ensure the team is engaged and focused?
- How can one ensure top management's continual sponsorship?
- What is the internal plan of communication and review?
- What is the external plan of dissemination (through road shows, workshops, seminars, training programs, workouts)?

Critical factors

No business makes a decision without relying on past data, and in that respect, analytics prevails to some degree or other in every business. There exists studies and evidence on the benefits of business analytics in an organization (International Data Corporation, 2003). Analytical projects improving manufacturing had a median return on investment (ROI) of 277%; those involving financial management had median ROI of 139%, and those involving customer relationship management had a median ROI of 55%. Similarly, the median ROI of predictive analytics projects was 145% compared to non-predictive (deterministic, exploratory) projects at 89%. The implementation of business analytics is demonstrated when it is developed and its potential is visualized by means of smaller-scale pilots with tests of incremental financial impact. Come what may, the sponsor or the manager (user) will never actualize the benefit until it is implemented in practice. Core competencies are the essential capabilities that create a firm's sustainable competitive advantage. A business analytics solution can be deployed and used to obtain its full impact potential provided it is done with caution and due diligence while understanding the limitations of both the solution as well as the data environment better.

The implementation of an analytics solution has often been a challenge for an industry. Both availability and access to business metadata and residing systems data are desired. An executor is someone who delivers an analytical implementation solution by deploying a scalable data mart, which renders a compatible data platform and computes the desired parameters efficiently. This is on account of a data-driven approach, and hence the task of collating data to gather information and then applying it on relevant attributes is a ridiculous task and can throwup numerous hurdles. Further, all business analytics applications need to integrate data better with their customers' (clients') system so as to make it easy to be deployed and used by the business users or their customers. There is no magic to the art of implementing an analytics solution, and it requires careful framing of business problems, and also their magnitudes, and achieving goals as milestones. Having reference financial measures for comparison can help reach a consensus on items, which justifies the implementation and derives success in the sponsor's view.

Where can an analytics implementation go wrong? For example, how can typical business manager mistakes be gauged? A few of the previously documented reasons of analytics failure include lack of top management support, a weak project manager, no stakeholder involvement and/or participation, weak commitment from the project team, lack of requisite knowledge or skills in team members, and the availability and commitment of subject matter experts. The process owner can foresee these challenges and prepare himself to achieve better outcomes.

There exist four factors or essential requisites for the successful implementation of an analytical application. These four factors we feel are the biggest drivers of implementation. Therefore, one could view them as four pillars supporting implementation as depicted in Figure 9.1.

Sponsorship support of senior and top management

Without buy-in from the top management, it is hard to find the cultural changes necessary to bring in the adoption of an analytically friendly environment in an organization. A single functional head, such as a marketing head or risk head, could try engineering these efforts, but he will be successful only to a limited extent. The foremost reason is that analytics is a cross-functional practice that needs facilitation from top management. A functional leader will find it tough and will have to fight with gigantic efforts to garner support from peers and subordinates to achieve the outcome. How can one obtain buy-in from top management? Evidence of the positive contribution of analytics in competitors' businesses should be identified by reviewing their practices and documentation. To gather evidence of competitors' practices, one can collect responses from common suppliers, common dealers, common customers, or regulatory filings. Value-adding activities include sales, marketing, promotion of products, campaign, outbound telemarketing, etc. An executor has to choose one of the functional activities to demonstrate its benefits. The non-value-adding activities, which cannot be directly related to customers or sales, include HR, finance, production, and administration, which are support functions. Senior management would be more enthusiastic to find top-line improvement initiatives on value-adding activities than bottom-line benefits to start with. Further, with the consent of management, a quick response survey of responders could be carried out among peers, clients, and direct reports on their opinions. Employees do not resist change so long as they perceive that change will cause a positive difference to their work life. It takes longer to realize the positive impact down the line. Analytics is no different from any other strategic change initiative that organizations pursue and implement constantly from time to time to transform them towards a worthy and valuable business.

Enterprise-wide approaches to solution implementation

Analytics needs to be executed or managed in an organization with an enterprise-wide adoption approach so as to have a unified version of truth or facts that are accessible and acceptable to all users in business. The purpose of an enterprise-wide approach is to ensure that managers do not make decisions on certain lines of the organization without obtaining a trade-off view across other related lines. For example, the decision to make a new product release with qualitative changes to a product will require significant related investments on re-training its onsite field sales team or conducting a user-awareness program. This is because the key message has now changed and needs rejuvenation with emphasis during every contact or interaction with the user or customer. Any decision to increase interest revenue by increasing credit line amounts for customers will definitely result in higher default rates (credit risk) and, hence, needs to be compared against alternatives. This also means that the data that is used for analytics is defined, stored, and interpreted in a consistent manner. This also means that implementation metadata can be attempted that combines the specific aspects from different business systems into a common architecture. The executor has to build and develop a data mart that denotes the common denominator of the business, which is sourced from one or more systems. Analytics should never denote multiple versions of the truth or collect standalone statements of unrelated facts.

Competency on a functional analytics capability

Distinctive competency, such as pricing, energy efficiency, quality focus, agile design, new product launch, acquisition efficiency, channel management, sales force optimization, responsive operations, customer service, revenue management, etc., needs to be developed to achieve the necessary scale and impetus to penetrate analytics horizontally. If the strategic decisions commonly taken by the company are judgmental, experience based, and cannot be driven scientifically, then it will be difficult even to propose a "business analytics", and there are plenty of examples of such situations in organizations. Careful attention to measures of distinctive capabilities by exploiting and exploring newer (alternative) engagement mix is required to further understand such capabilities. An enterprise can become a market leader when it takes care of three major functions – new product development, customer intimacy, and operational excellence – in that order. One example is the use of credit-scoring tools, which undertake credit approval or rejection decisions and are used across all industries such as hospitals, manufacturing, automobiles, insurance, and so on. The presence of functional analytics strength can reduce the time of execution. Another example is inventory management, which is used across industries and includes stock broking. This definitely requires skills of domain knowledge in the logistic field and the application of tools to support decision making.

Demonstrating value in analytics

The host of approaches and tools discussed in previous chapters needs to be evaluated for financial impact, and hence, financial analytics can go a long way in helping stakeholders arrive at potentials to permeate within the business. If a company cannot find any incremental financial impact from the new solution, it will not support the investment. Therefore, all such attempts to demonstrate value must start with smaller tests and then scaled up to fully-fledged ones. Such an approach is also called a pilot approach, which is done on a sample or a specific chosen unit of the organization, and then the results are shared across the other functional units, thus disseminating its success. Thinking big and dreaming grand are good. However, one must start with a smaller set of sub-populations to learn key challenges before being able to demonstrate the complete implementation benefits. Such pilots are to be done with the right set of functionally skilled people and tools and data environment. Further, not all of the total value impact can be derived at one go, and hence the incremental impact is separately measured in each stage

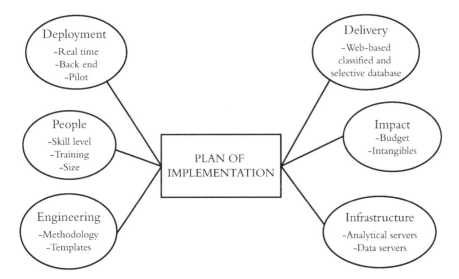

FIGURE 9.1 Plan of analytics implementation

and internally communicated. Therefore, the analytical implementation plan must be phased by splitting the goals and impact of each stage separately. The value in the application of analytics lies in development of the tools that have been discussed in previous chapters.

Of the four most critical factors, the buy-in of senior management can actually make all other factors work in support of the direction towards implementation. To conclude, if one assumes that circumstances are not conducive, that the environment is not supportive, or that there exists little data to generate sparkling facts, then the manager could explore evidence of successful, positive, incremental financial impact specifically demonstrated at competitors' businesses. Managers should highlight the robustness of such evidence by rejuvenating the reliability, repeatability, and scalability of these results across competitors. Human resources must put in place the right incentive systems to reward teamwork and also recruit, train, and evaluate the employees needed to create a flexible workforce that can successfully operate in analytics implementation.

Thought process in implementation

A more effective approach is to start with the problems or opportunities faced by the organization and to develop an understanding of what information is likely to be useful to managerial decisions. An understanding of these problems permits organizations to determine effectively the analytics that are most likely to be useful in improving organizational effectiveness. These analytics then determine which metrics are relevant to the analysis and which data elements need to be incorporated into the analysis. The difference in these two approaches is spectacular. The

TABLE 9.1 Business roles in implementation

Designation	Key responsibility
Sponsor	Monitor processes ensure that all operations are handled. Work planning for the entire unit, keeping in mind shift rotation.
Senior project manager	Ensure the delivery happens at the end of the transaction in a successful manner and to the satisfaction of the customer.
Functional manager	Responsible for ensuring good service to the branch customers. Benchmark turnaround times on servicing and implement best practices. Develop and implement a service plan. Communicate service initiatives and expectations to staff.
Team leader	Responsible for allocating and engaging team members and aligning members towards the consumer of analytics, training of team members and preparing periodic trackers, conducting appraisals, translating requirements, setting up the data and systems for access and executing on the sampling plan.
Team member	Taking initiatives for self-learning, gathering requirements from the client, data preparation, fitting of techniques, execution and generation of reports, submission for review by team leader.

TABLE 9.2 Implementation plan of analytics

Analytics type	Final stakeholders	Objectives	Duration
Ad hoc	Process owner	1. Give shape and crystallize an idea into a business report from raw data 2. Visualize the part of a big idea using refined data	3 months
Short term	Business owner	1. Take ownership of routinely generating information from a given owner from raw data using similar methods 2. Build and implement a new criteria filter or model for incremental positive gains	3 months
Very long term	SBU owner	1. Handle the burden of generating routine business reports that collate a union of measures and is shared across multiple stakeholders 2. Develop a mode that is tested as a pilot for the entire period	6 months
Very long term	Group owner	1. Multiple reports, multiple FTEs (full-time employees), multiple stakeholders and pretty standardized business specifications that are shared across more than one SBU of the business 2. Models that have been translated into rules or engines installed into one or more aspects of the customer life cycle processes such as approval, acquisition, closure, upgrading, optimization, fulfilment, inventory management, etc. A multiplicity of models that have simplified the complexity of tasks and are deployed to make real-time decisions	9 months

latter one is targeted at specific managerial decision situations, while the former does not have this focus.

Managers can take two approaches, depending on the nature of the business problem. First, for a known problem with a known solution (e.g. improving the success of campaigns), the company could take a hypothesis-based approach by starting with the outcome (e.g. cross-sell/up-sell to existing customers), piloting and testing the solution with a control group, and then scaling up broadly across the customer base. Second, for a known problem area with an unknown solution, fraud for example, the company could take an exploratory approach to look for patterns in the data to find interesting correlations that may be predictive; for instance a bank found that the use of a fixed IP (internet location) at which online forms were filled out was highly correlated with fraud. Once insights are uncovered, the next step is to create business rules, which may be nested by mapping the metadata.

The following steps in the cycle of implementation can be examined:

- Communicate a plan with a sense of exigency
- Break down big tasks into smaller steps with infrastructure and business requirements listed separately
- Set specific goals for teams and members and create a culture of accountability
- Have a plan of escalation and feedback for defects with time lines for resolution
- Plan periodic interim reviews, interim documentation, and reviews of forecasts
- Assign skilled personnel for teams and rotate members as and when the need arises
- Avoid over-communicating (an enthusiastic response) interim results until they are validated
- Share numbers in the form of monetary impacts for all stakeholders
- Celebrate interim success with the team
- Sign off on the implementation with well documented submissions of deliverables

Delivery mode

We describe the modes of delivery (propagation) of analytical reports that the user may opt to view or access in one form or other. For example, the information could be stored in analytical data marts permanently for a large number of users, or it could be generated on the fly for a few users as they need it. The generated information could be archived only after storing for a few periods. Delivery of business analytics could be internal score cards or dashboards, which are tools for the visitor. Delivery refers to the methods of rendering the output into the user's mailbox or an intranet portal for consumption by the manager. Alternatively, users could view these metrics in a static report, a snapshot view, a fixed template, a dynamic view or a dashboard, or a stored database (web stream). Further, such streams could be accessed in the form of mobile applications. Therefore, it can be seen that dashboard reports could vary by granularity or by the type of metrics that the particular role is interested in viewing. Certain metrics or reports could be confidential and hence should only be seen by the respective roles with appropriate security layers. The following section describes examples of analytic work flow by describing the flow of requests from a given role from a given work stage number to a given work stage number.

The responsibility of delivery of reports (dashboard) could lie on whoever has access to the report or has access to the data that can generate the report. Before acting on an action item, it is natural for someone to ask for clarification, and hence, the workflow is a two-way communication.

For the remainder of the chapter, we will describe implementations in banking, in insurance, in the telecom industry, in retail, and in manufacturing.

Implementation in banking

The banking industry uses analytics for a variety of customer benefits and is constantly challenged by the disruptive alternatives available to customers. It is a regulated industry that complies with domestic and external regulators and has to generate periodic statements for disclosure. Therefore, analytics need to be integrated significantly with the investment in its efforts to create a variety of statements for regulatory compliance, which includes Basel reports, credit acts, etc. It also deals with private, individual customer transaction information, and due caution is needed in picking and processing such information or its application to creating analytics that may be disseminated or shared by the business. Since banking is a business of irreversible transactions, whether dealing with customers or agents, operational mistakes are costly and are affected in real time; thus, both genuineness and accuracy are critical in banking.

Banks are financial intermediaries; perform the transformation of short-term liabilities into a mix of both short- and long-term assets; and are subjected to market, operations, and credit risk. Cross-functional integration of SBU-specific data is a bigger challenge, since individual divisions may be operating on a standalone basis or in silos. Therefore, the imperatives and nature of initiation in banking are explained in Table 9.3.

TABLE 9.3 Initiatives in banking implementation of analytics

Focus area/proof of concept	Period/ nature	Metric	Allocation of investment costs	Team size	Data
Interest rate analytics	Short	Margin, spread	Corporate	Small	Internal
Marketing analytics	Long	ROI	Sales	Large	Internal and external
Re-engineering customer service	Short	Repeat purchase	Marketing	Small	Internal

Implementation in insurance

Insurance is a direct sales-oriented product that booms with finer targeting of policy offers to households or entities with greater chances of renewal after the first year and also larger chances of renewal after the second year, respectively. The chances of renewal for existing policyholders, premium rates, maturity, and product type initially proposed vary a lot across buyers. These are products that are held lifelong and where no alteration can be made, and they are less flexible than banking products. Insurance is a protection product that promises to insulate a portion of financial damages against the likely loss from an event during the life of the insurer. Insurers add to their bundle of products, which results in claims from customers due to natural or unnatural disasters. Since the core value proportion of insurance is related to the events that may happen during the life of the insurers, the manner in which an insurer devises its renewal rate strategy must be based on life events that occur with the insured. For example, the death of a member may follow the birth of a new member, which are life events. A rise in income follows a job change or relocation to a new city by the policyholder. The dimensional view of a household can point to the specific needs that arise for that household. Typical cash-rich insurers have short-term cash inflows and long-term cash liabilities with operational expenses in the form of commissions. Periodic cash inflows are transformed into long-term investments. Insurance is regulated by solvency norms and deals in the private information of their customers. Therefore, subjected to market risks and operational risks, the insurance industry has put care into disclosure norms. The same unit or division deals with a multiplicity of products, many times targeted at the same households, and hence data integration is not a challenge for the managers. Customer service history can be integrated with renewal rate information for better results by taking advantage of alternate sales channels. A gradual migration of a sales channel from a direct sales, agent-based medium to a B2C online, postal, or alternate channel can reduce costs drastically.

Therefore, the imperatives and nature of initiation in insurance are explained in Table 9.4.

TABLE 9.4 Initiatives in insurance implementation of analytics

Focus area/proof of concept	Period/ nature	Metric	Allocation of investment costs	Team size	Data
Renewal rate	Short	Margin, spread	Corporate	Small	Internal
Lapse rate	Long	ROI	Sales	Large	Internal and external
Actuarial analytics	Short	Repeat purchase	Marketing	Small	Internal
Premium rate analysis	Short	Price	Marketing	Small	Internal
Claim analytics	Short	Claim frequency	Marketing	Small	Internal
Catastrophe risk	Short	Expected losses	Marketing	Small	Internal

Implementation in manufacturing

Manufacturing embodies a series of processes undertaken in the form of parallel or sequential operations on raw material or intermediates to transform them into finished goods. This engages and utilizes fixed or portable installations of equipment, machines, devices, modular assets, people, and energy, surrounded by a system to add value to inputs. Manufacturing has a higher share of fixed costs, often with immobile assets that may not be liquidated easily. Operating costs are in better control and so are the variable costs that can be minimized by curtailing production activity. The cycle of conversion is longer, and inventory is stored for much longer in warehouses with higher commitment costs. The entire life cycle of manufacturing deals with uncertainties with respect to availability, pricing, and delivery of raw material; to variable costs of processing that are dependent on fuel energy and skilled labour rates, taxation, and transportation costs; and lastly, to the willingness of the market to pay a fixed sale price. Therefore, the supply chain is critical to manufacturing. Savings or cost reduction by increasing efficiency and productivity, reducing downtime, improving quality, and forward purchasing of raw materials are the end strategies in this business.

Therefore, the imperatives and nature of initiation in manufacturing are explained in Table 9.5.

Implementation in telecom

Telecom is a business where investment in networks and infrastructure is huge and devolves into large fixed and operating costs in the form of towers, backup power supplies, control stations, and technical personnel all over the nation. The break-even point can be too long for many businesses but can be reduced by immediate and super-fast acquisition of subscribers. This means the marketing team is on its

TABLE 9.5 Initiatives in manufacturing implementation of analytics

Focus area/proof of concept	Period/ nature	Metric	Allocation of investment costs	Team size	Data
Inventory analytics	Short	Margin, spread	Corporate	Small	Internal
E-finance supply chain	Long	ROI	Operations	Large	Internal and external
SKU rationalization	Short	Cost	Operations	Small	Internal
Order management	Short	Cost	Operations	Small	Internal
Supplier/ customer return analysis	Short	Cost	Operations	Small	Internal

TABLE 9.6 Initiatives in telecom implementation of analytics

Focus area/proof of concept	Period/ nature	Metric	Allocation of investment costs	Team size	Data
Survival analysis	Short	Repurchase	Corporate	Small	Internal
Yield management	Long	Revenue	Sales	Large	Internal and external
Segmentation	Short	Average revenue per user (ARPU)	Marketing	Small	Internal
Value-based migration	Long	ROI	Marketing	Large	Internal and external

toes from day one. The telecom business must work on a basic value proposition to have a large base of subscribers that delivers minimum sustainable revenue. Subsequently, the operator can devise value-added services and the gradual migration of basic subscribers towards upgraded services such as 4G, media on demand, etc. Inorganic growth by means of acquiring targets that fit the value criteria and scanning for better targets to assume larger market share are not ruled out.

Therefore, the imperatives and nature of initiation in telecom are explained in Table 9.6.

Implementation in retail

Retail chains are shorter-cycle investments that take shape with the joint stakes of partners or franchisees and do not involve landlocked capital. Choice of store locations is extremely important. Similarly, sourcing destinations could be joined with shoppers adjacent to high-density residential hubs within the metro city. The onus of holding high-priced inventory of a wide variety of SKUs can be daunting, and working capital management is not as difficult. Unlike many other sectors, retail chains are low-levered trading companies that could be easily perplexed by discount wars, competitive pressure, changes in consumer confidence, and life style changes. Comparatively lower margin rates at the product level are all the more challenging. Retail businesses strive to increase their asset turnover ratio and push high-margin luxury items assorted with daily needs. Operating expenses (opex) should be targeted for reduction while increasing scale by adding stores will increase capex. Therefore, SKU rationalization, store-level choice selection, movement analysis seeking, reward behaviour, store-level promotion and brand promotion analysis, retention of skilled low paid employees, etc., are key areas of implementation challenges. Further, a larger volume of transactional and purchase history data needs to be mined and discovered for value.

Therefore, the imperatives and nature of initiation in retail are explained in Table 9.7.

160 Implementing business analytics

TABLE 9.7 Initiatives in retail implementation of analytics

Focus area/proof of concept	Period/ nature	Metric	Allocation of investment costs	Team size	Data
Survival analysis	Short	Margin, spread	Corporate	Small	Internal
Reward management	Long	ROI	Operations	Large	Internal and external
SKU rationalization	Short	Cost	Operations	Small	Internal
Customer satisfaction	Short	Cost	Operations	Small	Internal
Store profitability	Short	Cost	Operations	Small	Internal

Applied question

Assume that you are a project manager in a cement plant. Devise a research methodology to collect data for demonstrating the evidence of effective deployment of an attrition management solution for its implementation in the cement plant from the following information.

The cement plant has five divisions, namely raw materials, clinkers and grinding, R&D, ready mix and distribution, and packaging and marketing. The attrition rates for the divisions are given as 25% for raw materials, 27% for clinkers and grinding, 1% for R&D, 29% for ready mix and distribution, and 21% for packaging and marketing.

The attrition rates sorted in increasing order are, namely 1% for R&D, 21% for packaging and marketing, 25% for raw materials, 27% for clinkers and grinding, and 29% for ready mix and distribution. Since R&D has the lowest attrition rate, it is excluded from the study plan here. The rest of the divisions require further collection of data using a 5-point Likert scale to conduct a root cause analysis and also for the prioritization of the intervention program.

Assuming 50% response rate against a total employee size of 1,000, the maximum sample sizes for conducting the feedback survey of responders from these departments are described here:

$$\text{Packaging and marketing} = \frac{1.96^2 \times 0.21 \times (0.79) \times 1000}{0.03^2 \times 999 + 1.96^2 \times 0.21 \times (0.79)} = 414$$

$$\text{Raw materials} = \frac{1.96^2 \times 0.25 \times (0.75) \times 1000}{0.03^2 \times 999 + 1.96^2 \times 0.25 \times (0.75)} = 444$$

$$\text{Clinkers and grinding} = \frac{1.96^2 \times 0.27 \times (0.73) \times 1000}{0.03^2 \times 999 + 1.96^2 \times 0.27 \times (0.73)} = 457$$

$$\text{Ready mix and distribution} = \frac{1.96^2 \times 0.29 \times (0.71) \times 1000}{0.03^2 \times 999 + 1.96^2 \times 0.29 \times (0.71)} = 468$$

The schedule questionnaire is as follows:

1 – Most likely, 2 – Likely, 3 – Not sure, 4 – Not likely, 5 – Least likely

1. Are you planning to leave the company in next 6 months to 1 year?
2. Are you happy with the current benefits and compensations plan offered?
3. Are you engaged in your current role?
4. Do you have the freedom to make decisions and act independently?
5. Is your supervisor encouraging and supportive and treating you fairly?

The mean or median attitude for each item and each department are computed to arrive at the attrition score. The individual contributions of items are ranked to identify the stronger causes from the weaker causes. The attitude scores are ranked in descending order to prioritize the department that needs an urgent intervention. The implementation team can introduce suggested changes to the roles or the organization of employees to improve overall attitude.

References

Evelson, B. (2008, November 21). Topic Overview: Business Intelligence. Forrester Research.

International Data Corporation. (2003). *The Financial Impact of Business Analytics: Key Findings* (IDC #28689). Framingham, MA: International Data Corporation.

Luhn, H. P. (1958). A Business Intelligence System. *IBM Journal, 2*(4): 314.

Ross, J.W., P. Weill, and D.C. Robertson. (2006). *Enterprise Architecture as Strategy*. Boston, MA: Harvard Business Press, 2006.

Rud, O. (2009). *Business Intelligence Success Factors: Tools for Aligning Your Business in the Global Economy*. Hoboken, NJ: Wiley & Sons.

10

USE CASES AND BUSINESS APPLICATIONS

This chapter is intended to explain to business managers real-life examples of use cases and applications of a variety of situations where business analytics has come to the aid of the business. These use cases are specific to a sector and situation and may not be applicable to another situation and sector. A use case is defined as a test of the practical, known arts that are commonly used and applied by an individual ordinarily familiar with the art. The instances described are by way of example only and should not be used to limit the scope of use. Although the use cases have been described in terms of a particular application, one with ordinary skill in the art can extend its uses and modify them without departing from the spirit, or exceeding the scope, of the presented instance. Accordingly, it is understood that the descriptions herein are provided only to facilitate comprehension of the test case and should not be altered to limit the scope.

Business case

Business use cases cover examples of the "how" in real-life situations, such as scheduling in manufacturing, product management, product engineering, and pricing, prepared with a certain level of detail for execution. Such cases need to be prepared across a variety of sectors that describe the nuances of handling clichés in business data and engaging in the understanding of end uses. Use cases are not standard operating procedures (SOPs) that ordinarily describe key steps. On the other hand, use cases are specific to the situation and the manner in which analysts handle the nuances.

The tenets of a good business use case model are:

- Use cases should conform to the exact nature of the business need.
- Every activity within the business analysis should be included in at least one use case.
- A use case must make an activity easier to understand.

- A use case describes steps to assist the analyst.
- Each use case must be unique.

Use cases in banking

A business can make a good model with only five segments because, with too many segments, the number of observations per group falls, which leads to lower confidence in estimates. The choice and design of variables in segmentation are selected appropriately so that they are less interactive among themselves and more representative of basic demographic traits, endowments, and entitlements.

Further, credit discrimination occurs when a creditor treats one applicant less favourably than other applicants on the basis of sex, marital status, race, colour, religion, national origin, age, receipt of income from public assistance programs, and so on. One approach, a top-down segmentation strategy, is a companywide common strategy approved by top management and is a first step to treating customers consistently across all channels/regions.

A few cases of targeting are discussed here.

Credit marketing

Credit marketing segmentation, which has unique challenges for a leading bank, is described here. The basis of value creation, the gains from the product use of customers, is the life of the credit relationship.

It appears that the four groups are heterogeneous as compared to other groups and homogenous within each group. Heterogeneity is due to the nature of differences observed among these groups of samples created. Homogeneity is observed in the nature of similarity among these groups.

Technique

Net present value (NPV) is derived from a balance forecast model to obtain the projected revenue in a future time period. The regression models can provide the forecast estimates of Balance for the future time period during the life of the

TABLE 10.1 Expected segment NPV summary

Segment	% (volume)	NPV ('000 Rs.)	NPV/ account (Rs.)	ΔNPV over BAU (Rs.)
C	22 (6,600)	1569	238	29
D	29 (8,700)	1530	176	−33
B	14 (4,200)	1585	377	168
A	35 (10,500)	1590	151	−58
All	100 (30,000)	6274	209	0

Note: The maximum incremental value against leaders is explained by their lowest savings rate and delinquency.

product. These models select three variables, namely the previous balance amount of the account, the month of the books on the accounts, and the time period since delinquent as the determinants of future balance. The model parameter estimates are different for each of the four segments. These parameters are used to arrive at the cash flows for each segment by multiplying the parameters with the projected estimates of outstanding balance (from the regression models). The cash flows are discounted to current time period (at 10%) to arrive at the expected NPV summarized at segment level, as shown in Figure 10.1.

Results

A pie chart is a simpler method to figure out the distribution of segments. As shown in Figure 10.1, the implementation of the segmentation model on test data of 30,000 accounts results in the distribution of four segments in robust groups of C (22%), D (29%), B (14%), and A (35%). The size of each segment is a good representation from the population drawn. Base NPV (net present value) is the NPV per account that is realized when no segmentation schema is applied.

Without the model, the base (average) profitability from the acquired base would be lower. The gain in the test model scenario over a random scenario stands at Rs. 168 ($3.00) and Rs. 29 ($0.500) for the top two segments, respectively.

The average NPV for a segment is the ratio of the present value of cash flows for the segment to the number of accounts in that segment. The base NPV is the average NPV calculated as the portfolio total to the total number of accounts (30,000). The drivers (characteristics) for each of the four groups include home ownership, occupation, age of the relationship, balance amount, fees, and payment amount, which includes a balanced mix of transaction, delinquency, and demographic attributes.

Table 10.2 provides the segments profile on the general characteristics of the customers. A closer look at the profile amongst the segments reflects behavioural differences across the segments.

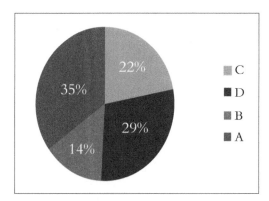

Legend: C: Chasers; D: Followers; B: Leaders; A: Laggards.

FIGURE 10.1 Distribution of segments

TABLE 10.2 Segment profile

Segment and name	Customer age (years)	All trade balance (Rs.)	Annual income (Rs.)	Outstanding balance (Rs.)	Savings balance (Rs.)	Delinquent amount (Rs.)
C : Chasers	27	27,759	3,33,268	22,207	1,66,556	262
D : Followers	46	1,31,787	3,66,630	1,83,315	36,66,300	0
B : Leaders	29	66,229	7,94,749	1,44,607	3,97,375	604
A : Laggards	52	47,206	8,04,428	4,02,214	8,04,4280	0

Response score

Response scores are used to target prospects/customers for a bank's product offer. Response scores and net response scores are widely used in marketing as targeting tools. Response scores are built on the responses obtained on the results of past mailings or past offers made.

A customer or prospect's response is observed based on their response during the response window. The response window is defined for every campaign. In the case of outbound telemarketing (OBTM), inbound telemarketing (IBTM), web marketing, and e-marketing, responses are obtained instantaneously whereas in the case of direct mail, responses are obtained within a span of 6–8 weeks.

Channels, such as OBTM, IBTM, web marketing, etc., are important distinguishers of the response behaviour. Therefore, it is a standard practice to build channel-specific response scores instead of a generic response score across all channels.

Net response scores are another category of response scores, which are built on approved accounts.

A response score can be used in conjunction with or without prospect segmentation. The response score when implemented in top deciles or top demi-deciles helps differentiate prospects with higher likelihoods of response. An offer score is another type of response score specific to each offer.

Technique

The steps in building a propensity model on prospect attributes are detailed here. Creating target variables such as propensity or response indicators is used as the dependent variable. Unlike a digital campaign where responses can be matched against mail codes, propensity can be inferred from the activities in the customer data at two different points in time. If a customer has acquired a credit card in the interim period, when he did not hold one 6 months back, then the customer is stated to have had a propensity for credit cards 6 months ago. Another example is an increase in the number of home equity relationships over a 6-month period. If there is an increase in the number of relationships and they are greater than 3, then the propensity is stated to be positive (1) instead of none (0).

The response score profile report in Table 10.3 provides the sample details of customer response data, while Tables 10.4 through 10.6 interpret customer data. Table 10.7 analyzes customer affinity for various offers.

TABLE 10.3 Response score profile

Demi-decile	# (%)	Actual (%)	Predicted (%)	Model variables				Name	Offers targeting
				Max (credit limit)	Average (outstanding balance)	# of relationships		
1	20,000 (5)	6%	8%	18,000	10,000	17	High look-alike	Medium risk, medium return
2	16,000 (5)	5%	6%	14,000	9,000	13	High look-alike	Medium risk, medium return
3	11,000 (5)	4%	5%	9,000	6,000	8	Medium look-alike	High risk and High return
4	29,000 (5)	3%	4%	7,000	4,500	6	Medium look-alike	No offer
5	35,000 (5)	2%	3%	1,500	1,000	2	Low look-alike	No offer
Total	111000 (25)							

Note: Demi-decile refers to 20% of the sub-population.

TABLE 10.4 Response segmentation report

	# (%)	Age range	Income range	Max credit limit range	Average outstanding balance range	# of relationships range	Name of the segment	Offers targeting
Segment 1	20,000 (20)	21–22	< 5,000	> 18,000	> 10,000	> 17	Active and young low income	Medium-risk, high-return offer
Segment 2	16,000 (16)	38–55	> 9,000	14,000–18,000	9,000–10,000	13–17	Active and middle	Medium risk, medium return
Segment 3	11,000 (11)	33–38	6,000–9,000	9,000–14,000	6,000–9,000	8–13		
Segment 4	29,000 (29)	< 21	4,500–6,000	7,000–9,000	4,500–6,000	6–8	Young and high income	High risk and high return
Segment 5	35,000 (35)	> 55	< 5,000	< 1,500	< 1,000	< 2	Old and dormant	No offer
Total								

TABLE 10.5 Classification table report

Number of actual 1s	Number of actual 0s	Number of predicted 1s	Number of predicted 0s	Sensitivity	Specificity	False positive rate
140	240	120	220	75	45	45
130	260	125	240	65	55	40
100	300	95	320	75	65	85

Note: Sensitivity = number of true positive 1s / (number of true positives 1s + number of false negative 0s); specificity = number of true negative 0s / (number of true negative 0s + number of false positive 1s).

TABLE 10.6 Segment optimization report

Test	Segment	Size	Cumulative size	Total cost of segment ($)	Cumulative cost of segments ($)
	Segment 1	20,000	20,000	40,000	40,000
	Segment 2	16,000	36,000	32,000	72,000
	Segment 3	11,000	47,000	22,000	94,000
	Segment 4	29,000	76,000	58,000	152,000
	Total	76,000	76,000	152,000	
Control		35,000	35,000		70,000

Note: Test and Control are drawn separately for the campaign.

TABLE 10.7 Offer affinity analysis

Name of the segment	AA	AB	BA	BB	CA	CC
No. of prospects	1,000	1,000	1,000	1,000	1,000	1,000
No. of responders	120	100	102	102	122	112
Mean response score (10–1000)	750	710	690	640	540	520
Response rate (%)	12	10	10.2	10.2	12.2	11.2
Approval rate (%)	0.5	0.5	0.5	0.5	0.5	0.5
No. of approved accounts	60	50	51	51	61	56
Acquisition rate (%)	6	5	5.1	5.1	6.1	5.6
Offer affinity	Offer 1	Offer 1	Offer 2	Offer 2	Offer 3	Offer 3

Note: Offers are ranked by the value it brings to the prospects.

A product overlap report across all products helps in determining the cross-sell status. Further, these overlaps could also be summarized across channels and using measures such as the number of products or relationships held (of a specific product) or the percentage of products cross-held (for a specific product). Based on the overlaps in product holding, the cross-sell status is determined for a time period, when the overlap did not exist. As such, a cross-sell status could be populated as 1 for specific cross-product holdings or multiple cross-product holdings, and 0 for otherwise.

A regression model is used to project the net income for a specified time period. The inputs to the model are:

- Segment type
- Duration (years) of net income
- % of new accounts to the cross-sell program
- Contact rate
- Acceptance rate
- No. of months billed
- Revenue from fee
- Marketing fulfilment cost per sale (CPS)
- Other marketing cost per sale
- Net revenue
- Annual adjustment factor for net revenue

Loss of consumer card income

A consumer bank was experiencing a significant decline in credit card receivables over a 1-year period. Customer payment rates were climbing up over the past 12 months (vis-à-vis previous months), leading to a fall in interest income. The major proportion of the fall in interest income was due to a drop in balances associated with high APRs (annual percentage rates).

The purpose of the analysis is to understand the source of balance erosion and its impact on profitability and to locate internal and external factors causing the balance erosion, in order to contain the payment rate and maintain net credit margin at a fixed level.

Technique

A waterfall on the balance amounts revealed that only 3% of accounts accounted for over 80% of the balance erosion. This meant that attention could be focused on a smaller size (only 3%) without impacting the bulk of the portfolio. More detailed introspection on the 3% of accounts showed that these customers were shifting their balances using balance transfers or cash on card or home improvement loans.

A payment rate model was suggested to identify the top 3% of customers who were most likely to pay off their card balances in the next period. The payment rate model used variables such as age on book, previous delinquency, utilization, HELOC (home equity line of credit) relationships, inflation, etc.

Two strategies were proposed to contain the net receivables at a fixed level:

- Revise the APR rate for customers who were most likely to pay off balances
- Offer cash loans to accounts with existing mortgage balances

The model was tracked using test control mode. Lower card pricing resulted in a 30% drop in balances lost. Although absolute profitability was lowered due to lower pricing, the balances retained helped offset this loss, leading to overall gains in profitability.

Results

It was found that, by offering alternative cash loan products, the test cells had a 45% higher acceptance to cash. Further, by reducing APR, net receivables were also maintained. The business was advised to extend this approach against preventing poaching of balances by competitors.

Use cases in insurance

An insurance business must attempt to choose a universal schema of segmentation rather than create a whole bunch of segments for each product, division, cluster, function, and season. There are examples of generic segmentation that have been used in retail banking, remittances, payment industry, insurance, telecom, courier logistics, travel industry, and also FMCG or SME. The criteria used to decide to purchase a protection product will vary for each customer. Therefore, for one segment price will be important; for another value, another brand, another kind of content, and so on. To influence purchases for each situation, the marketing manager must be aware of what benefits turn his or her customer segments. Any uncertainty here could cause the customer to return to next stage to consider the information.

Results

Table 10.8 explains insurance clusters and their usability to the industry.

There are differences in purchase behaviour based on a household's life stage (Elliott 1960). ACXIOM USA's seventy PersonicX clusters are organized into twenty-one distinct life stage groups that have reached similar life events, such as having a baby, retirement, getting married, a new income, or buying a home. A balanced mix of demographic elements (e.g. age, presence of children, occupation, marital status, length of residence); socio-economic elements (e.g. income, types of credit cards, homeowner/renter, home market value, home equity); purchase behaviour (mail order buyer, mail order donor); vehicle ownership; lifestyle elements (internet use, club member, social presence, travel, online investing, home improvement); and so on. Primarily, within the household, it captures age of eldest child, marital status, home ownership, household income, location, net worth, etc.

In value-based segmentation, a telecom company may have more than 50% of their customers changing value segments depending on the costs of service to the customer. Customers with high turnover do not fit the value proposition. New

TABLE 10.8 Life stage clusters for insurance marketing

Cluster	Cluster name	Description	Insurance offering
1	Summit Estates	Wealthiest of all clusters; late 30s to early 60s	Investment insurance
2	Established Elites	Professionals and self-employed in their 40s	Single pension plan
3	Corporate Connected	Well-educated corporate executives	Investment insurance plan
4	Top Professionals	Well-educated and established professionals spend on outing	Term insurance
5	Active and Involved	Represents financially secure households; enjoy the outdoors	Health, investment
6	Casual Comfort	Childless couples and singles in their 30s	Motor, term
7	Active Life Styles	Established couples with teenage kids, minivans and mortgages	Credit protection
8	Solid Surroundings	Educated couples and singles that have substantial net worth and no children at home	Home mortgage insurance
9	Busy Schedules	Soon-to-be retirees living in their own homes are enjoying the fruits of their lifetime labour; interested in maintaining their health and fitness	Household assets insurance
10	Careers and Travel	30s and 40s; mostly established homeowners in a mix of houses and condominiums	Travel insurance, household
11	Schools and Shopping	Activities tend to be geared toward work, home, or kids	Health policy, term
12	On the Go	Affluent working couples with young children; homeowners, mainly in single-family houses	Critical health policy, household insurance
13	Work and Play	Predominantly white collar workers or professionals; mostly homeowners living in smaller cities and surrounding areas	Hybrid policy, pension
14	Career Centred	Well educated and dedicated to their careers; long-term homeowners in their communities	Term, health, pension
15	Country Ways	Upper incomes and middle-to-upper net worth; enjoy rural life	Pension plan
16	Country Enthusiasts	Entrenched in their rural communities; upper-middle incomes and no children enable them to save and spend on their personal interests	Single pension plan
17	Firmly Established	Homeowners, tend to have multiple vehicles, often inclusive of a minivan	Investment insurance plan, motor

(Continued)

TABLE 10.8 Continued

Cluster	Cluster name	Description	Insurance offering
18	Climbing the Ladder	Enjoy upper-middle range incomes; almost all homeowners with above-average net worth, living in upscale suburban neighbourhoods	Term insurance, pension
19	Country Comfort	Self-employed, with mixed-age children; families bond over outdoor activities and enjoy the land and water around them	Health, pension
20	Carving Out Time	Homeowners in mostly upscale neighbourhoods	Motor, investment
21	Children First	Raising children; evenly split between married couples and singles; live in suburban areas; some pursuing higher education	Credit protection, term
22	Comfortable Cornerstones	Late 40s and early 50s, living in outer suburbs and towns; married with no children in the home; administrative fields	Home mortgage insurance
23	Good Neighbours	50s and early 60s; upper-middle income empty nesters enjoying a wide range of social activities	Household assets insurance
24	Career Building	Young singles with no children in the home; mix of mobile renters and first-time homeowners; living in condos and single-family houses	Travel, pension
25	Clubs and Causes	Retired and approaching-retirement singles and couples in their late 60s and early 70s; live comfortably in outer suburbs and towns	Health policy
26	Getting Established	Enjoy upper-middle incomes and tend to live in more urban areas; their location often requires renting in multiple-family dwellings	Critical health policy
27	Tenured Proprietors	Large, upper-middle income families located in cities	Hybrid policy
28	Community Pillars	Upper-middle incomes and net worth; very comfortable in their advancing age	Health, term
29	City Mixers	30s to 50s with no children in the home working in a broad spectrum of white-collar jobs	Pension plan

30	Out and About	20s; mainly high school grads; own their homes and tend to live in suburbs and towns around the country	Single pension plan
31	Mid-Americana	Right at national averages in terms of education and income, although home values result in above-average net worth	Investment insurance plan
32	Metro Mix	Mid-40s to mid-60s, and with middle incomes, this group of family dwellings	Term insurance
33	Urban Diversity	50s, middle-income, white-collar professionals taking advantage of urban life, enjoying the income	Health
34	Outward Bound	Home ownership dominates this cluster; likely to have trucks and trailers to haul ATVs	Motor
35	Working and Active	Singles are all homeowners who work middle-class incomes and net worth	Credit protection
36	Persistent and Productive	Older singles and couples are notable for their active grandparent presence of children of all ages	Home mortgage insurance, critical health
37	Firm Foundations	Homeowners are blue- and white-collar workers, supporting their families while establishing roots in their communities	Household assets insurance, investment endowment
38	Occupational Mix	Blue-collar bastions in the country, proportion of minorities	Term life pension
	Setting Goals	Mean age of 25, setting goals represents one of the youngest of the clusters; leisure time is heavily influenced by their young children and living within their means	Health policy
39	Great Outdoors	Young empty-nest couples living in very rural areas; low-key, traditional pursuits that revolve around the home and enjoying the land around them	Health and term life
40	Rural Adventure	30s and 40s, living in rural towns with no spouse and no children	Hybrid and travel policy
41	Creative Variety	Homeowners in their 20s or early 30s climbing the career ladder	Endowment and investment and health

(Continued)

TABLE 10.8 Continued

Cluster	Cluster name	Description	Insurance offering
42	Work and Causes	Singles in their late 40s to early 50s; homeowners, most well established in single-family dwellings	Pension plan, investment endowment policy
43	Open Houses	Lower-to-middle income singles; late 50s to early 60s; are homeowners	Single pension plan
44	Offices and Entertainment	Single individuals that are renters are looking forward to purchasing first homes soon	Investment insurance plan
45	Rural and Active	30s and early 40s, have no children; mostly lower-middle income homeowners living in the rural areas	Term insurance, household
46	Rural Parents	Rural parts working women and the homes they own	Term life and endowment
47	Farm and Home	Blue-collar families living in the rural areas lower-middle category for income and net worth	Motor
48	Home and Garden	Long-standing tenure in their communities and their homes in the suburbs	Credit protection, home insurance, term life, pension
49	Rural Community	Oldest of all the clusters, mean age of 76; socially active lives	Health
50	Role Models	Mean age of 70; this group is less than 30% retired; lower-middle incomes and own their suburban homes	Critical health
51	Stylish and Striving	Late 30s to mid-50s, single, and have no children in the home; relatively mobile renters	Term, pension
52	Metro Strivers	Single parents stressed by urban life on a small budget	Investment, endowment
53	Work and Outdoors	Singles in their mid-50s; homeowners living in rural parts	Investment, pension, endowment
54	Community Life	Small-town couples in late 40s to mid-60s; long-time homeowners	Hybrid policy, health, household, motor
55	Metro Active	Singles without children, all homeowners	Household insurance, term, health
56	Collegiate Crowd	Mean age of 20; youngest of all the clusters	Term plan
57	Outdoor Fervor	Mean age of 24; youngest clusters in small towns and more rural areas	Term

58	Mobile Mixers	Highly mobile, diverse groups of people that are single renters in their early 30s; low income	Investment endowment travel plan
59	Rural and Mobile	Single and highly mobile renting in the most rural areas of the country	Term insurance, travel
60	City Life	Students living densely populated and expensive cities	Health, travel, credit protection
61	Movies and Sports	Singles and married couples, with children, mostly renters, with incomes below national averages	Motor, accident, term
62	Staying Home	Single, downtown-metro renters; upper-middle-aged	Life and health policy
63	Practical and Careful	Elderly singles living in rural areas renters, with little net worth accrued	Pension, health
64	Hobbies and Shopping	Elderly singles living on modest incomes in small towns and suburbs	Pension, health
65	Helping Hands	Mean age of 84, enjoy relaxing hobbies and stay up-to-date	Pension, health
66	First Steps	Students found in many college towns; childless and highly mobile	Term
67	Staying Healthy	Incomes below national averages, long tenures in their homes; more densely populated areas	Term, health
68	Productive Havens	Mid-20s to mid-40s homeowners with lower incomes, mostly childless	Term policy
69	Favorably Frugal	Singles with a mean age of 39; renters in the second-tier cities	Term, pension
70	Solid Surroundings	Mix of affluent, well educated couples and singles with substantial net worth and no children at home	Health, travel

Source: ACXIOM USA 2014.

customers are classified as Silver customers for the first 3 months unless they spend higher to become Gold customers, which is up a grade. If the value is based on the average spending over the last 3 months, then a segmentation model is chosen for finding the costs and benefits. The trade-off between the sources of acquisition and the alignment of the performance of customers towards achieving the expected outcome is critical.

Use case in manufacturing

Job scheduling

The scheduling of jobs is a critical step in manufacturing, and the data gathered from customer orders and resource availability from the operations head are used to generate the work sequence of jobs. Sequencing is critical in job scheduling to determine the order in which jobs or customers are processed in the waiting line at the counter. When combined with expected processing time, this allows a company to estimate the start and finish times of each job.

Two of the priority sequencing rules, namely first come, first served (FCFS) and earliest due date (EDD) methods, are as follows. First come, first served is more common whereas, in the EDD method, jobs with the earliest due date are the ones to be processed. The due date is the day of the start of assembly and not the day of finishing. The performance measures are the flow time and the days past due for the job.

Flow time is the amount of time a job spends in the service of system and is the sum of the waiting time and the time spent between operators and delays including breakdowns. For each job arriving at the associates' desks, the flow time (T_{FLOW}) is referred to as throughput time or time spent in the system, including servicing time ($T_{SERVICE}$):

> Flow time (t) = finish time (T_F) + time since the job arrived at the counter (T_A)

The objective is to sequence the order of jobs to prepare associates in such a manner that the total flow time for m numbers of jobs is minimized.

The first job scheduled starts at time 0. Past due or tardiness is the measure that can be expressed as the amount of time by which a job has missed a due date. The percentage of total requests processed over time that missed their due dates can be measured. Minimizing the past due measure supports competitive priorities to minimize the cost of missing dates and to raise the quality of on-time delivery. The first come, first serve (FCFS) rule is applied for scheduling, which must take into account high-priority requests.

The finish time is the start time to which the processing time is added. The finish time then becomes the start time for the next job in the series, assuming that the next job is available for immediate processing. The days past due is 0 when the due date is equal to or exceeds the finish time. The days past due for a job is 0 if its due date is equal to or exceeds the finish time. For example, Job 3's flow time is its scheduled finish time of 65 days plus the 5 days since the order arrived, or 70 days. The days past due and average flow time performance measures the FCFS schedule.

Other alternatives to FCFS scheduling do exist but do not result in optimal outcomes.

TABLE 10.9 Scheduling of jobs in manufacturing (days)

Order	Start	Processing	Finish	Due	Past due	Received	Flow time
1	0	25	25	29	0	15	40
2	25	16	41	27	14	12	53
3	41	10	51	48	3	10	61
4	51	14	65	68	0	5	70
5	65	12	77	80	0	0	77
Average past due = $(\frac{0+14+3+0+0}{5})$							3.4
Average flow time = $(\frac{40+53+61+70+77}{5})$							60.2

Use cases in telecommunications

Yield management

Yield management is a revenue-driving technique highly ranked and recommended for the competitive telecom sector. For many subscribers, one may use behavioural data to arrive at the likelihood of them using the network at peak hours versus off-peak hours. Deployment of yield management models can reduce the payback period and improve the viability of communication service providers (CSPs) that have invested in large capital expenditures (capex). Large investments with much longer breakeven periods could be justified by the net revenue from yield management. This will provide a much healthier operating ratio compared to their peers.

The objectives are to demonstrate that caller optimization can lead to revenue enhancement and higher capacity utilization and that network resilience is enhanced by dropping calls from the peak period to the off-peak period.

Technique

A yield model projects the proportion of users who will transfer their call to one period given a discount (d). The basic yield management model is a dynamic revenue maximization problem. The model uses congestion pricing to maximize the net revenue with random, discrete, and exponential arrivals of callers.

The assumptions are that callers are ready to move to on-demand services over real-time services when prices are lowered; that the maximum feasible rate arrival of requests for which the probability of blocking requests rate is below 1%; that, by lowering prices, customers will call more often and demand will increase significantly due to price sensitivity; that callers arriving during peak periods will be transferred by at most one period; and that the arrival process is stationary.

One solution is to shift demand during periods of congestion to periods of lower demand by lower price. This lower price can act as an incentive for users to forego current use to a subsequent time period. The base yield model will maximize the yield over dynamic prices for a given network parameter of the CSP, such as bandwidth, activity rate, connection rates, etc. over a horizon (T). These shifts in demand will be an exogenous input to adjust the dynamic prices for the individual segments.

The resulting impact will compared by the trade-off between capex, operating costs, cash flows due to the implementation of dynamic pricing, over a horizon (T).

Takagi (1993) and Keon and Anandalingam (2005) suggest that the probability distribution of the number of users in a system follows the Poisson distribution.

The maximum number of connections is a fixed integer c:

$$P[N = n] = \frac{\rho^n / n!}{\rho \sum_{i=0}^{c} \rho^i / i!}$$

where the traffic intensity ρ is the product of the arrival rate of requests λ and the average call duration h:

$$\rho = \lambda h$$

The average number of call requests and the blocking probability B for the queue are:

$$\mu = \rho(1 - B(\rho, c)),$$

where c = number of call connections which is the ratio between total amount of available bandwidth by the bandwidth required per connection:

$$B(\rho, c) = \frac{\rho^c / c!}{\sum_{i=0}^{c} \rho^i / i!},$$

where i is the individual call request that varies from 0 to c.

The maximum arrival rate (demand) is dependent on the blocking rate b (%) and hence is given as:

$$B(\rho, c) \leq b$$

Blocking probability (B) follows an Erlang loss formula where B is the blocking rate. A higher blocking rate implies that more calls will be transferred to the subsequent period. Delayed users from period t will use the service in period $t + 1$. The average call duration can be shorter during peak and off-peak demand.

The objective function of the service provider is to maximize the total yield from the system over time periods ($1 = < t = < M$):

$$\text{Max} = (1 - B)\lambda_t \rho h - \sum_{t=1}^{M} \lambda_t T_t a_t \times d_t)$$

Subject to:

$$\lambda_t(1 - a_t \times (d_t)) + \lambda_t^d \leq \lambda^*,$$

where $a_t(d_t)$ is the proportion of users who have accepted for discount rate d_t;

$\lambda^* = \dfrac{\rho^*}{h}$, which is the maximum possible demand rate that can be served;

$\lambda_t^d = \lambda_{t-1} a_{t-1} \times (d_{t-1})$;

λ_t^d = arrival rate of call requests in period t of users who have accepted lower rate; and

λ_t = arrival rate of fresh requests for service in the current period.

$\lambda_t = \sum\limits_{j} \lambda_{t,j}$, and

j is the number of segments from 1 to m and $\lambda_{t,j}$ is the demand in each segment.

$$\lambda_{t,j} = F_t(X_{i,t}) = a_0 + b_0 F_1 + b_1 F_2, \ldots$$

where F_1, F_2 are the factors impacting demand (namely income, population density, urbanization, migration, etc.).

Let's consider one scenario with peak levels of demand, which is compared against the random scenario $\lambda(k)$ and the time-value of consumption $\beta(k)$. The fixed price is 10 cents per minute per connection, and the holding time is fixed at 5 minutes. For a given capacity of 250 connections, in the peak scenario, the demand is higher in the

TABLE 10.10 Variation in traffic density (ρ^*)

Parameter	Blocking probability (P_b)	Number of connections
ι	0%	250.0
	1%	228.3
	2%	235.8
	3%	241.4
	4%	246.2
	5%	250.5
	6%	254.6
	7%	258.4
	8%	262.2
	9%	265.9
$\rho\star$	10%	269.6
	$B(\rho,c) = \dfrac{\rho^c / c!}{\sum\limits_{i=0}^{c} \rho^i / i!}$	

initial 2 hours and grows over 2–4 hours, and delayed users can be accommodated in the 4–6 hours slot. In a random scenario, the unit price (β) changes from 0.5 to 0.3 and arrival rate demand changes from 0 to 6 hours.

The prescribed blocking probability is altered from 1% to 10% for each of the problems mentioned earlier, running 1,000 simulations of each to arrive at average performance measures. For each demand scenario, one can simulate the case with no discounting as a measure of baseline performance. Every simulation was initialized with a 6-hour period of simulated time at the maximum arrival rate of requests per minute (e.g. for 1% of cases, the simulations were initialized with an arrival rate of $\frac{228.3}{5} = 45.66$. With peak demand during peak periods, the increased revenue derived through reduced blocking offsets more than half of the discounts paid out. Therefore, managers can enhance yield management or revenues by changing the rate of blocking from 1% to 10%.

TABLE 10.11 Yield from traffic intensities

Blocking probability	Net revenue yield gain	Revenue loss	Number of connections
1	−10	20	228.3
2	−5	10	241.4
4	0	50	246.2
6	0	0	254.6
8	0	0	262.2
10	0	0	246.2

TABLE 10.12 Balanced traffic after acceptance

Scenario	Time (hours)	Arrival rate per minute (λ)	Unit price of consumption (β)	Proportional acceptance rate of discount (b)
	0–2	50.0	0.5	0.067
	2–4	55.0	0.4	0.056
	> 4	35.0	0.3	0.047
Balanced traffic	> 6	35.0	0.3	0.047
	0–1	54.77	0.5	0.067
	1–2	54.21	0.5	0.056
	2–3	44.19	0.4	0.047
	3–4	54.51	0.4	0.047
	4–5	49.19	0.3	0.047
	5–6	46.42	0.3	0.047
Random	> 6	35	0.3	0.047

Subscribers' segmentation

A multi-pronged benefit can be derived by using subscriber data (call data record [CDR] data) to build usage segmentation. An example using such information that provides complete use of caller details is described here. A list of variables can be used as variables for the calls subscribers originated and received over a fixed time period.

Technique

The call records were split into groups of subscribers using a K-means (Euclidean distance) model, which is a method of clustering using transformation of call data records. A list of variables used for calls originated and received over some time period includes:

1. Average call duration
2. Average number of calls received per day
3. Average number of calls originated per day
4. Percentage of daytime calls (9am–6pm)
5. Percentage of weekday calls (Monday–Friday)
6. Percentage of calls to mobile phones
7. Average number of SMS received per day
8. Average number of SMS originated per day
9. Percentage of international calls
10. Percentage of outgoing calls within the same operator
11. Number of fixed area codes called
12. Number of roaming calls made
13. Average roaming bill amount ($)
14. Average monthly bill amount ($)
15. Average value-added services (VAS) amount ($)

Results

For the six major segments, the profile of subscribers is described as follows:

Segment 1 (pure collegiate): subscribers with a relative low number of voice calls. Their average call duration is also lower than average. However, their SMS usage is relatively high. These subscribers do not call too many different numbers and have the lowest bill amount.

Segment 2 (suburbanites): subscribers with a relative high number of fixed number contacts. These subscribers make calls to different domestic locations.

Segment 3 (urban outgoers): subscribers that make a relatively high number of voice calls. Their SMS usage is low. They also make more international phone calls.

Segment 4 (ordinary): average subscribers. None of the attribute values is high or low. Their profile matches with the average population.

TABLE 10.13 GSM clusters

Cluster	No. of call duration	No. of calls received per day	No. of calls originated per day	No. of weekend calls	No. of calls during week day business hours	No. of calls made to land phones	No. of SMS received per day	No. of SMS originated per day	No. of international calls	No. of outgoing calls within the same operator	No of specific location codes called	Duration of calls received	Duration of calls made	No. of commercial special messages sent	Data/video down load duration	Other VAS services duration
1	95	1.2	2.8	4.5	88	72	2.3	4.5	1.8	11.3	6.1	13.5	66.3	1.8	9	5
2	121	1.7	4.1	3.7	86	73	1.6	3.7	1.9	17.8	9.5	40.5	65.9	1.9	10	6
3	121	2.5	4.9	2.9	84	71	1	2.9	2.9	15.1	6.6	26.9	66	2.9	11	7
4	126	1.6	4	3.6	87	71	1.5	3.6	1.9	15	6.2	24	65.7	1.9	7	6
5	96	1.1	3.5	2.9	88	92	0.8	2.9	1.8	12.4	6.1	23.1	65.2	1.8	8	5
6	155	2.1	4.1	4.6	87	73	2.4	4.6	2.9	14.8	6.9	22.7	65.7	2.9	6	4

Note: Averages are reported for all variables.

Segment 5 (rural): subscribers that do not receive many voice calls. The average call duration is low. They also receive and deliver fewer SMS messages.

Segment 6 (elites): subscribers that make and receive many voice calls. They also send and receive many SMS messages. The duration of their voice calls is longer than average. The percentage of international calls is high. They are highly active globetrotters and premier subscribers.

Here in this demonstration, Segment 4 and Segment 5 don't conform to the goals of meeting greater revenue targets and hence can be excluded from the implementation stage of the study. Further, the marketer can focus on the remaining Segments (1, 2, 3, and 6) to build suitable value propositions for targeting subscribers.

Use case in food services

Food service refers to businesses where customers arrive during a fixed time of the day for a short duration and expect fulfilment to happen fairly quickly.

Service aspects of the transaction, especially delivery time, influence both customer satisfaction and the purchase behaviour of customers (Verma, Thompson, and Louviere 1999). Timely service has been widely accepted as a key to success in the service industry because it is the first interaction in the sequence of experiences of customers (e.g. Bitner 1992). Firms can use improved service time as a means of differentiation based on convenience (Lund and Marinova 2014). Secondly, customer satisfaction acts as a proxy for service performance and provides information value to customer purchase behaviour. Interpurchase time may get elongated, and the transaction amount may fall when satisfaction is impacted due to increasing delivery time. The objectives are to investigate the impact of service performance on customer purchase behaviour and to ponder the impact of service performance deterioration on the interpurchase time of customers.

Technique

Delivery time is indicated as the service performance measure in this analysis and is better controlled than other measures of service performance (e.g. number of service failures, telephone CSR service quality, frontline employee interactions, product quality, etc.). Gupta and Morrison (1991) and Lund and Marinova (2014) suggested a simultaneous equation model to control for heterogeneity bias and within-individual selection bias in satisfaction ratings by using a random effects model specification.

The probability/willingness of a customer to provide his/her feedback on the table is based on the number of transactions undertaken by the customer and also the interpurchase time.

Similarly, the probability of assigning a fixed choice of rating value (1 to m) is also impacted by his/her number of transactions and interpurchase time. The purchase amount of a transaction is impacted by satisfaction rating. This case helps determine the degree to which a multi-cuisine helped restaurant can afford to slip from higher rating values to increase delivery time in this model.

The logistic regression model of a customer agreeing to provide a rating is given as:

$$P_i = \exp^{\mu SAT_j} / \sum \exp^{\mu SAT_j}$$

where P_j represents the probability of agreeing to give a rating and SAT_i represents the satisfaction of customer j.

The multinomial logit model of selecting a rating value (1–5) is expressed as:

$$P_i = \exp^{\mu SAT_i} / \sum \exp^{\mu SAT_i}$$

where P_{ij} represents the probability of selecting an alternative from a set of choices containing five possible choices. SAT_j represents the satisfaction rating of customer i;

$SAT_{ij} = \alpha + \beta_1 AMT_{ijt} + \beta_2 NTR_{ijt} + \beta_3 TIME_t + \varepsilon$;
SAT_{ijt} are observed satisfaction ratings;
AMT_{ijt} is the purchase amount;
NTR_{jt} is the number of transactions; and
INT_{ijt} is the interpurchase time in the data, explanatory variables for rating incidence, satisfaction rating, and interpurchase time, respectively.

The interpurchase time INT_{ijt} is impacted by the point-in-time satisfaction level of the customer, which also drives his/her decision to agree to give a rating:

$$INT_{ijt} = \alpha + SAT_{ij} + \varepsilon$$

and

$$AMT_{ijt} = \alpha + NTR_{ijt} + \varepsilon$$

To explore the effect of a delay in service by simulating delivery time, where delivery time increases by k percent each period, we use:

$$TIME_t = (1 + k) \times TIME_{t-1}, \text{ where } k = 5, 10, 15, \ldots 50$$

For each iteration, performance inconsistencies based on the simulated delivery time are updated to determine whether the customer will spend the purchase amount with an increase in $TIME_t$.

Customers purchase less frequently as delivery time increases. For example, if service performance worsens by 20% from the previous service encounter, then the expected customers' interpurchase time increases by approximately 1.6%. The decreasing effect of service performance on interpurchase time indicates that the disapproval effect overrides the effect of performance on interpurchase time. The proportion of highly satisfied customers (i.e. satisfaction rating = 5) substantially decreases

TABLE 10.14 Parameter estimates from satisfaction models

Model estimates for purchase amount

Equation	Estimates	P-values
Rating incidence		
Disconfirmation	0.0341	−0.026
Performance inconsistency	0.0110	−0.0617
Number of transactions since last rating	−0.0652	0.0016
Satisfaction rating		
Disconfirmation	−0.5883	0.0524
Performance inconsistency	−0.0940	0.1263
Interpurchase time		
Satisfaction rating	0.0078	0.0031
Disconfirmation	−0.0262	−0.0141
Performance inconsistency	0.0389	−0.0341
−log (likelihood)		2967.1
AIC		5958.2
Number of observations	141,301	

from more than 90% to approximately 77% (with a 50% increase in delivery time). Higher satisfaction leads to quicker purchases. This links objective performance to customer repurchase behaviour through customer satisfaction and therefore provides implementable suggestions. Higher customer satisfaction also leads to higher purchase amounts.

The results in parameter estimates shown in Table 10.14. The results show that cross-individual selection is not significant. Similarly, purchase amount, as a robust measure of business outcome, is driven by the number of transactions that result in a rating. Similarly, it is driven by disconfirmation and also predicted satisfaction.

Improving customer satisfaction in a multi-cuisine chain

A leading restaurant chain intends to re-engineer itself driven by customer feedback collected and implemented periodically and also scale across many of its locations. The scale chosen is a qualitative scale that effectively depicts the human element in feedback. The happiness of a customer cannot be expressed in numbers. The challenge is to compile and translate the criteria of customer satisfaction from feedback information.

Technique

Five-point Likert scale questionnaires were used to collect feedback on a variety of service items and qualitative feedback as comments/remarks. Qualitative checking of data involved parsing, running spell check, transforming that data into a uniform shape, and concatenating as required. Comments or remarks were summarized by

TABLE 10.15 Causes of food quality dissatisfaction

Themes	Count	Percent	Cumulative percent	Rank
Price/service tax and ambience	1,358	22%	22%	1
Taste is not good	802	13%	34%	2
Order takes a long time	747	12%	46%	3
Overall experience	582	9%	56%	4
Small portions	574	9%	65%	5
Food is not hot	522	8%	73%	6
Card machine not working	493	8%	81%	7
Staff not friendly	440	7%	88%	8
Items not available	405	6%	94%	9
Not enough counters open	175	3%	97%	10
Tables not clean	174	3%	100%	11
Total	6,272	100%		

analyzing the frequency, choice, and tone of words. The pattern of occurrences of words was observed to create additional indicator variables to be used in the analysis. Table 10.15 provides a detailed summary of the rank for each attribute converged into actionable insights.

The benefits included identifying the pain or prioritization area, which requires timely action; identifying necessary and essential wants as core experiences; identifying desirable, preferred, or delighting attributes that customers would rejoice; and fighting "fires" and burning issues that cannot be compromised.

Results

The rankings of all the reason codes were identified based on descending proportions. The key determinants of customer satisfaction ratings are price/service tax and ambience, bad food taste, orders taking a long time, overall experience, small food portions, cold food, card machine not working, unfriendly staff, unavailable items, not enough open counters, unclean tables, and so on. The top reasons were "price and ambience," which along with "service time" and "food taste" contributed to over 46% of the dissatisfaction. A Pareto chart could be plotted to graphically represent cumulative proportions against their respective reason codes.

Use case in logistics

Radio cab fleet size determination

With the advent of technology-enabled radio cab services, a growing neighbourhood service of digital cabs invites registration from self-operated and self-owned cab drivers for taxi service. The total fleet includes a mix of self-owned and agency-owned cabs, and new agencies are inducted into the fold to enhance their capacity as a routine process. Usually, the cab service would receive quite a few calls for outstation highway drops and many calls during the day for within-city local drops and local pickups that include many rounds to domestic or international airports, interstate bus depots, and the train terminus. The weekdays are filled with shorter jaunts for business customers within the city. Occasional weekend cab users hire cabs from entertainment engagements, family gatherings, or parties back to their homes in the late evening. The cab agency may get a good deal by joining up with hotels to provide fixed-rate services to the hotels' patrons. For example, POLA Cab Company has over 700 registered fleet cars who are self-service providers and drivers by themselves and 200 self-owned cabs that both operate inside Bangalore and also conduct religious trips up to 100 miles away at Tirupati or for entertainment trips up to 110 miles away at Koorg. Since the influx of cab agencies with much lower entry costs, the market has become too competitive now, and it is a challenge to retain franchisees.

Further, pricing has to be done on a reasonable basis as compared to competitors. Pricing also has to be rationalized or altered when it comes to making it worthwhile for franchisees to deliver a high-quality, on-time service to passengers. With increasing population density and vehicular traffic, the lead time to respond to a call increases day by day and so does overall capacity utilization. Cab businesses now face the need to rationalize the fleet size for each user segment that it offers, which includes, vanilla cabs without air conditioning; air-conditioned cabs; and SUVs for corporate teams, family outings, and airport services. Not all radio cabs are substitutable across segments, and rising fuel and insurance costs and waiting times have also made it imperative to rethink alternatives to business operations and planning.

In Table 10.16, we suggest ways to parameterize the problem with the cab company.

Technique and results

If the system capacity is increased by incurring a cost of $300,000, the probabilities of increased, sustained, or decreased use are estimated to be 0.2, 0.5, and 0.3, respectively. POLA Cabs cannot prevent congestion, inconveniences, or other factors that may reduce usage. Breakeven is not nearby, and the annual losses for all the three situations prevail.

TABLE 10.16 Operating parameters of the cab company

Operating parameters (monthly)	Number	Unit costs (monthly)	USD	Unit costs (monthly)	USD
Fleet size (own)	300	Fixed operating costs (including finance from the bank)	500	Variable costs of fuel, maintenance, and servicing	500
Fleet size (franchise)	700	Fixed operating costs (need not include finance from the bank)	200	Variable costs without fuel or maintenance that include servicing users	100

188 Use cases and business applications

$$\text{Maximizing expected pay-offs} = \Sigma\Sigma \, (\text{Prob}_{ij} \times \text{Net Income}_{ij})$$

Where net income = revenue − expenses
and subject to $N_{i(\text{Owned})} + N_{i(\text{Hired})} \leq 183$
For example, $N_{i(\text{Owned})} = 80$ and $N_{i(\text{Hired})} = 103$, with an option of revision in prices:

Revised price (per trip) $P' = P$ (price per trip) $(1 + \Delta)$ where $\Delta = 0.2$

Choice making starts with the calculation of expected payoffs as depicted in the Table 10.17, with the decision tree for the POLA Cab Company.

TABLE 10.17 Fleet expansion choices for the cab company

Outlay	Net income	Usage	Pricing	Payoffs ($)
			No change	500
	500	No change	Higher	700
			Lower	300
			No change	200
	800	Reduced	Higher	500
			Lower	100
	1,200	Higher	No change	1,200
			Higher	1,500
0			Lower	800
	1,200	No change	No change	1,000
			Higher	1,500
			Lower	700
	1,000	Reduced	No change	1,000
			Higher	1,500
			Lower	700
			No change	1,800
			Higher	2,200
300	1,800	Higher	Lower	1,200
	1,200	No change	No change	1,200
			Higher	1,500
	800	Reduced	Lower	600
			No change	800
			Higher	1,400
			Lower	500
			No change	1,000
50	1,000	Higher	Higher	1,500
			Lower	700
Usage probability	Probability of no change = 0.3; probability of reduced = 0.7; probability of higher = 0.0
Price revision probability	Probability of no change = 0.5; probability of higher = 0.2; probability of lower = 0.3

Note: Numbers in parenthesis represent the associated probabilities with the events. For example, 0.3 denotes that the chances of lowering prices are only 30%.

TABLE 10.18 Daily scheduling of cabs

Segment	Weekday							Total duty hours
End use	M	T	W	Th	F	S	S	
Business and corporate	x	x	x	x	x	x	x	
Work and school	x	x	x	x	x	x	x	
Leisure and recreational and others	x	x	x	x	x	x	x	
Residence and airport	x	x	x	x	x	x	x	
Business and corporate	x	x	x	x	x	x	x	
Work and school	x	x	x	x	x	x	x	
Total no. of cabs	183	183	183	183	183	183	183	
Total no. of drivers	190	190	190	190	190	190	190	
Driver 1	0	1	1	1	1	1	1	
Driver 2	1	0	1	1	1	1	1	
...,								
Driver 189	1		0	1	1	1	1	
Driver 190	1	1	1	1	1	1	0	

Note: No. of drivers includes relievers at 4% of the expected demand; x rostered for duty.

Table 10.17 shows the event probability and the payoff for each of the alternative event combinations. The first decision is whether to expand capacity. The second and third decision nodes are reached only after 2 years. The second decision node is reached when capacity is not expanded initially and there is decreased use whereas the third decision node is reached when the capacity is not expanded initially and there is higher use.

The maximization of cumulative expected payoff using a linear programming problem will result in a series of schedules and payoffs. The associated expected payoffs against the combination of segments and passenger activity are given in the following example.

Therefore, the business problem for POLA Cabs boils down to modelling the excess demand for cabs or calls. One may simplify this problem of scheduling by giving a solution of hourly seasonal demand for calls so that the owner can schedule cabs accordingly with the given constraints. Therefore, managing POLA Cabs is a problem of forecasting, scheduling, optimizing, and pricing the product together with splitting the fixed and operating costs separately. The unit-level forecast model is described here.

The method of calculating capacity is based on reordering new cabs, which involves calculating usage rate per day and lead time, which is the amount of time between placing the order and receiving the service.

$$R = A \times T,$$

where R = reorder level, A = average daily usage rate, and T = lead time in minutes.

From this formula, it can be easily deduced that an order for new cabs (replenishment of materials) should be made when the level of inventory is just adequate to meet the needs of production during lead time.

Forecasting and scheduling

Linear regression with additive seasonality is the technique to determine hourly demand for fleets. "Hour of the day" and "day of the week" seasonality must be taken into account. Forecasts can be generated at an hourly level for the entire day at the start of the day. Multiplicative factor of safety is preferred to ensure capturing of peak demand. Scheduling is done by allocating cabs, and starting from the first hour, cabs in transit available in the next hour are taken into account when calculating supply. The working hours of a driver and the distribution of loads across cabs are taken into account, while measuring the demand across segments.

The daily forecast U_{it} are given as:

$$U_{it} = \alpha_0 + \alpha_{it} U_{it-1} + \Sigma \beta_{it} D_{it} \ldots + \varepsilon_{it},$$

where U_{it} is demand for cabs for a given segment i on any given day, D_{it} is the dummy for the day of the week. U_{it-1} is the demand for previous day, α_{it} denotes the trend, and β_{it} is the adjustment for seasonality. This univariate model needs to be estimated using OLS after ensuring the random error ε_{it} is not stationary nor reflects heteroscedasticity.

How many cabs are required to be allocated and scheduled for segments and end use, which varies seasonally?

The manager maximizes the expected payoff, subject to capacity constraints of the availability of numbers of cab hours (no. of scheduled cabs × no. of rostered drivers):

$$\Sigma p_i V_i$$

This is possible by reducing idle capacity, which must put drivers on the roster for a certain number of driving hours (8 hours per day) and must distribute the passenger load uniformly across all such cabs. Drivers can be hired or de-rostered off duty with a few hours of notice.

Let N = number of drivers and D = demand for drivers (number of cabs scheduled for the day) i and let $W = 1$ when the driver is working and $W = 0$ when he is not scheduled for the day. Let $H = 8$ hours of working for one driver at a stretch with a 48-hour per-week maximum. Using the assignment method, one can assign $N - D_i$ drivers off on Day 1 and assign the next $N - D_i$ off and continue until all days have been scheduled.

Therefore, revenue maximization (R_{ij}) is a simple linear programming problem.

Use cases and business applications

TABLE 10.19 Allocation of cabs to segments

End use	Probability (%)	No. of Trips	Probability (%)	Expected no. of trips	Trip time	Probability (%)	Expected trip time (m)	Fleet size
Business and corporate	25				< 20	15	3	46
					20–40	52	20.8	
					41–60	28	16.8	
		0–5	37	1.85	> 60	5	3	
					< 20	15	43.6	46
					20–40	52		
					41–60	28		
		5–10	55	5.5	> 60	5		
					< 20	15	43.6	46
					20–40	52		
					41–60	28		
		10–20	7	1.4	> 60	5		
		> 20	1		< 20	15	43.6	46
					20–40	52		
					41–60	28		
				0.2	> 60	5		
Expected		Total	100	1.28		100		183
Work and school	20		100	1.46		100		183
Leisure and recreational and others	5		100	1.41		100		183
Residence and airport	50		100	1.61		100		183
Business and corporate	25		100	1.84		100		183
Work and school	20		100	2.10		100		183
	100			Expected total				183

Note: Total fleet size is the sum total of expected fleet uses over the week.

The on-duty and off-duty periods of driving for each employee over a certain time period (1 week) to specific work days or hours must be adjusted to create capacity to customer demand.

Use case in retail stores

SKU rationalization

SKU-based analytics is a process whereby sales results are adjusted according to the distribution levels of the particular product groups being analyzed. In our example, SKU rationalization was undertaken for a retail chain having a wide distribution of SKUs.

Technique

Rather than a product-centric view of which SKUs were contributing marginally to overall revenues and profits, a customer-centric view was implemented, involving complexity while maintaining customer satisfaction. Approximately 30% of SKUs were rationalized with minimal impact to revenues, profitability, and customer retention. This framework reduced business. The business had over 5,000 SKUs across a few unique product platforms. Each platform had SKUs across many style groups and colours.

Style groups and colours were investigated for marginal contributions to revenues. It was found that only a few key style groups and colours accounted for over 90% of revenues. It was found that key style groups and colours remained consistent year-on-year and that customer repurchases on deleted style groups and colours were not significantly impacted the following year.

Recommendations were made to rationalize marginal style groups and colours, leading to approximately 30% SKU reduction and significant cost savings in business complexity and working capital.

Brand visibility for a consumer durables player

Business situation

A consumer durables store had set up stores in two new metropolitan areas in India. The brand already had presence in older metropolitan areas. However, the company was not getting the desired attention in the new areas. The market share remained in single digits and nowhere to breakeven at store level.

The objective was to develop a mixed media strategy to improve brand awareness of the consumer durables stores in the new metropolitan areas.

Technique

Despite high spend in media, the brand had very little awareness. The reasons for this were many: the primary driver medium was print, which was expensive and had low reach among the target. The copy – both print and television – was large, which reduced the overall exposure of the brand. Alternate channels were to be suggested.

There was very little use of outdoor and point-of-sale (POS) areas, which was a disconnect with the consumers at the POS.

Using media analytics, the primary medium of promotion was shifted to TV with the mix of print to create impact. This helped to differentiate the store from its competition, which were primarily print media driven. Visibility increased because of the better reach and cost efficiency of television as a medium. A combined pushing strategy of scheduling was recommended. This, with the short duration of copies, took the share of voice (SOV) of the brand to extremely high levels, which helped in establishing the brand. POS (point of sale) was effectively used for selling attributes. Outdoor space was recommended to improve the overall branding visibility.

Result

- Brand achieved 80% spontaneous awareness in 3 months of the campaign (up from 48%).
- The major brand health metrics such as, top-of-mind (TOM), spontaneous, and awareness recorded a more than 100% increase.
- The strategy was continued in subsequent campaigns with minor tuning. At the end of 2 years, the brand had the highest top-of-mind (TOM) and became a leader in the largest category it operated in.

Survival analysis

Survival analysis is well developed in the medical and biological sciences and has also been widely used in industry and in engineering for failure studies. The aim is to make predictions on failure or survival times for observed cases. The distribution of survival frequency in a life table is also used in actuarial analytics to determine insurance premiums. Survival analysis can be applied to sales transactions to validate patterns in customer purchasing data and allow managers to evaluate purchase frequency, purchase value, and other important factors. Approximately 20% of customers do not make further purchases in later periods, which increases with the drop in the number of purchases. The sample preparation for the survival analysis via various promotional offers over different time periods is subjected to separate survival models.

Technique

If the attributes of the promotional campaign (teasers, channel, validity redemption features) are controllable, they can be used as variables for customers acquired over different time period and can be combined together. Overall frequency can be divided into thresholds, and different levels of frequencies can be selected by capping the extreme value (of frequencies) based on their number of visits to the store in 1 year. As threshold increases, customers with a higher frequency of purchases are included, which generates more data and thus improves prediction.

The Kaplan-Meier survival probability at any particular time is calculated by the following formula:

$$S_t = \left(\frac{\Delta_O}{N_O}\right),$$

where Δ = (number of subjects active at the beginning − number of subjects currently inactive) and N_o = number of subjects active at the start.

TABLE 10.20 Survival analysis

Threshold	0	1	2	3	4	5	6	7	8	9
Active	60,202	59,669	57,989	55,280	51,708	47,450	43,033	38,388	34,111	30,089
Sluggish	58,185	57,786	38,101	27,191	18,855	12,862	8,583	5,762	3,894	2,680
Dead	36,064	24,985	13,537	8,001	5,113	3,456	2,401	17,32	1,352	1,035
Total	154,451	142,440	109,627	90,472	75,676	63,768	54,017	45,882	39,357	33,804

The total probability of survival until that time interval is calculated by multiplying all the probabilities of survival at all time intervals preceding that time (by applying the law of multiplication of probability to calculate cumulative probability). For example, the probability of a subject surviving 2 days after a purchase transaction can be considered to be the probability of surviving the 1 day multiplied by the probability surviving the second day given that customer survived the first day. This second probability is called a conditional probability.

Customers are selected given these criteria and are divided into three classes:

- *Active customers*: customers who have made frequent visits and purchase from the store more than five visits in the target period.
- *Sluggish customers*: customers who mark down purchasing and visits from one to five times in the target period.
- *Inactive customers*: customers who have ceased purchasing and no longer visit the store in the target period.

The shift in threshold value leads to an increase in the proportion of active customers, while the proportion of rare and dead customers decreases. It is prudent to identify the group of sluggish customers and the reason they cease purchasing or become stagnant in the future. The purchase histories of all customers from the beginning of purchase until their last purchase are desirable over the observation window. Indicator variables are created based on a 1-year time span for each customer, which is divided into 12 monthly intervals each. The variables that give the highest prediction accuracy are:

- Sales per visit ($)
- Number of categories purchased
- Number of visits
- Average number of days between visits
- Category share of daily necessities (staple)
- Category share of cigarettes (entertainment)
- Category share of car care products (lifestyle)
- Travel distance (time) of the store from home or office (convenience)
- Day and time of purchase (seasonality)
- Model of payment (cash or credit)

TABLE 10.21 Usage of products by customers over time

Cohort group	Quarter 1	Quarter 2	Quarter 3	Quarter 4
Month 1	1,050	1,050	1,050	1,050
Month 2	1,075	1,075	1,075	1,075
Month 3	1,080	1,080	1,080	1,080
Month 4	1,095	1,095	1,095	1,095
Total	15,000	15,000	15,000	15,000

The product manager will focus on keeping the proportion of sluggish customers at a fixed level by managing one of the control variables, such as repeat foot traffic or category placement and assortments in the store. A decision tree model using a supervisory learning technique can locate significant drivers of sluggishness among customers.

Use case in human resources

Workforce scheduling

Modern-day businesses are subjected to variable workforce demand during the weekend, and managers must meet them by hiring or making a productivity-enhancing choice. There are two strategies for workforce planning, including laying off employees to match the demand forecast level over the planning horizon. The challenges are the loss to productivity and time due to constant changes in the workforce. For example, the alternate level strategy is the manager's choice to keep the workforce constant and alter their utilization to match the demand forecast level via overtime, undertime, and vacation planning. A constant workforce can be sized at many levels, or a smaller workforce can be planned for slack periods. Overtime can be used in peak hours.

Managers can choose to have a large workforce so as to minimize the planned use of overtime during peak hours or instead have a smaller workforce and rely on overtime.

A chase strategy involves the scheduling of manpower as per the real-time need of the business unit.

In order to minimize undertime, the use of overtime must occur in the peak period, which is the shifting of demand in a levelling strategy.

The maximum overtime that the manager can use is 20% of the regular time capacity.

Number of employees allocated = $1.2 \times W = 18$ during peak periods, which gives rise to $W = \frac{18}{1.2}$, or 15 employees.

For example, the manager must choose how many part-time workers to maintain the payroll and develop a staffing plan that minimizes total costs. The manager

TABLE 10.22 Workforce scheduling

Month	1	2	3	4	5	6	Total
Forecast demand	6	12	18	15	13	14	78
Workforce	6	12	18	15	13	14	78
Overstaffing	0	0	0	0	0	0	0
Overtime	0	0	0	0	0	0	0
Utilized time	6	12	18	15	13	14	78
Hires	0	6	6	0	0	1	134
Layoffs	4	0	0	3	2	0	9
Time costs	12,000	24,000	36,000	30,000	26,000	28,000	156,000
Overstaffing costs	0	0	0	0	0	0	0
Hiring costs	0	6,000	6,000	0	0	1,000	13,000
Layoff costs	2,000	0	0	1,500	1,000	0	4,500
Layoff	0	0	0	0	0	0	0
Total cost	14,000	30,000	42,000	31,500	27,000	29,000	173,500

Level strategy

Month	1	2	3	4	5	6	Total
Forecast demand	6	12	18	15	13	14	78
Workforce	15	15	15	15	15	15	90
Overstaffing	9	3	0	0	2	1	15
Overtime	0	0	3	0	0	0	3
Utilized time	6	12	15	15	13	14	75
Hires	5	0	0	0	0	0	5
Layoffs	0	0	0	0	0	0	0
Time costs	12,000	24,000	30,000	30,000	26,000	28,000	150,000
Overstaffing costs	0	0	0	0	0	0	0
Hiring costs	5,000	0	0	0	0	000	5,000
Layoff costs	2,000	0	0	1,500	1,000	0	4,500
Layoffs	0	0	0	0	0	0	0
Total cost	17,000	24,000	39,000	30,000	26,000	28,000	164,000

Note: Level strategy eliminates the need for hiring.

can divide the year into 6 periods of 2 months long when each part-time labourer can work for 20 hours ($H \leq 20$) per week on regular time, but the actual number can be less. Instead of paying undertime, each worker's day is shortened during slack periods.

The demand forecast for distribution centres is given in the following. Let 6 facilities limit the hiring to 10 staff members. No back orders are possible.

Overtime cannot exceed 20% of the regular time capacity (4 hours) in any period. At most, any part-time employee can work $1.2 \times 20 = 24$ per week.

TABLE 10.23 Manpower scheduling for the week

Week	1	2	3	4	5	6	Total
No. of workers	6	12	18	15	13	14	78

Regular wage rate = $2,000 per time @ 20 hours/week
Hires = $1,000 per person
Overtime wages = 150% of the regular time rate
Layoff = $500 per person

Use case in health care

Cardiac recovery costs

Cardiac recovery costs describes the percentage of customers who abandon a service mid-way and can be measured at weekly or monthly intervals. Churn is calculated in a simple and accurate manner, such as the ratio of the number of churns during a period divided by the number of customers at the beginning and the number of customers at the end. For example, customer lifetime value (CLV) implies that we cannot focus only on profits but also on costs, and, hence the ratio between the customer acquisition cost (CAC) and customer lifetime value is very related.

The instances of heart ailments that lead to malfunctioning of the organ beyond the age of 45 is rising consistently among males. Clinical models developed on clinical histories of individual subjects can help pre-empt the failure risk of the organ based on diagnostic attributes. The diagnostic score of an individual subject can put him into a high-risk category for further treatment such as admission into an intensive care unit (ICU). An expected cost of treatment and recovery can be arrived at. Although clinical data is hardest to obtain, the efforts are highly remunerative when the symptomatic and non-symptomatic subjects are lucidly distinguished using a logistic regression technique. The symptomatic elements discussed in the literature (Gordon and Kannel, 1971) were identified for male subjects and include:

- Dyspnoea (ordinary and nocturnal)
- Hepatomegaly
- Pleural effusion
- Loss of weight
- Vital capacity
- Vein distension
- Rales
- Cardiomegaly
- S3 gallop
- ICV pressure
- Biochemistry

198 Use cases and business applications

After the diagnosis, which is based on the failure risk assessed, the recommended recovery options include:

- Internal admittance in ICU
- Internal admission under observation and surgery
- Internal admission under observation and medication
- External release under medication (flexible diuretic regimen)
- External release with follow-up treatment (care)
- External release with education and counselling

Each of these options is organized by descending cost of the option. A pooled logistic regression model estimated the heart failure risk profile using the diagnostic attributes to obtain the probability of failure, which can be associated with an expected recovery.

For example,

$$\text{Probability(failure)} = \alpha + (\beta_1 \times \text{age}) + (\beta_2 \times \text{LVH}) + (\beta_3 \times \text{vital capacity}) + (\beta_4 \times \text{heart rate}) + (\beta_5 \times \text{systolic blood pressure}) + (\beta_6 \times \text{coronary disease}) + (\beta_7 \times \text{valve disease}) + (\beta_8 \times \text{diabetes}) + (\beta_9 \times \text{cardiomegaly})$$

This model provides a simple formula for estimating the probability of heart failure when specific risk factors are present.

The ratio of each diagnostic attribute reflects the relative importance of an anomaly. The receiver operating characteristics (ROC) of the model can provide

TABLE 10.24 Logistic regression model for males

Variables	Description	Units	Beta	Wald-Chi-square	P-value
Intercept			−7.3611	168	< 0.001
Age	Subject age	10 year	0.0313	146	< 0.001
Left ventricular hypertrophy (LVH)	Left ventricular hypertrophy	Yes/no	0.8428	144	0.003
Vital capacity	Pulmonary function	100CL	−0.003	124	0.002
Heart rate	Oxygen deficiency	10 bpm	0.0144	118	0.03
Systolic BP	Maximum arterial pressure of left ventricle	20 mm HG	0.0067	168	< 0.001
Congenital heart defect (CHD)		Yes/no	1.5333	146	< 0.001
Valve disease	Plaque build up	Yes/no	0.8868	116	0.17
Diabetes	FBS levels	Yes/no	0.2383	162	< 0.001
Cardiomegaly	Enlargement of the heart	Yes/no	0.7968	185	< 0.001

TABLE 10.25 Follow-up cost of multi-disciplinary heart failure

Cost domain	Cost ($)
Intervention	216
Caregivers	1,164
Other medical care	1,257
Re-admission	2,178
Total	4,815

Note: All costs are for 3 months of follow-up, and annual costs are $1,960 per case.

predictive benefits over a random scenario of basic care as can a separate regression controlling for risk factors such as sex, age group, location with coronary history, etc. The longer observation period in the sample can help arrive at longer prediction period, which is for 1 year.

For patients with about a 5% probability of risk, coronary care would cost $2.04 million per year of life saved. Intermediate care would cost $139,000 per year of life saved. At probabilities of about 20%, the cost to save a year of life would be much higher. On average, the incremental cost is approximately about $40,000 over a random scenario.

References

ACXIOM USA. (2014). *Life Stage Clustering System: "PersonicX," An Explanation of the Development of the PersonicX Clustering System*. Little Rock, AR: ACXIOM, USA. Reprinted by permission of ACXIOM, USA.

Bitner, M.J. (1992), Servicescapes: The Impact of Physical Surroundings on Customers and Employees. *Journal of Marketing, 56*. 57–71.

Cho, J., A. Aribarg, and P. Manchanda. (2015, October 1), *The Value of Measuring Customer Satisfaction*. Ross School of Business Paper No. 1283. Retrieved from http://ssrn.com/abstract=2630898 or http://dx.doi.org/10.2139/ssrn.2630898.

Clark, D.D. (1997). Internet Cost Allocation and Pricing. In: J.P. Bailey and L.W. McKnight (eds.), *Internet Economics*. Cambridge, MA: MIT Press.

Cunningham, M.A., T.H. Lee, E.F. Cook, D.A. Brand, G.W. Rouan, M.C. Weisberg, and L. Goldman. (1989). The Effect of Gender on the Probability of Myocardial Infarction among Emergency Department Patients with Acute Chest Pain. *Journal of General Internal Medicine*, 4, 392–398.

Elliott, J. (1961). *Equitable Payment: A General Theory of Work, Differential Payment, and Individual Progress*. London: Heinemann Educational.

Fiebach, N., E.F. Cook, T.H. Lee, D.A. Brand, G.W. Rouan, M. Weisberg, and L. Goldman. (1990). Outcomes of Patients with Myocardial Infarction Who Are Initially admitted to Stepdown Units: Data from the Multicenter Chest Pain Study. *American Journal of Medicine, 89*, 15–20.

Gibbens, R.J., and F.P. Kelly. (1999). Resource Pricing and the Evolution of Congestion Control. *Automatica*, 35, 1969–1985. Available from http://statslab.cam.ac.uk/~frank/evol.ps.

Gordon, T., and W. B. Kannel. (1971). Premature Mortality from Coronary Heart Disease: The Framingham Study. *Journal of the American Medical Association, 215*(10): 1617–1625.

Gupta, A., D. O. Stahl, and A. Whinston. (1997). A Stochastic Equilibrium Model of Internet Pricing. *Journal of Economic Dynamics and Control 21*: 699–702.

Gupta, S., and D. G. Morrison. (1991, Summer). Estimating Heterogeneity in Consumers' Purchasing Rates. *Marketing Science, 10*(3), 264–269.

MacKie-Mason, J. K., and H. R. Varian. (1994). *Pricing the Internet.* Upper Saddle River, NJ: Prentice Hall.

Kannel, W. B., R. B. D'Agostino, H. Silbershatz, A. J. Belanger, P. W. F. Wilson, and D. Levy. (1999). Profile for Estimating Risk of Heart Failure. *Archives of Internal Medicine, 159*(11): 1197–1204. Reprinted by permission of Authors.

Keon, N., and G. Anandalingam. (2006). A New Pricing Model for Competitive Telecommunications Services Using Congestion Discounts. *INFORMS Journal on Computing, 17*(2): 248–262. Reprinted with the permission of Authors.

Kimes, S. (1997). Yield Management: An Overview. In: I. Yeoman and A. Ingold, A. (eds.), *Yield Management: Strategies for the Service Industries.* London: Cassell.

Kimes, S. E. (2000). Revenue Management on the Links. *The Cornell Hotel and Restaurant Administration Quarterly*, 120–127.

Kimes, S. E., and E. Sheryl. (1989). Yield Management: A Tool for Capacity Constrained Service Firm. *Journal of Operations Management, 8*(4): 348–363.

Lee, T. H., G. Juarez, E. F. Cook, M. C. Weisberg, G. W. Rouan, D. A. Brand, and L. Goldman (1991). Ruling Out Acute Myocardial Infarction: A Prospective Multicenter Validation of a 12 Hour Strategy for Patients at Low Risk. *New England Journal of Medicine*, 324, 1239–1246.

Lee, T. H., L. E. Short, D. A. Brand, Y. D. Jean-Claude, M. C. Weisberg, G. W. Rouan, and L. Goldman. (1988). Patients with Acute Chest Pain Who Leave Emergency Departments against Medical Advice. *Journal of General Internal Medicine*, 3, 21–24.

Lund, D. J., and D. Marinova. (2014). Managing Revenue across Retail Channels: The Interplay of Service Performance and Direct Marketing. *Journal of Marketing, 78*(5): 99–118.

Madden, G. and S. J. Savage. (2000). Market Structure, Competition and Pricing in United States International Telephone Service Markets. *The Review of Economics and Statistics, 82*(2), pp. 291–296.

Takagi, H. (1991). Queueing Analysis: A Foundation of Performance Evaluation. In: *Vacation and Priority Systems*, vol. l. New York: North-Holland.

Verma, R., G. Thompson, and J. Louviere. (1999). Configuring Service Operations in Accordance with Customers' Needs and Preferences. *Journal of Service Research, 1*(3): 262–274.

Ward, A., J. Liker, J. Cristiano, and D. Sobek II. (1995, Spring). The Second Toyota Paradox: How Delaying Decisions Can Make Better Cars Faster. *Sloan Management Review*, 43–62.

White, L. D., T. H. Lee, E. F. Cook, M. C. Weisberg, G. W. Rouan, D. A. Brand, and L. Goldman. (1990). Comparison of the Natural History of New Onset and Exacerbated Chronic Ischemic Heart Disease. *Journal of the American College of Cardiology*, 16, 304–310.

Wysocki, B. (2004, April 9). Industrial Strength: To Fix Health Care, Hospitals Take Tips from Factory Floor. *The Wall Street Journal*, p. A1.

APPENDIX 1

Formulae and derivations

1 Base measures

Base measures are univariate measures, which use one variable at a time to report on a single statistic from the sample or population. Measures of central tendency are the most common examples of base measures in a normal distribution. However, in the case of non-normal distribution, the base measures would be non-parametric statistics. In the following section, we will discuss base measures that can be generated by an analyst from data.

1.1 Count: the number of items present in a given variable such as number of observations, the number of customers that own a product, the number of households residing at a given street, etc.

- Number of new customers
- Number of new and open customers
- Debit balances of new and open customers
- Credit balances of new and open customers
- Number of open customers
- Debit balance open customers
- Credit balance open customers
- Number of new and closed customers
- Number of closed customers
- Number of products
- Number of valid accounts
- Number of closed accounts
- Total number of customers
- Number of responses
- Total costs incurred
- Number of leads

- 1.2 Mode: the most frequent value of a variable, such as the most occurring character in a field or attribute. For example, "James" is the most common first name of all customers in a store, "Cheese Slice" is the most common bread assortment that visitors buy in a departmental store, and "45" is the most common age for males to undergo cardiomegaly.
- 1.3 Median: the value of an observation that is the midpoint between the top value and bottom value for a variable. It is equidistant from both ends when the number of observations is odd (not divisible by 2) but could be the nearest higher value when the number of observations are even (e.g. the median income of US households in 2013 was $51,939).

2 Computed measures

Computed measures are univariate measures that involve the addition, aggregation, ratio, or division of two or more values to report on a single statistic from data.

- 2.1 Ratio: the division of two variables or the two values of a single variable or the division of a variable by a fixed number; for example, average monthly sales is equal to the total annual sales divided by 12 (for 12 months).
- 2.2 Mean: the ratio between the sum of the values of all observations divided by the number of observations in a sample, also known as the average value.
- 2.3 Class mean: the mean of the group (the ratio between the sum of values of all observations divided by the number of observations in that group), when the data are classified by groups.
- 2.4 Horizontal ratio: the ratio created by dividing the values of one variable of a given column against the corresponding values of another variable against another column in the same row. For example, the unit purchase value of a product category is the division of the value of the product by the quantities of that product category.
- 2.5 Vertical ratio: the ratio created by dividing the values of one variable of a given column against a fixed value of the same or another variable in the same column. For example, the purchase share of a product category is the division of the purchase value of the product category by the total value of all product categories in the same column.
- 2.6 Frequency distribution table: a table (plot) of the frequency count of a given item (class) reported against the name of the item (class), for example the number of items of inventories, angles equalling 25, channels equalling 45, frames equalling 45, lying in the stock etc.
- 2.7 Cumulative probability distribution: the frequency count appearing for each item added together one by one. The ratio between the cumulative frequency count and the size of sample (sub-populations) gives rise to cumulative probability.

3   Monte Carlo Simulation

    This is a technique of generating artificial values of one or more variables where the distribution of the variable is assumed normal and random. For example, one can simulate a situation on the basis of past historical data. For example, let $Y = F(X_1, X_2, \ldots X_n)$, where each of the X is a random number. For each trial, the values of X is $X_{11}, X_{21} \ldots X_{N1}$ that gives rise to Y_1 and for m trials X are $X_{1m}, X_{2m} \ldots X_{Nm}$, that gives rise to Y_m. The observations so generated with values of Y_1 to Y_m can be analyzed by central tendency measures for reporting one or more statistics for business use.

4   Moving average

    Moving average forecast is a trend that smooths out a forecast indicator over the horizon. A simple moving average is calculated by summing up the indicators during a fixed consecutive time period and then dividing that sum by the number of time periods. The number of time periods to include in the denominator could be two, three, or more. For a weighted moving average, the indicators are weighed by the weights w_i before summing them up to compute the average.

5   Residual error structure

    Understanding the error structure in a model is critical to arrive at best and unbiased estimators with minimum variance in analytical models. The asymptotic properties of estimators are realized with fairly large samples.

    5.1 Root mean squared error (RMSE): the most common standard of goodness-of-fit, when errors are squared
    5.2 Mean absolute error (MAE): the average of the absolute values of the errors, when errors are not squared
    5.3 Mean absolute percentage error (MAPE): better to use when errors vary over a wide range due to compound growth more suited for errors in percentage terms
    5.4 Mean error (ME): indicates whether forecasts are random or biased should be close to 0

The specification of a model is

$$Y_t = X_i\beta + \varepsilon_t$$

where $\varepsilon_{it} = \rho e_{it-1} + v_{it}$ and

where the residual error ε_t follows autocorrelation of degree one among itself.

The addendum to the error, v_{it}, is assumed to have constant variance and uncorrelated among itself and $0 < \rho < 1$.

When we have a simple equation with a few consecutive time periods, the error terms might be correlated across time and the errors and can take three forms:

1 When the fixed effect is λ_i, then $\varepsilon = \lambda_i + v_{it}$.
2 When the transitory effect is λ_i, then $\varepsilon_{it} = \rho\varepsilon_{it-1} + v_{it}$.
3 When the fixed and transitory is λ_i, then $\varepsilon_{it} = \lambda_i + u_{it}$, where $u_{it} = \rho u_{it-1} + v_{it}$.

Therefore, the analyst must conduct statistical tests as appropriate to validate the presence or absence of these parameters in the model specification.

Variance of ε_{it} is decomposed into three components:

$$\text{Var}(\varepsilon_{it}) = \text{Var}(\lambda_i) + \rho^2\text{Var}(u_{it-1}) + \text{Var}(v_{it})$$

Table A.1 provides exemplary estimates of the residual error variance.

TABLE A.1 Exemplary estimates

ρ^2	.165
$\text{Var}(\rho_i)$	.224
$\text{Var}(u_{it-1})$	.083
$\rho^2\text{Var}(u_{it-1})$	.014
$\text{Var}(v_{it})$	.069
$\text{Var}(e_{it})$	.307

APPENDIX 2

TABLE A.2 Sample test data on banking customers

acctno	date_opened	date_opened	no_dependents	gender	marital_status	education	$ credit_limit	Home_type	Last_Payment_Amount	delnq_mar	delnq_feb	Occupation	$ Total Fees and Charges
580	2/26/2006	2/26/2006	0	M	S	G	375000	RENTED	14000	1	1	1	0
760	9/16/2002	9/16/2002	3	M	M	G	150000	others	30500	1	1	1	0
089	11/3/2004	11/3/2004	2	M	M	G	150000	others	0	0	1	1	0
556	11/27/2003	11/27/2003	3	M	M	P	150000	others	24129	1	1	1	0
580	5/31/2002	5/31/2002	3	M	M	P	100000	others	10787	1	1	1	0
257	6/27/2003	6/27/2003	2	M	M	P	150000	OWNED	30000	1	1	1	0
653	11/3/2003	11/3/2003	2	M	M	M	100000	others	9000	2	1	1	0
760	6/10/2005	6/10/2005	1	M	S	M	100000	others	0	2	2	1	349.9
255	9/7/2004	9/7/2004	1	M	M	M	130000	others	390	1	1	1	0
610	6/23/2003	6/23/2003	0	F	M	G	150000	others	2220	1	1	1	0
636	2/28/2006	2/28/2006	0	F	M	G	277000	others	7871	1	1	1	0
682	3/3/2003	3/3/2003	2	M	M	G	150000	PATERNAL	10000	1	1	15	0
807	3/1/2006	3/1/2006	1	M	M	M	100000	others	0	0	1	1	0
219	2/24/2003	2/24/2003	2	M	M	P	150000	RENTED	7118	1	1	15	0
652	11/21/2004	11/21/2004	2	M	M	P	140000	others	0	1	0	1	0
900	1/19/2006	1/19/2006	2	M	M	M	180000	others	1194	1	0	1	0
908	12/23/2004	12/23/2004	0	M	M	M	140000	others	13000	1	1	1	0
235	8/8/2002	8/8/2002	3	M	M	G	125000	OWNED	20000	1	1	1	555.1
257	5/6/2004	5/6/2004	3	M	M	G	140000	others	10948	1	1	1	0
750	5/15/2003	5/15/2003	1	M	M	G	150000	others	400	0	0	1	0
063	4/7/2003	4/7/2003	0	F	S	G	100000	PATERNAL	4122	0	1	15	0
857	1/25/2005	1/25/2005	1	M	M	G	112000	others	5471	1	1	14	0
907	1/31/2005	1/31/2005	1	M	M	P	112000	others	5704	1	1	1	0
095	7/20/2004	7/20/2004	3	M	M	G	105000	RENTED	4250	1	1	1	199.94
418	5/24/2005	5/24/2005	2	M	M	G	161000	others	4359	1	1	1	0

806	1/28/2005	1/28/2005	3	M	M	G	116000	others	2600	1	1	15	0
689	7/12/2005	7/12/2005	0	M	S	G	125000	others	0	1	1	1	0
206	11/11/2005	11/11/2005	0	M	S	G	119000	others	4160	1	1	15	0
933	9/27/2004	9/27/2004	0	F	M	M	150000	others	5800	1	0	1	599.83
458	6/16/2006	6/16/2006	2	M	M	M	155000	others	38593	1	1	15	0
557	7/5/2005	7/5/2005	1	F	M	M	170000	others	2000	1	1	1	0
005	12/9/2002	12/9/2002	1	M	M	G	105000	others	0	1	0	1	0
542	7/28/2005	7/28/2005	2	M	M	M	150000	others	0	1	1	15	0
490	10/23/2002	10/23/2002	0	M	S	P	155000	PATERNAL	10000	1	1	15	444.97
056	5/4/2004	5/4/2004	2	M	M	P	150000	others	22261	1	1	15	0
648	7/13/2006	7/13/2006	3	M	M	G	112000	others	10980	1	1	1	0
804	9/3/2005	9/3/2005	3	M	M	G	100000	others	5151	1	1	15	0
046	10/12/2004	10/12/2004	2	M	M	G	159000	others	8250	1	1	15	0
657	7/16/2005	7/16/2005	1	M	M	M	130000	others	0	0	0	1	0

APPENDIX 3

TABLE A.3 Sample test data on GSM subscribers

PROBE ID	CALL ID	SIDE	CLASS ID	CODE ID	START	END	DURATION	RELEASE
	11116111506-4	WDC	3	5	11/06/2014 11:14:10	11/06/2014 11:15:44	0:01:34	NORMAL
	11116111506-4	NYC	3	4	11/06/2014 11:10:15	11/06/2014 11:11:29	0:01:14	NORMAL
	11116111506-4	MIAM	2	5	11/06/2014 11:04:12	11/06/2014 11:05:17	0:01:05	NORMAL
	11116111506-4	NYC	2	3	11/06/2014 11:14:10	11/06/2014 11:15:04	0:54:00	NORMAL
	11116111506-4	CHG	3	4	11/06/2014 11:14:20	11/06/2014 11:15:10	0:50:00	NORMAL
	11116111506-4	CHG	3	5	11/06/2014 11:14:30	11/06/2014 11:15:19	0:49:00	NORMAL
	11116111506-4	CHG	2	3	11/06/2014 11:14:00	11/06/2014 11:14:44	0:44:00	NORMAL
	11116111506-4	NYC	2	5	11/06/2014 11:14:20	11/06/2014 11:15:11	0:51:00	NORMAL
	11116111506-4	NYC	3	4	11/06/2014 11:14:20	11/06/2014 11:15:09	0:39:00	NORMAL
	11116111506-4	NYC	3	4	11/06/2014 11:14:20	11/06/2014 11:15:02	0:42:00	NORMAL
	11116111506-4	NYC	2	3	11/06/2014 11:14:30	11/06/2014 11:15:12	0:42:00	NORMAL
	11116111506-4	NYC	2	3	11/06/2014 11:14:40	11/06/2014 11:15:20	0:40:00	NORMAL
	11116111506-4	NYC	1	4	11/06/2014 11:14:50	11/06/2014 11:15:	0:41:00	NORMAL
	11116111506-4	NYC	1	5	11/06/2014 11:14:55	11/06/2014 11:15:31	0:40:00	NORMAL
	11116111506-4	NYC	1	5	11/06/2014 11:14:59	11/06/2014 11:15:53	0:54:00	NORMAL
	11116111506-4	NYC	1	3	11/06/2014 11:14:49	11/06/2014 11:15:28	0:39:00	NORMAL
	11116111506-4	DLW	1	3	11/06/2014 11:14:39	11/06/2014 11:15:17	0:38:00	NORMAL
	11116111506-4	DLW	3	4	11/06/2014 11:14:19	11/06/2014 11:14:55	0:36:00	NORMAL
	11116111506-4	DLW	3	4	11/06/2014 11:14:01	11/06/2014 11:14:35	0:35:00	NORMAL
	11116111506-4	NYC	3	4	11/06/2014 11:14:05	11/06/2014 11:14:39	0:34:00	NORMAL
	11116111506-4	NYC	3	3	11/06/2014 11:15:05	11/06/2014 11:15:37	0:32:00	NORMAL
	11116111506-4	NYC	2	3	11/06/2014 11:14:09	11/06/2014 11:14:49	0:40:00	NORMAL
	11116111506-4	NYC	2	4	11/06/2014 11:14:10	11/06/2014 11:15:04	0:54:00	NORMAL
	11116111506-4	NYC	2	5	11/06/2014 11:14:06	11/06/2014 11:15:44	0:50:00	NORMAL
	11116111506-4	NYC	3	5	11/06/2014 11:14:08	11/06/2014 11:14:57	0:49:00	NORMAL

(*Continued*)

TABLE A.3 Continued

PROBE ID	CALL ID	SIDE	CLASS ID	CODE ID	START	END	DURATION	RELEASE
	11116111506-4	NYC	3	3	11/06/2014 11:14:08	11/06/2014 11:14:52	0:44:00	NORMAL
	11116111506-4	NYC	2	3	11/06/2014 11:14:10	11/06/2014 11:15:01	0:51:00	NORMAL
	11116111506-4	NYC	2	4	11/06/2014 11:14:18	11/06/2014 11:14:57	0:39:00	NORMAL
	11116111506-4	NWK	3	4	11/06/2014 11:14:30	11/06/2014 11:15:12	0:42:00	NORMAL
	11116111506-10	NWK	3	4	11/06/2014 11:14:50	11/06/2014 11:15:32	0:42:00	NORMAL
	11116111506-4	NWK	3	3	11/06/2014 11:14:56	11/06/2014 11:15:36	0:40:00	NORMAL
	11116111506-4	NYC	3	3	11/06/2014 11:14:57	11/06/2014 11:15:44	0:41:00	NORMAL
	11116111506-4	NYC	3	4	11/06/2014 11:14:10	11/06/2014 11:15:44	0:40:00	NORMAL
	11116111506-4	NYC	2	5	11/06/2014 11:14:10	11/06/2014 11:15:44	0:54:00	NORMAL
	11116111506-4	NYC	2	5	11/06/2014 11:14:10	11/06/2014 11:15:44	0:39:00	NORMAL
	11116111506-4	NYC	2	3	11/06/2014 11:14:10	11/06/2014 11:15:44	0:38:00	NORMAL
	11116111506-4	NYC	2	3	11/06/2014 11:14:10	11/06/2014 11:15:44	0:36:00	NORMAL
	11116111506-4	NYC	2	4	11/06/2014 11:14:10	11/06/2014 11:15:44	0:35:00	NORMAL
	11116111506-4	NYC	3	4	11/06/2014 11:14:10	11/06/2014 11:15:44	0:54:00	NORMAL
	11116111506-4	NYC	3	4	11/06/2014 11:14:10	11/06/2014 11:15:44	0:50:00	NORMAL
	11116111506-4	NWK	3	3	11/06/2014 11:14:10	11/06/2014 11:15:44	0:49:00	NORMAL
	11116111506-4	NWK	2	3	11/06/2014 11:14:10	11/06/2014 11:15:44	0:44:00	NORMAL
	11116111506-4	NYC	2	4	11/06/2014 11:14:10	11/06/2014 11:15:44	0:51:00	NORMAL
	11116111506-4	NYC	1	5	11/06/2014 11:14:10	11/06/2014 11:15:44	0:39:00	NORMAL
	11116111506-4	NYC	1	5	11/06/2014 11:14:10	11/06/2014 11:15:44	0:42:00	NORMAL
	11116111506-4	NYC	1	3	11/06/2014 11:14:10	11/06/2014 11:15:44	0:42:00	NORMAL
	11116111506-4	NYC	1	3	11/06/2014 11:14:10	11/06/2014 11:15:44	0:40:00	NORMAL
	11116111506-4	NYC	1	4	11/06/2014 11:14:10	11/06/2014 11:15:44	0:41:00	NORMAL
	11116111506-4	NYC	3	4	11/06/2014 11:14:10	11/06/2014 11:15:44	0:40:00	NORMAL
	11116111506-4	NYC	3	4	11/06/2014 11:14:10	11/06/2014 11:15:44	0:54:00	NORMAL
	11116111506-4	NYC	3	3	11/06/2014 11:14:10	11/06/2014 11:15:44	0:39:00	NORMAL
	11116111506-4	NWK	3	3	11/06/2014 11:14:10	11/06/2014 11:15:44	0:38:00	NORMAL

111116111506-4	NWK	3	4	11/06/2014 11:14:10	11/06/2014 11:15:44	0:36:00	NORMAL
111116111506-4	NWK	3	5	11/06/2014 11:14:10	11/06/2014 11:15:44	0:35:00	NORMAL
111116111506-4	NWK	3	5	11/06/2014 11:14:10	11/06/2014 11:15:44	0:40:00	NORMAL
111116111506-4	NWK	3	3	11/06/2014 11:14:10	11/06/2014 11:15:44	0:40:00	NORMAL
111116111506-4	NWK	3	3	11/06/2014 11:14:10	11/06/2014 11:15:44	0:40:00	NORMAL
111116111506-4	NWK	3	4	11/06/2014 11:14:10	11/06/2014 11:15:44	0:40:00	NORMAL
111116111506-4	NWK	3	4	11/06/2014 11:14:10	11/06/2014 11:15:44	0:40:00	NORMAL
111116111506-4	NYC	3	4	11/06/2014 11:14:10	11/06/2014 11:15:44	0:40:00	NORMAL
111116111506-4	NYC	3	3	11/06/2014 11:14:10	11/06/2014 11:15:44	0:40:00	NORMAL
111116111506-4	NYC	2	3	11/06/2014 11:14:10	11/06/2014 11:15:44	0:40:00	NORMAL
111116111506-4	NYC	2	4	11/06/2014 11:14:10	11/06/2014 11:15:44	0:40:00	NORMAL
111116111506-4	NYC	3	5	11/06/2014 11:14:10	11/06/2014 11:15:44	0:40:00	NORMAL
111116111506-4	NYC	3	5	11/06/2014 11:14:10	11/06/2014 11:15:44	0:40:00	NORMAL
111116111506-4	NYC	3	3	11/06/2014 11:14:10	11/06/2014 11:15:44	0:40:00	NORMAL
111116111506-4	NYC	2	3	11/06/2014 11:14:10	11/06/2014 11:15:44	0:40:00	NORMAL
111116111506-4	NWK	2	4	11/06/2014 11:14:10	11/06/2014 11:15:44	0:40:00	NORMAL
111116111506-4	NWK	1	4	11/06/2014 11:14:10	11/06/2014 11:15:44	0:40:00	NORMAL
111116111506-4	NWK	1	4	11/06/2014 11:14:10	11/06/2014 11:15:44	0:40:00	NORMAL
111116111506-4	NWK	1	3	11/06/2014 11:14:10	11/06/2014 11:15:44	0:40:00	NORMAL
111116111506-4	NYC	1	3	11/06/2014 11:14:10	11/06/2014 11:15:44	0:40:00	NORMAL
111116111506-4	NYC	1	4	11/06/2014 11:14:10	11/06/2014 11:15:44	0:40:00	NORMAL
111116111506-4	NYC	3	5	11/06/2014 11:14:10	11/06/2014 11:15:44	0:40:00	NORMAL
111116111506-4	NYC	3	5	11/06/2014 11:14:10	11/06/2014 11:15:44	0:40:00	NORMAL
111116111506-4	NYC	3	3	11/06/2014 11:14:10	11/06/2014 11:15:44	0:40:00	NORMAL
111116111506-4	NYC	3	3	11/06/2014 11:14:10	11/06/2014 11:15:44	0:40:00	NORMAL
111116111506-4	NYC	3	4	11/06/2014 11:14:10	11/06/2014 11:15:44	0:40:00	NORMAL
111116111506-4	NYC	3	4	11/06/2014 11:14:10	11/06/2014 11:15:44	0:40:00	NORMAL
111116111506-4	NWK	3	4	11/06/2014 11:14:10	11/06/2014 11:15:44	0:40:00	NORMAL
111116111506-4	NWK	3	3	11/06/2014 11:14:10	11/06/2014 11:15:44	0:40:00	NORMAL
111116111506-4	NWK	3	3	11/06/2014 11:14:10	11/06/2014 11:15:44	0:40:00	NORMAL
111116111506-4	NWK	3	4	11/06/2014 11:14:10	11/06/2014 11:15:44	0:40:00	NORMAL

(*Continued*)

TABLE A.3 Continued

PROBE ID	CALL ID	SIDE	CLASS ID	CODE ID	START	END	DURATION	RELEASE
	11116111506-4	NYC	3	5	11/06/2014 11:14:10	11/06/2014 11:15:44	0:40:00	NORMAL
	11116111506-4	NYC	3	5	11/06/2014 11:14:10	11/06/2014 11:15:44	0:40:00	NORMAL
	11116111506-4	NYC	3	3	11/06/2014 11:14:10	11/06/2014 11:15:44	0:40:00	NORMAL
	11116111506-4	NYC	2	3	11/06/2014 11:14:10	11/06/2014 11:15:44	0:40:00	NORMAL
	11116111506-4	NYC	2	4	11/06/2014 11:14:10	11/06/2014 11:15:44	0:40:00	NORMAL
	11116111506-4	NYC	3	4	11/06/2014 11:14:10	11/06/2014 11:15:44	0:40:00	NORMAL
	11116111506-4	NYC	3	4	11/06/2014 11:14:10	11/06/2014 11:15:44	0:40:00	NORMAL
	11116111506-4	NYC	3	3	11/06/2014 11:14:10	11/06/2014 11:15:44	0:40:00	NORMAL
	11116111506-4	NYC	2	3	11/06/2014 11:14:10	11/06/2014 11:15:44	0:40:00	NORMAL
	11116111506-4	NWK	2	4	11/06/2014 11:14:10	11/06/2014 11:15:44	0:40:00	NORMAL
	11116111506-4	NWK	1	5	11/06/2014 11:14:10	11/06/2014 11:15:44	0:40:00	NORMAL
	11116111506-4	NWK	1	5	11/06/2014 11:14:10	11/06/2014 11:15:44	0:40:00	NORMAL
	11116111506-4	NWK	1	3	11/06/2014 11:14:10	11/06/2014 11:15:44	0:40:00	NORMAL
	11116111506-4	NYC	1	3	11/06/2014 11:14:10	11/06/2014 11:15:44	0:40:00	NORMAL
	11116111506-4	NYC	1	4	11/06/2014 11:14:10	11/06/2014 11:15:44	0:40:00	NORMAL
	11116111506-4	NYC	3	4	11/06/2014 11:14:10	11/06/2014 11:15:44	0:40:00	NORMAL
	11116111506-4	NYC	3	4	11/06/2014 11:14:10	11/06/2014 11:15:44	0:40:00	NORMAL
	11116111506-4	NYC	3	3	11/06/2014 11:14:10	11/06/2014 11:15:44	0:40:00	NORMAL
	11116111506-4	NYC	3	3	11/06/2014 11:14:10	11/06/2014 11:15:44	0:40:00	NORMAL
	11116111506-4	NYC	3	4	11/06/2014 11:14:10	11/06/2014 11:15:44	0:40:00	NORMAL
	11116111506-4	NYC	3	5	11/06/2014 11:14:10	11/06/2014 11:15:44	0:40:00	NORMAL
	11116111506-4	NJ	3	5	11/06/2014 11:14:10	11/06/2014 11:15:44	0:40:00	NORMAL
	11116111506-4	NJ	3	3	11/06/2014 11:14:10	11/06/2014 11:15:44	0:40:00	NORMAL
	11116111506-4	NJ	3	3	11/06/2014 11:14:10	11/06/2014 11:15:44	0:40:00	NORMAL
	11116111506-4	NJ	3	4	11/06/2014 11:14:10	11/06/2014 11:15:44	0:40:00	NORMAL
	11116111506-4	NJ	3	4	11/06/2014 11:14:10	11/06/2014 11:15:44	0:40:00	NORMAL
			3					NORMAL
			3					NORMAL

APPENDIX 4

TABLE A.4 Sample test data on household purchases from stores

HHID	REGION	URB	HHSIZE	INCOME	SHP_FREQ	SHP_STOR	SHP_GROC	SHP_GROU	SHP_NONF	SHP_NONU	SHP_SPEC	SHP_SPEU
10218	1	2	7	30806	2	1	150	1	15	1	20	1
10321	1	2	6	50000	2	1	100	1	10	1	0	
10338	1	2	6	100000	4	1	700	2	150	2	60	2
10634	1	2	4	64584	3	1	300	2	100	2	120	2
11221	1	1	5	40000	2	1	400	2	25	2	0	
11312	1	2	4	40000	2	1	100	1	15	1	0	
11613	1	2	4	20100	3	1	40	1	5	1	20	1
11627	1	2	3	24500	3	1	135	1	3	1	45	1
11822	1	2	3	50000	3	1	200	2	50	2	100	2
11825	1	2	4	30000	3	1	400	2	70	2	0	
11833	1	2	3	12313	3	1	300	2	0		100	2
12816	1	1	3	54000	4	1	200	2	50	2	20	2
13564	2	1	8	11460	3	1	65	1	20	1	200	2
13928	2	2	6	100000	1	1	400	2	25	2	200	2
14301	2	1	4	50000	2	1	50	1	0		10	2
14514	2	1	3	30000	1	1	80	1	8	1	3	1
15737	2	2	3	35000	3	1	300	2	100	2	0	
15843	2	1	3	75000	1	1	300	2	0		0	
16205	3	2	3	50000	3	1	250	2	0		50	2
16316	3	2	3	24000	4	1	100	2	50	2	20	2

16364	3	2	4	26300	4	1	60	1	5	1	45	1
16712	3	2	6	55300	1	1	250	1	150	1	175	2
16830	3	2	4	66545	2	1	300	1	20	1	10	1
16875	3	2	5	44300	4	1	400	2	50	2	15	2
16900	3	1	5	21428	2	1	120	1	9998		0	
17147	3	1	4	49250	3	13	500	2	50	2	0	
17149	3	1	3	42900	4	13	250	2	75	2	40	2
17334	3	1	5	75356	2	1	60	1	10	1	0	
17816	3	2	4	64732	2	1	140	2	40	2	60	2
18345	3	1	4	91191	2	1	120	1	10	1	30	2
18351	3	1	3	25000	3	1	300	2	100	2	10	2

APPENDIX 5

TABLE A.5 Sample test data on learning in manufacturing

Trial run	Batch number	Cumulative average cost (in dollars)	Cumulative production (in units)	Cumulative training time
1	1	120	10	11
1	2	140	10	8
2	3	95	20	54
2	4	125	20	25
3	5	80	40	100
3	6	75	40	80
4	7	65	80	220
4	8	50	80	150
5	9	55	160	410
5	10	40	160	500
6	11	40	320	660
6	12	38	320	600
7	13	32	640	810
7	14	36	640	750
8	15	25	1280	890
8	16	25	1280	800
9	17	20	2560	990
9	18	24	2560	900
10	19	19	5120	1155
10	20	25	5120	1000

APPENDIX 6

TABLE A.6 Sample test data on general insurance

policy ID	eq_site_ limit	hu_site_ limit	fl_site_ limit	fr_site_ limit	tiv_2011	tiv_2012	eq_site_ deductible	hu_site_ deductible	fl_site_ deductible	fr_site_ deductible	line	construction
	498960	498960	498960	498960	498960	792149	0	9979	0	0	Residential	Masonry
	1322376	1322376	1322376	1322376	1322376	1438164	0	0	0	0	Residential	Masonry
	190724	190724	190724	190724	190724	192477	0	0	0	0	Residential	Wood
	0	79521	0	0	79521	86854	0	0	0	0	Residential	Wood
	0	254282	0	254282	254282	246144	0	0	0	0	Residential	Wood
	0	515036	0	0	515036	884419	0	0	0	0	Residential	Masonry
	0	19260000	0	0	19260000	20610000	0	0	0	0	Commercial	Reinforced Concrete
	328500	328500	328500	328500	328500	348374	0	16425	0	0	Residential	Wood
	315000	315000	315000	315000	315000	265822	0	15750	0	0	Residential	Wood
	705600	705600	705600	705600	705600	1010843	14112	35280	0	0	Residential	Masonry
	831498	831498	831498	831498	831498	1117791	0	0	0	0	Residential	Masonry
	0	24059	0	0	24059	33952	0	0	0	0	Residential	Wood
	0	48116	0	0	48116	66755	0	0	0	0	Residential	Wood
	0	28869	0	0	28869	42827	0	0	0	0	Residential	Wood
	0	56136	0	0	56136	50657	0	0	0	0	Residential	Wood
	0	48116	0	0	48116	67905	0	0	0	0	Residential	Wood
	0	48116	0	0	48116	66939	0	0	0	0	Residential	Wood
	0	80192	0	0	80192	86421	0	0	0	0	Residential	Wood
	0	48116	0	0	48116	73799	0	0	0	0	Residential	Wood
	0	60947	0	0	60947	62467	0	0	0	0	Residential	Wood
	0	28869	0	0	28869	42728	0	0	0	0	Residential	Wood
	0	13410000	0	0	13410000	11700000	0	0	0	0	Commercial	Reinforced Concrete
	0	1669114	0	0	1669114	2099128	0	0	0	0	Residential	Masonry
	0	179562	0	0	179562	211373	0	0	0	0	Residential	Wood
	0	177744	0	0	177744	157171	0	0	0	0	Residential	Wood

0	17758	0	17758	16949	0	0	0	Residential	Wood
0	130130	0	130130	101758	0	0	0	Residential	Wood
0	42855	0	42855	63593	0	0	0	Residential	Wood
0	786	0	786	662	0	0	0	Residential	Wood
0	170362	0	170362	177176	0	0	0	Residential	Wood
0	1431	0	1431	1861	0	0	0	Residential	Wood
0	129913	0	129913	101693	0	0	0	Residential	Wood
0	366286	0	366286	507164	0	0	0	Residential	Masonry
0	22513	0	22513	28637	0	0	0	Residential	Wood
0	9247	9247	9247	10880	0	0	0	Residential	Wood
0	96165	0	96165	69358	0	0	0	Residential	Wood
0	11096	0	11096	12738	0	0	0	Residential	Wood
218475	218475	218475	218475	199030	4370	0	0	Residential	Wood
1400904	1400904	1400904	1400904	1772984	0	0	0	Residential	Masonry
4365	4365	4365	4365	4438	87	0	0	Residential	Wood
4365	4365	4365	4365	6096	87	0	0	Residential	Wood
39789	39789	39789	39789	58107	0	0	0	Residential	Wood
24867	24867	24867	24867	18970	0	0	0	Residential	Wood
213876	213876	213876	213876	261435	0	0	0	Residential	Wood
69435	69435	69435	69435	93674	1389	0	0	Residential	Wood
14922	14922	14922	14922	12333	0	0	0	Residential	Wood
165546	165546	165546	165546	239135	0	0	0	Residential	Wood
72837	72837	72837	72837	86638	0	0	0	Residential	Wood
72837	72837	72837	72837	98148	0	0	0	Residential	Wood

(Continued)

TABLE A.6 Continued

policy ID	eq_site_ limit	hu_site_ limit	fl_site_ limit	fr_site_ limit	tiv_2011	tiv_2012	eq_site_ deductible	hu_site_ deductible	fl_site_ deductible	fr_site_ deductible	line	construction
	19440	19440	19440	19440	19440	30659	0	389	0	0	Residential	Wood
	9945	9945	9945	9945	9945	11551	0	199	0	0	Residential	Wood
	0	255879	0	0	255879	345895	0	0	0	0	Residential	Wood
	0	153527	0	0	153527	138229	0	0	0	0	Residential	Wood
	0	255879	0	0	255879	177340	0	0	0	0	Residential	Wood
	0	102351	0	0	102351	95133	0	0	0	0	Residential	Wood
	0	155490	0	0	155490	145140	0	0	0	0	Residential	Wood
	0	137234	0	0	137234	114920	0	0	0	0	Residential	Wood
	0	123596	0	0	123596	183015	0	0	0	0	Residential	Wood
	0	107111	0	0	107111	88219	0	0	0	0	Residential	Wood
	0	96309	0	0	96309	85911	0	0	0	0	Residential	Wood
	0	104032	0	0	104032	168444	0	0	0	0	Residential	Wood
	338945	338945	338945	338945	338945	485817	0	0	0	0	Residential	Wood
	272349	272349	272349	272349	272349	414566	0	0	0	0	Residential	Wood
	129690	129690	129690	129690	129690	129636	0	0	0	0	Residential	Wood
	123210	123210	123210	123210	123210	120346	0	0	0	0	Residential	Wood
	0	3699	0	0	3699	3939	0	0	0	0	Residential	Wood

GLOSSARY

ABC system   A method for classifying inventory items according to their dollar value to the firm based on the principle that only a few items account for the greatest dollar value of holding.

Active customer accounts per credit representative or collector   Active customer accounts / number of total credit representatives or collectors

Agent balance to surplus   Collectible balance from agents (brokers) / surplus

Agent expense ratio   Commission and expense / net premium written

Aggregate planning   The process of determining the quantity and timing of production over an intermediate time frame

Arrival rate   The rate at which customers arrive at a service facility during a specified period

Average accounts per customer   Total number of accounts / total number of customers

Average credit balance per customer   Total closing credit balance / total number of open customers

Average days delinquent   The average time from the invoice due date to the paid date

Average duration of promotion   Average time duration of promotion from one band to another

Average expenses per closed customer   Total account expenses for closed accounts / total number of closed customers

Average number of accounts held per closed customer   Total number of accounts of closed customers / total number of closed customers

Average number of products held   Total number of unique products / total number of open customers

Average number of products held per closed customer   Total number of unique products of closed customers / total number of closed customers

Glossary

Average outstanding (days) (Closing balance of total receivables × number of days in period) / credit sales for that period

Average pre-closure balance Amount (pre-closure) from closed customers / number of closed customers

Average revenue per closed customer Total account revenue for closed accounts / total number of closed customers

Average time to closure per closed account Total account age on book for closed accounts

Back ordering Ordering an item that is temporarily out-of-stock

Bad debt to sales Percentage of credit sales that were written off to bad debt / credit sales

Balance delay The total idle time of an assembly line

Balanced score card A performance assessment that includes metrics related to customers, processes, and learning and growing, as well as financials

Batch production The low-volume production of customized products

Benefits expense per full-time employee (FTE) Total benefits expense for all employees / number of FTEs

Bill of material (BOM) A list of all the materials, parts, and assemblies that make up a product, including quantities, parent–component relationships, and order of assembly

Book leverage Book value of debt / book value of equity

Breakeven analysis A technique that determines the volume of demand needed to be profitable takes into account the trade-off between fixed and variable costs

Capacity The maximum capability to produce

Carrying costs The cost of holding an item in inventory that adds opportunity costs, storage, rent, cooling, lighting, and interest costs

Cash conversion cycle (CCC) Cumulative no. of days between collecting cash and disbursing cash for all discrete unit operations / total number of discrete unit operations

Cash flow ratio Operating cash flow to net premium written amount

Ceded premiums Premiums are charged to income over the terms of the respective policies and the applicable term of the reinsurance contracts with third party reinsurers. Ceded unearned premiums represent the unexpired portion of premiums ceded to CAR and other reinsurers.

Change in closed accounts (Number of closed accounts in current period − number of closed accounts in previous period) / number of closed accounts in previous period

Change in credit balance from open customers (Credit balances from open customers in current period − credit balances from open customers in previous period) / credit balances from open customers in previous period

Change in net writings (Current year net premium written − prior year net premium written) / net premium written prior year

Change in number of closed customers No. of closed customers in previous period

Change in number of open customers (Number of open customers in current period − number of open customers in previous period) / number of open customers in previous period

Collection efficiency Beginning receivables + (credit sales) − ending total receivables × 100

Conservation ratio (CR) How much of business underwritten in the previous years is getting renewed each year, for the entire life insurance industry

Continuous production The production of a very high-volume commodity product with highly automated equipment

Continuous replenishment Supplying orders in a short period of time according to a predetermined schedule

Cost of Capital Net yield to maturity of debt issues + risk premium on equity

Cost of deal conversion Cumulative sales & marketing cost of all deals closed / total no. of sales account deals closed

Cost of sales and marketing Total cost of sales and marketing / total operating expenses

Cumulative lead time The total length of time required to manufacture a product; also, the longest path through a product structure

Current reserve deficiency to surplus (Reserves required − actual reserves) / surplus

Cycle counting A method for auditing inventory accuracy that counts inventory and reconciles errors on a cyclical schedule rather than once a year; how well a machine or worker performs compared to a standard output level

Cycle time The time between successive product completions

Days average collection rate The average time from the invoice date to the date paid

Days in cash-to-cash cycle time Cumulative no. of days in receiving cash to deploying cash in discrete operations / no. of discrete unit operations

Days of maturity of debt Maturity in days × debt volume / total debt

Days sales outstanding (DSO) Number of days from invoice date to reporting date × (invoice amount / net credit sales for the month in which the sale occurred):

Σage category / credit sales j × 30

Where age category i is:

Age category i	Credit sales period j
Current age (current delinquent)	Current
1–30 days	Previous first quarter
30–60 days	Previous second quarter
61–90 days	Previous third quarter
90–120 days	Previous fourth quarter

Days to sales cycle close Cumulative days to close sales accounts / no. of sales accounts

Delivery time for all supply orders Cumulative delivery times in days of all supply orders / total no. of suppliers

Direct compensation expense per FTE Total direct expense for all employees / number of FTEs

Dividend yield Annual dividend / stock price

Drum buffer rope A concept in a theory of constraints where the *drum* sets the pace of production, a *buffer* is placed in front of the bottleneck, and the *rope* communicates changes

Earnings before interest and tax (EBIT) Earnings before gross interest expense and taxes but after minority interest and equity interest in subsidiaries

Earnings before interest, taxes, depreciation and amortization (EBITDA) EBIT + depreciation + depletion + amortization

Employee development program participation rate Number of employees opted and participated and awarded development certificate / total number of employees

Employee total compensation expense per FTE Total compensation for all employees / number of FTEs

Employees in sales and marketing No. of employees in sales and marketing / total number of employees

Equity value Equity stock price × common shares outstanding

Expected value Expected value a weighted average of decision outcomes in which each future state of nature is assigned a probability of occurrence

Fill rate The portion of orders placed by a customer with a supplier distribution that are filled within a day

Firm value Equity value + long-term debt + short-term debt − cash

Flow time The time that it takes for a job to "flow" through the system; that is, its completion time

Gross margin for all channels Gross revenue − operating costs / gross revenue for all channels

Herfindahl$_{Geography}$ Σ (premium written in ith cluster / total premium written)^2

Herfindahl$_{LOB}$ Σ (premium written in jth line / total premium written)^2

High-risk accounts List of potential bad debt accounts, for example, a minimum $2,000 over 60 days and a total due of $5,000

Human capital expenses Total cost of human capital / total expenses of all functions

ICOV Interest coverage EBIT / gross interest expense

Interchangeability Interchangeable parts the standardization of parts initially as replacement parts

Intermodal transportation Combines several modes of transportation

Investment yield Net investment income / average of cash and investment assets for current and previous period

Item master file   A file that contains the inventory status and descriptive information on every item in inventory

Load   The standard hours of work assigned to a facility

Load leveling   The process of balancing underloads and overloads

Job   A set of tasks that comprise the work performed by employees that contributes to the production of a product or delivery of a service

Job rotation   The horizontal movement between two or more jobs

Letter of Credit (LC)   A bank's guarantee that a buyer's payment to a seller will be received on time and for the correct amount. In the event that the buyer is unable to make payment on the purchase, the bank will be required to cover the full or remaining amount of the purchase

Level production   An aggregate planning strategy that produces units at a constant rate and uses inventory to absorb variations in demand

Liability ratio   Liability to liquid assets ratio

Line balancing   A technique that attempts to equalize the amount of work assigned to each workstation on an assembly line

Load level   The process of smoothing out the work assigned across time and the available resources

Loss experience ratio   Loss experience ratio = annual losses incurred / net premiums earned

Market leverage   Market value of debt / (market value of debt + market value of equity held publicly)

Mass customization   The mass production of customized products

Mass production   The high-volume production of a standardized product for a mass market

Master production schedule (MPS)   A schedule for the production of end items (usually final products)

Material requirements planning (MRP)   An inventory control and production planning system for generating purchase orders and work orders of materials, components, and assemblies

Modular bill of material   A special bill of material used to plan the production of products with many optional attributes

Net credit margin   The net of credit outstanding and the payments made by the customer

Net operating margin   (Gross sales − total operating costs) / gross sales

Net premium ratio   Net premium written/surplus

New product launch costs   Cost of all new product launches / total no. of product launches

New product launch time   Cumulative time for new product launches / total no. of new launches

Net interest margin (NIM)   The difference between interest income and interest expense; can also be expressed as the ratio of expenses to average earning assets

No. of likes / comments in social media channels   No. of likes/comments in social media channels by posts

No. of new branches   No. of new branches or offices or stores or ATMs or customer touch points

No. of new followers across social media channels   No. of new followers across social media channels

No. of referrals in social medial channels   No. of referrals in social media channels

On-demand delivery   Requires the supplier to deliver goods when demanded by the customer

Operating cash flow   Net income + depreciation, depletion, and amortization plus changes in deferred taxes plus other non-cash charges

Operating cost per employee   Total dollars spent per employee / number of employees

Operating expenses   Operating or converting expenses / total expenses of the company for all functions

Operations   A function or system that transforms inputs into outputs of greater value

Order imbalance   The difference between the cumulative buy quantity and cumulative sell quantity at each eligible price point. If there is a single volume-maximizing price at which the absolute unfilled/unmatched quantity, the order imbalance is minimum that price is the opening price

Ordering costs   The cost of replenishing the stock of inventory including requisition cost, transportation and shipping, receiving, inspection, handling, and so forth

Overall operation ratio   Loss and loss adjustment expense ratio + expense ratio − investment income ratio

P/cash ratio   Price/cash flow stock price/operating cash flow per share

P/E ratio   Price/earnings stock price/EPS or equity value/net income (see also EPS)

Pay off   The outcome of a decision

Payout   Percent payout annual dividend / EPS

Percent (%) accounts payable   Cumulative amount of supplier payments outstanding / gross sales

Percent (%) sales returns   Cumulative sales amount returned and rejected / gross sales

Percent (%) supplier service request resolution   No. of supplier request resolved / total no. of suppliers received

Percent (%) accounts receivable   Cumulative amount of customer credit sales / gross sales

Percent (%) asset utilization to revenue   Amount of assets / gross revenue

Percent (%) channel migration   No. of customers switching one channel to another / total no. of customers in all channels

Percent (%) employee productivity   Gross operating / total no. of employees

Percent (%) employee retention   1 − employee turnover = 1 − (no. of employees resigned and retired / total no. of employees)

Percent (%) employees trained No. of employees trained / total no. of employees

Percent (%) employees in operations No. of employees in operations or conversion / total no. of employees

Percent (%) employees in research and development No. of employees in research and development / total no. of employees

Percent (%) global suppliers No. of global suppliers / total no. of suppliers

Percent (%) gross margin on cost of goods sold Gross revenue − cost of goods sold / gross revenue

Percent (%) HR benefits cost to total employee costs Total cost of human capital benefits / total employee costs

Percent (%) material quality for all supply orders No. of suppliers orders procured with satisfactory quality norms / total no. of suppliers orders

Percent (%) sales account receivable Cumulative amount of credit account sales / gross sales

Percent (%) sales new account receivable Cumulative amount of credit sales from new accounts / gross sales

Percent (%) SME suppliers No. of SME suppliers / total no. of suppliers

Percent (%) suppliers expired No. of suppliers agreements expired / total no. of supplier agreements

Percent (%) suppliers trained No. of suppliers trained / total no. of suppliers

Percent (%) training cost Costs of training / total employee costs

Performance appraisal participation rate No. of employees who participated in the appraisal cycle / total no. of eligible employees for appraisal during the cycle

Performance rating distribution No. of converted deals closed / total no. of products

Persistency The proportion of an insurance company's already written policies remaining in force, without lapsing or being replaced by policies of other insurers

Product lifecycle management (PLM) Engine that manages the product development process, product lifecycles, and design collaboration with suppliers and customers

Point of sale (POS) Point at which the customer transaction takes place

Postponement Moving final assembly or product customization into the warehouse or distribution centre

Premium ratio Gross premium /surplus

Price to earnings ratio Stock price / earnings per share = net profit / no. of outstanding shares held publicly

Price/book value Price / book value per share

Process A group of related tasks with specific inputs and outputs

Process chart A tool that uses standardized symbols to chart the flow of activities involved in a process

Process flowchart A flowchart that illustrates, with symbols, the steps for a job or how several jobs fit together within the flow of the production process

Process planning The conversion of schedules into workable instructions for manufacturing, along with associated decisions on component purchase or fabrication, process, and equipment

Procurement Purchasing goods and services from suppliers

Product depth Ratio of number of products to product family and number of families

Product layout A layout that arranges activities in a line according to the sequence of operations to assemble a particular product

Productivity The ratio of output to input

Profit after tax Net profit after tax / gross revenue

Promotion rate Number of employees promoted to next level / no. of employees eligible for promotion

Queue A single waiting line that forms in front of a service facility

Recruitment cost of new employees Total recruitment costs of new employees / no. of new employees

Recruitment time for new employees Cumulative recruitment time in months for new employees / no. of new employees

Reorder point A level of inventory in stock at which a new order is placed

Reserve development ratio Reserve development to surplus 1 year reserve development / prior year surplus, where 1 year reserve development = previous losses outstanding + payments towards those losses made − the reserve at the end of the prior year

Resolution time customer service request resolution Cumulative resolution time for all customer services in days/ total number of service request resolved

Return on revenue Pre-tax operating income / net premiums earned

Revenue from products in each line to total products Revenue from product lines / total revenue from all products

Revenue per customer Revenue from product / total revenue of target markets

Return on capital (ROC) Measure of the profitability of a firm expressed as a percentage of funds acquired from investors and lenders on invested capital = net income / (equity + long-term debt)

Return on equity (ROE) (Surplus current year − surplus previous year) / average surplus of current and previous year

Return on investment (ROI) The division between benefit or return of an investment by the cost of the investment = gain − cost of investment / cost of investment

Return on total assets (ROTA) A ratio between the earnings before interest and taxes (EBIT) against its total assets = EBIT / total assets

Safety stock An amount added to the expected amount demanded during the lead time (the reorder point level) as a hedge against a stock out

Satisfied employee No. of satisfied employees (fulfilling cut-off score) / total no. employees

SCOR The supply chain operations reference model

Sequencing The process of assigning priorities to jobs so that they are processed in a particular order

Service level The probability that the amount of inventory on hand during the lead time is sufficient to meet expected demand

Service time The time required to serve a customer; the time period divided by service time yields the service rate

Shortage costs Temporary or permanent loss of sales that will result when customer demand cannot be met

Spread (bid /offer) The difference between the bid and the offer rate. The bid/offer spread is a measure of liquidity and counterparty risk

Strike price The price at which an asset can be purchased or sold, which is determined at the time the option contract is formed

Supplier on-time delivery Cumulative no. of on-time delivery of supply orders procured / total no. of suppliers received

Surplus aid to surplus Ceding commission ratio × ceded unearned reinsurance premium/surplus

Talent inventory No. of employees satisfying talent requirements / total no. of employees

Tardiness The difference between a job's due date and its completion time for jobs completed after their due dates

Transfer price Re-sales price × (1 − margin) / sale price, where resale price is when the interim output is sold to unrelated customers, and margin is expected

Transshipment Intermediate shipping points between the sources and final destination

Unit cost of all suppliers Cumulative cost of all suppliers orders procured / total no. of suppliers received

Unit cost of global vendors Cumulative cost of all global vendors / no. of global vendors

Unit cost of SME suppliers Cumulative cost of all SME suppliers / no. of SME suppliers

Value chain A series of activities from supplier to customer that add value to a product or service

Value at risk (VaR) and conditional VaR (CVaR) Used in related context, and CVaR is calculated as the expected value of all simulated data points that exceed the VaR. The values exceeding 99th value in a particular time bucket are considered when computing CVaR and will indicate economic capital required beyond the 99% confidence level

Vendor-managed inventory (VMI) Vendor-managed demands within the facility of buyer